ISBN 0-918-110-16-5
Folio Magazine Publishing Corporation,
Six River Bend, Post Office Box 4949,
Stamford, Connecticut 06907-0949
Printed in the United States of America

Typeset in Times Roman, on an Apple© Laserwriter™ Plus
by The Printed Word of Evanston, Illinois

STRATEGIC PLANNING
FOR MAGAZINE EXECUTIVES

How to take the guesswork out of

magazine publishing decisions

A Monograph on Advanced Magazine Planning Techniques

by

Richard M. Koff

ABOUT THE AUTHOR

Richard M. Koff consults with publishers and other corporations concerning the strategic and tactical problems they face in starting and running their companies, and in evaluating and negotiating for their purchase or sale. He was Vice President, Business Manager, Assistant Publisher, and a Member of the Office of the President of Playboy Enterprises, Inc., over a period of 11 years. Earlier, he spent 11 years with McGraw-Hill Publishing Company in editorial positions.

A licensed engineer with a graduate degree, Koff is the inventor and patent holder of several adult toys and art designs. He is the author of *"Home Computers,"* published by Harcourt-Brace Jovanovich in March, 1979; *"How Does it Work?,"* published by Doubleday and now in its twentieth printing; *"Christopher,"* a juvenile science fiction novel published by Dawne-Leigh in September, 1981 and currently distributed by Bantam in paperback. His series of articles on magazine and book publishing strategy which ran in *Folio: The Magazine For Magazine Managment,* was expanded to book-length and published by *Folio Magazine Publishing* Corporation as *"Strategic Planning for Magazine Executives."* This book is an updated and expanded version of that original. Wiley & Sons brought out his *"Using Small Computers to Make Your Business Strategy Work"* in June, 1984, and a computer program, "The Business Simulation Model" in February, 1985. He coauthored *"Increasing Your Wealth in Good Times & Bad,"* published by Probus in March, 1985.

Articles under his byline have appeared in *Playboy, Cowles Educational Encyclopedia, Nature & Science, Graphic Arts Monthly* and *Restaurant Hospitality.* He was the subject of a full-length feature in *Successful Business* magazine and is a three-time winner of the Jesse H. Neal Award for Editorial Achievement, given by the American Business Press, Inc.

He has written a number of computer software programs for magazine, newsletter and book publishers, as well as an investment strategies program. All are currently marketed by Sheridan Software.

He is Adjunct Professor at Northwestern University's Medill School of Journalism, has led seminars at Stanford University's Publisher's Conferences on magazine management, at New York University's School of Continuing Education, at the Midwest Planning Association, at Magazine Publishers Association workshops, and at the Society of Business Press Editors. He is a regular lecturer at Folio: Show, Face to Face and Publishing Week Conferences for publishing executives.

CONTENTS

Preface to the Second Edition   1

1. Introduction   3
2. What Kind of Publisher Are You?   7
3. What is Strategic Planning?   15
4. The Computer as a Tool   31
5. Advertising   39
6. Subscriptions   67
7. Single-copy Sales   85
8. Other Income   103
9. Costs   109
10. At the Margin   123
11. Spreadsheet Model Design   137
12. A City Magazine   153
13. Staying on Top   161
14. Balancing Revenue Streams   171
15. The Face of Failure   181
16. Challenge I: A Subscription Magazine   189
17. Challenge II: A Newsstand Magazine   205
18. Challenge III: Controlled Circulation   217
19. Tracking the Results   231

Appendices

A. Curve fitting Program Listings   233
B. Discount Rates for Cashflow   247
C. Packaged Application Programs   253

PREFACE TO THE SECOND EDITION

The computer that sits on my desk today cost about one tenth of what I paid for one in 1977. It is one quarter the size, has ten times the memory capacity, and runs four times as fast.

By 1979, I was carrying a "luggable" computer into Folio: seminar rooms to demonstrate word processing and spreadsheets (WordStar and VisiCalc, in those days). It was like magic. I would display an advertising rate card on the screen and then recalculate every cell with the press of a single button.

"Watch closely," I would say. "There is nothing in my hands. There is nothing up my sleeve." Invariably, a gasp would go through the room when the numbers rippled through the table almost too fast to be seen.

Today, you really can't function as business manager, advertising director, circulation director or editor without some familiarity with spreadsheets, data base managers and word processors. And it is the rare publisher who hasn't tried setting up a spreadsheet to answer the critical questions faced every year when budget time rolls around. How much do I dare raise subscription prices? What about the advertising CPM? Is the newsstand promotion really working for us?

We have the tools now——plenty of computer power, statistical programs, spreadsheets, programming languages——as never before to take control of our publishing destinies. It only needs a theory, a method of approach, what the programmers call an "algorithm" to solve the problem. That's what this book was originally and what it still is.

The book is chock-full of new material——it is half again as big as the first edition. Much of the new material comes from my experience in leading seminars on strategic planning, sponsored by Folio: year after year. To the hardy participants who braved those early, stumbling years, who asked the questions, made the suggestions, and raised my level of awareness and competence, I give very sincere thanks.

Much other new material comes from a rich literature on the theory of management and business strategy that has been published in recent years. In particular, I recommend Michael E. Porter's books, *The Harvard Business Review* and, of course, Peter Drucker.

Finally, I have added appendices that provide program listings for curve fitting (probably the biggest stumbling block to do-it-yourself strategic modeling) and a genuinely new approach to risk assessment.

Despite the passage of time since it was initially published, this book remains at the forefront of sophisticated publishing management. It is as advanced as anything you will find on the subject. The book is also at the forefront of publishing production——it has been written and edited on a word processor, its graphics were generated by computer, and the text was typeset and made into pages on a laser printer. Five years from now we will look back on this process as slow, primitive and costly, but today it is an amazing advance over what we have been using to reproduce the printed word.

——RMK
4/1/87

Chapter 1

INTRODUCTION

Publishers are the most skeptical readers in the world—it's an occupational disease—and I know because I was one. That explains why we regard the new techniques of management science as good copy for our magazines, but we would never be so naive as to think they could be applied to our own businesses.

When this curious myopia is pointed out to publishers the answer invariably is that, "We're different. We don't sell soap or television sets." Or, "We're just too complicated to fit into your neat theories, and anyway, we don't have any data because our new business manager just started last week and he is going to need some time to get his feet under him."

But we don't have the luxury to be so provincial when there is so much national and international competition for advertising dollars from an incredible number of magazines as well as the competition for reading time from magazines, cable television, video cassettes, compact audio disks, soft cover books, newspapers, and electronic data bases.

Investors, stockholders, and our own board members look at our ailing financial statements and wonder when our magazines are going to catch up with the rest of the business world. They are beginning to suspect that publishing doesn't have to be quite as much a seat-of-the-pants navigation as we have been claiming.

They are correct. I do not argue that new magazines can be created by a management theory any more than a meaningful poem can be written on a computer. But there are a number of techniques and analytical tools available that can help us manage our magazine better and more profitably. Not the least among them is one that goes under the name of strategic planning.

Strategy is a military word—which doesn't recommend it to most publishers—and it may have a distinctly Machiavellian connotation as well. But current experience is that, if anything, strategic thinking will open up exciting and creative alternatives that might otherwise never have been considered.

Strategic planning first asks you to rough out some objectives for yourself and your company. It is an old saw that if you don't know where you're going, all destinations are equally likely—and that includes bankruptcy. So goals, or objectives, have the virtue at least of establishing a preferred direction of travel.

Next, you take a close look at your market and the preferences and prejudices of its customers. This may require a fairly extensive study since magazines may have as many as three different groups of customers, and maybe more.

Then you do an audit of your own resources in people, dollars and magazines. Up to this point there is nothing remarkable or particularly original in the process, though we all would benefit from the discipline.

Now you let the information simmer in your mind as you look for a plan of action. This is the creative phase when you loose the strings on your imagination to explore all possible directions. In the next couple of chapters, we'll show how management theory can provide new visualization techniques to help assure that a good selection of alternatives is considered.

Invariably, some plan of action will surface. It's hard to know where it comes from. I tend to believe most creative solutions come from the unconscious and irrational mind—the right side of the brain, if the research in brain halves has any validity. Whether the solutions are practical or not is for the conscious, rational left brain to judge. They may be plans of action and reaction to a competitive situation; they may be an entirely new concept of a magazine; they may be a small twist on an existing magazine that repositions it relative to its audience or its competition. Whatever the idea, it is here that the truly original departures begin.

Having settled on one or more possible strategies you must next evaluate each in detail. This may mean pushing the accounting department into some weekend work. It will almost certainly involve you in hands-on hours with your personal computer. What you want to determine is the maximum that can be achieved, or lost, from each strategy. You are looking for what Wall Street calls upside potential and downside risk. If you know the potential of a group of alternative strategies, and also their requirements in resources and their risks, it becomes relatively easy to decide on which to pursue.

Put this way it sounds so simple, but magazines are complicated to analyze and understand. Most have at least two and often three or more revenue streams—advertising, subscriptions and single-copy sales. Each stream flows from a different market which is reached through different sales channels and techniques, and the product is delivered to its readers by two or more distinct distribution channels.

To make things more complicated, the revenue streams are highly interdependent. What happens to subscriptions affects single-copy sales as well as the number of advertising pages sold; what happens to advertising may affect the thickness of the book and thus the single-copy sales. Yet, in all, we are talking about the same basic product—a magazine.

It is this very complexity which makes magazines such prime candidates for strategic planning.

As an example, for seminar participants and clients I have devised a number of computer simulation games which, in this day of portable computers, can be played almost anywhere. In the simplest of the games players make three decisions—how much they will charge for advertising space in a particular magazine, how much they will spend to promote advertising sales, and how much circulation to acquire. When the three decisions have been made by the four competitors in this market, the computer calculates and then displays the resulting circulation, number of advertising pages sold, costs and profits of each contestant.

It is amazing how much the game reveals about the psychology of the players. There are two general types: One is what I call the caretaker. This is the careful decision maker. Prices or expenditures are changed only slightly, if at all. Caution is the watchword and while the result is rarely a disaster, neither is it ever a runaway success.

The other is the entrepreneur. This manager decides on a policy and exercises it aggressively. Perhaps prices are raised or cut dramatically, and promotion is doubled or tripled. Whatever action taken is done decisively and emphatically. This player usually wins big—or loses big.

The game mirrors life. Most publishers have not founded, nor do they own, the magazines they manage. Their powers are circumscribed because they report to a board of directors and a group of stockholders. Every critical decision will have to be defended. They are permitted to take few risks—no matter how strong the intuition. Playing safe works because the stockholders or board members never know what could have happened if a more aggressive policy had been pursued. And, playing safe, they are not likely to take the magazine down the drain, either.

Individuals who start magazines and retain majority ownership are more willing to take risks. When they are right they can be very successful—like Hugh Hefner and *Playboy*, Jann Wenner and *Rolling Stone,* Clay Felker and *New York*. When they are wrong they disappear.

The purpose of this book is to take some of the guesswork out of magazine publishing when the problems will respond to quantitative analysis, and to acknowledge and accept intuition as a legitimate, perhaps the only, way to make a decision. Yes, I believe in the intuition of publishers. Like good managers anywhere, the best publishers develop a sense of timing and of pattern that has to be relied on when the quantitative data isn't available, or when it would be too expensive or difficult to acquire.

No book can innoculate you with the inspiration and obsessive conviction that drives the successful entrepreneur; either you have that personality or you don't. But we will be making suggestions and offering approaches that will help get the creative juices flowing and perhaps, sometimes, make the courageous or unexpected path as attractive and reasonable as the safer one.

The next chapter is in the form of a questionnaire. Answer honestly and you will learn something about yourself as a magazine manager.

Chapters three and four provide an approach to strategic planning thinking, and review some of the techniques presently being used by the most sophisticated managers in business today.

Chapters five through nine examine aspects of magazine publishing in detail. They identify those business and publishing questions which are necessarily qualitative in nature and must be decided on the basis of intuition or personal preference, and separate out those that are quantitative and will respond to analytical treatment.

Chapters ten through fifteen show how to combine what you have learned about revenue streams and costs into a functioning model that will show the bottom-line outcome of your decisions. The model is a tool—pencil and paper, spreadsheet, or simulation model—that accepts as input your assumptions and test results, and returns the results in circulation and cashflow.

Chapters twelve through eighteen are a series of real-life examples of magazines. Each has reached a point in its life where critical decisions must be made and you are challenged to test your managerial ability by making the decisions yourself. The first few examples show you how; later, you are left on your own.

It is fun, but these are not games. While simplified to demonstrate particular points, the situations are real, the magazines they represent could exist (pretending they don't), and real publishers could save or lose their companies based on what they did in situations just like these.

Appendix A includes listings of three curve fitting programs written in Microsoft BASIC that can be entered into your own computer. Appendix B shows how to estimate a discount rate for discounted cashflow computations. Appendix C describes several packaged programs available now which are based on the methods described in this monograph.

Chapter 2

WHAT KIND OF PUBLISHER ARE YOU?

I hate quizzes; they always seem so sophomoric. But they provide a very real and quantitative measure of what is otherwise just another theoretical discussion. They turn a one-way lecture into a dialogue.

This one provides a personal inventory of you as publisher and manager. It is short and relatively painless but it will tell you a great deal about yourself, how you function and where your strengths and weaknesses are.

Circle one of the three answers to each question that most closely approximates how you feel. When you have completed all twenty questions you will be told how to total your scores and what they mean.

1. Do you have a business plan?

    A. Yes. It's detailed and runs for five years.
    B. Yes. It's informal but runs for two or three years.
    C. Yes. It's not written down but it is clear in my head.

2. How would the editor, advertising director and circulation director explain your magazine objectives and the strategy being used to get there?

    A. They'd point to the business plan. It's all there.
    B. They'd probably disagree, but it would make for a good discussion.
    C. That's easy. The ad director would say, "more pages;" the editor would say, "more circulation."

3. When was the last time you met with your editor and art director, and reviewed an entire issue page by page?

    A. We do it with every issue.
    B. About three months ago.
    C. The last time we did a complete redesign.

4. How much editorial material is in inventory?

    A. We like to keep three complete issues in inventory.
    B. If we scrambled we could probably put together one complete issue from inventory.
    C. None. We run a very tight operation here.

5. Are you ever late in closing an issue at the printer?

    A. About once every six months we may be a few days late.
    B. Never.
    C. Always, by a day or two. Sometimes more. It's the nature of our industry.

6. Can you estimate how many ad pages and how much circulation there is in your market?

    A. Sure, both this year and five years into the future.
    B. Sure, for this year. Who knows about next year?
    C. With the economy waffling the way it is, it's anybody's guess.

7. Do you personally call on all major advertisers?

    A. Yes.
    B. No, but the ad director does.
    C. No, but someone in the ad department does.

8. What is the toughest challenge your competitors offer?

    A. To stay ahead of them in our editorial content and look.
    B. To keep up with their flashy sales pitches.
    C. To hold our CPM under theirs and still make a profit.

9. How often do you do a detailed analysis of your monthly statements?

A. Every month, of course.
B. As often as I have time.
C. Whenever the numbers begin to look unhealthy.

10. Is the budget prepared before it is due?

A. Always.
B. We start it early but it usually doesn't get done until a
    couple of weeks after the new fiscal year begins.
C. Never made it on time yet.

11. Do you have a cashflow projection?

A. Yes. It is never more than a couple of months old.
B. Yes. It is updated every six months.
C. No. It never works out as planned anyway.

12. Do you know the profit margin of every copy sold either through
subscription or single-copy sale?

A. Yes, by source as well as effort.
B. Yes, by source.
C. Yes, roughly. Though response and sell-through vary by
    source and the condition of the economy.

13. Do you know the profit margin of every advertising page sold?

A. Yes. We have costs completely spelled out for every size
    and color combination.
B. Yes. I have a rule of thumb that works very well.
C. Yes, roughly.

14. Describe the ad sales staff.

A. They are bright, ambitious hustlers. They wear me out.
B. We have a few self-starters; the rest need a lot of supervision.
C. They are all hardworking and helpful.

15. How often do you have performance reviews with the editor, advertising director and circulation director?

    A. I try to do it every six months in a long, private meeting.
    B. Once a year at salary review time.
    C. When it's a new person and obviously in trouble. The others know how I feel about them.

16. What happens if it's clear they are not doing their jobs?

    A. We talk and try to agree on a performance criterion that can be used to measure improvement.
    B. I'll talk to the person at review time.
    C. If it's really bad I'll transfer some of the responsibilities over to others. The person in trouble usually gets the message and quits.

17. If the magazine had double the present circulation and advertising sales, how would the staff be different?

    A. The top people would be the same but they would have others working for them.
    B. I'd have some of the same top people but there are one or two that would have to be replaced by better managers.
    C. It would need all new people to handle that level of responsibility.

18. Are the data and statements reported to you by your accounting department, advertising department or business staff reliable?

    A. Of course not. I only believe half of it at best. They don't consciously lie, it's just that hard data is almost impossible to get.
    B. I'd guess most of it is out of date, but on the whole I would say it is pretty accurate.
    C. We've got an absolutely top notch information system now and I know I can rely on the statements.

19. How many new magazines have you been involved with in your professional career?

    A. Two or more.
    B. One.
    C. None.

20. You have a good second-tier job with an established publisher but are offered the top spot on a new magazine that has the potential to be a large, mass-market success. They want you to invest all your savings to show your commitment. Would you take the offer?

    A. Yes, if I judged the odds to be 3 to 2 in favor of success.
    B. Yes, if I judged the odds to be 8 or 9 to 1 in favor of success.
    C. No. I can't risk my life savings on a speculative venture no matter how good the odds.

Count three points for every "A" answer, two for every "B" and one for every "C." The questions are divided among five areas of concern to a publisher:

Planning (Questions 1 & 2)

A score below four means you have no interest in, or respect for, the business plan but update it only when you need to go to backers or the bank for money. This is a mistake because a business plan helps set specific objectives and direction. It forces you to make a systematic consideration of factors which then becomes a basis for better decision making. It is a means of measurement and control of the magazine—both quantitative and qualitative. Finally, it will tell you what your resource needs are right now and how they will change in the future so that you can be thinking more about funds, or hiring and training additional people, before the emergency hits.

Note that you don't have to be a "caretaker" to rely on a business plan. Entrepreneurs take more risks, it is true, but they prefer calculated risks and that means analysing the costs and potential returns of a contemplated plan of action. In short, a business plan.

Editorial (Questions 3 to 5)

A score below six means you are not paying enough attention to the quality of your product. Inventory can certainly get out of hand if editors are given free rein to buy whatever they want and even three issues worth of inventory may appear to be excessive, but it rarely is. Too little inventory means that each issue of the magazine is put together from what is available, not from what is best.

Chronic late closing indicates too little planning and foresight and obviously wastes money; but a perfect record indicates the editors have been browbeaten by the finance department and will too quickly sacrifice currency to cashflow.

Market (Questions 6 to 8)

Do you really know your customers and your competition? If you didn't get a score of six or more the answer is probably no. Remember to consider more than the two or three direct competitors. Any magazine your reader buys or spends time with is taking time away from you; any advertiser that wants to reach your reader should be using your pages, not some other magazine or some other medium. This may seem exaggerated but if you don't think in these terms you are automatically limiting your growth potential.

Money (Questions 9 to 13)

Magazine publishers who come up through the advertising or editorial departments tend to be weakest in these areas, yet there is no doubt here is where the profit controls come from. A score of less than ten in these five questions means you are not making the profits you could. Budgets, cashflow, and profit-and-loss projections, subscription analyses, newsstand and advertising margin analyses are early warning signals about the health of your magazine. You should be taking its pulse every month, at the longest. If you wait longer it is too late to make changes that can help.

Cashflow (question 11) is critical for magazines. If you can't pay the printer or make a subscription mailing at the right time, it's going to be nearly impossible to produce a successful magazine.

Personnel (Questions 14 to 17)

In the last analysis, a magazine is nothing without its people. Yes, once the format is set a magazine has an enormous inertia that is not likely to run down in a hurry, and there are many fine editors and advertising directors available to take your ideas and run with them. But do you have talent on the staff that can be relied on to do a little more than the minimum necessary, who can grow with the magazine? A score here of less than eight indicates you do not, and it is almost certainly your fault as manager and leader.

Are you willing to delegate the authority as well as the responsibility necessary to get the job done? Do you give department heads clear objectives and then the freedom to go about reaching the objectives?

Take a long time to think about question 17 because this is the pivot of all growth potential.

Entrepreneur or Caretaker? (Questions 18 to 20)

It is important to realize that the management style identified in the first 17 questions of this quiz has nothing to do with whether one is a natural entrepreneur or caretaker. Either will be a better manager if the total score is 35 or higher because he or she will have tighter control and more reliable information about the magazine. These last three questions don't have value judgment attached; The scores will simply separate the two personality types.

It's not hard to see how these three questions add up. If your score is seven or higher you are definitely an entrepreneurial personality—you tend to be a loner, have trouble working in large organizations, naturally gravitate to new magazine start-ups and are willing to play hunches if the rewards are high enough.

Entrepreneurs are not necessarily gamblers in the craps or blackjack sense. As a matter of fact, they may regard 50-50 odds as nowhere near high enough and consider Las Vegas a sucker trap. On the other hand, the entrepreneur will sometimes leave a job before a new one has been found and would always choose to be president of a small magazine rather than vice president of a larger one.

If you were the majority stockholder of a company would you hire an entrepreneur to run the company or would you prefer someone who will check back with the board of directors for all major decisions, will aim at steady, if slow, earnings growth and will build a strong second level management team ready to take over in emergencies?

A score of five or lower puts you in the caretaker class. You are a responsible executive and a good team player. You can delegate authority and take real pleasure in training younger executives and bringing them along. You have years of experience in publishing and take a lot of pride in doing your job well.

Entrepreneurs are usually, though not always, younger. They are more energetic, more willing to experiment, more accepting of change, brasher, ruder, more impatient, less people conscious and always in a hurry.

Caretakers are usually older; indeed, they may be the mature incarnation of an entrepreneur. By definition they are more conservative, careful, interested in preserving what has been accumulated or made. It's no wonder that new magazines rarely start in the large, old publishing houses. The very selection process that picks the leaders of these companies was specifically designed to eliminate risk-taking characteristics.

Knowing what kind of manager you are is not just a matter of passing interest. It is critical in the development of the strategic plan. Now we can get on with that subject.

Chapter 3

WHAT IS STRATEGIC PLANNING?

Every few years a new theory of management science is enthusiastically adopted by business writers and consultants. It would be cynical to suggest that, after all, writers need new things to write about and consultants need new things to consult about, but it is curious how the theories rise and fall as inevitably as the Dow Jones average. In recent years we've had portfolio management and experience curves, growth/share matrices, decision trees, zero-base budgeting, crisis management, management by objectives and many others.

While it is true there is a fad aspect to many of these theories, the fact is that we are getting better at managing our companies. We have to be as competition get tougher, resources become more expensive, and monopolies of ideas or markets become impossible in a shrinking world.

My preference, let me be quick to admit, is strategic planning —*planning* because it attends to the future and will be concerned about foreseeable and unforeseeable contingencies; *strategic* because it is concerned with setting realistic goals and the best we can do to get to those goals. In short:

Strategic Planning is the process of directing a magazine's resources toward selected objectives

In previous chapters you have read about my conviction that plans are necessary to the efficient management of a business. To me it seems to be one of those self-evident truths that need no defense or explanation. But there is legitimate objection to a too-rigid planner who resists change and therefore cannot take advantage of opportunity, and there is nothing to recommend a plan that is carefully prepared, read once, and then permanently consigned to a file. A good plan is one that can and must be lived with; its guideposts appear in the budget column of your monthly statements; its fallibility (or yours as planner, forecaster and manager) in the variations between actual and budgeted sales, costs and profits.

Formalized strategic planning theory was first applied to manufacturing companies. It appeared in the early 1960's with a line of reasoning that goes roughly as follows: The company with the highest market share is producing the largest volume and must be doing so at the lowest unit cost. It therefore generates highest profits from both the larger quantity sold and the higher profit margins possible.

In a growing market, the company with the highest market share can maintain or increase its share fairly easily with some plowing back of profits. In a static or declining market, it can reap large profits with almost no additional investment other than to maintain its equipment and position.

The theory was confirmed by statistical studies of hundreds of companies in many industries in which it was found that there is a high correlation of profits with market share, and this led to the creation of a matrix much admired by business strategists. The original looked something like Figure 3.1.

Note that we are concerned here not with entire companies whose products may vary considerably in market share and growth, but with strategic business units which are defined as one or more products and markets that share a common but distinctive set of economics.

You find the place on the two axes for your magazine and its market, and that will tell you which of the following strategies to follow. If you have a low market share in a low growth industry the best bet is to sell out. If you have a high market share in a low growth industry you are a cash cow which can be milked to provide funds for the stars and for the question marks. The stars need cash to maintain market share in a growing industry so that they, in turn, may eventually become cash cows. The question marks also may be turned into stars by the investment of cash to increase market share.

The theory has some relevance to the advertising side of our businesses where ratebase (guaranteed by circulation) and CPM (cost-per-thousand readers) are gages used by advertisers to measure magazine efficiency. It has little or none on the circulation side unless there are two or more almost interchangeable magazines in the field.

There are several other problems with this matrix. The most critical is in the market definition. Obviously, how you define your market has a lot to do with whether you have high or low market share and whether or not it is growing, so that looked at by one analyst a magazine may be a star, and by another, a dog. Furthermore, the publisher with the largest share of the market isn't necessarily the one producing and distributing its magazine at the least cost. Finally, magazines are not interchangeable the way refrigerators or electronic components may be, so that growth can depend on things other than the infusion of cash—no matter how well spent.

Still, the matrix insures that you consider all possible alternatives. It is

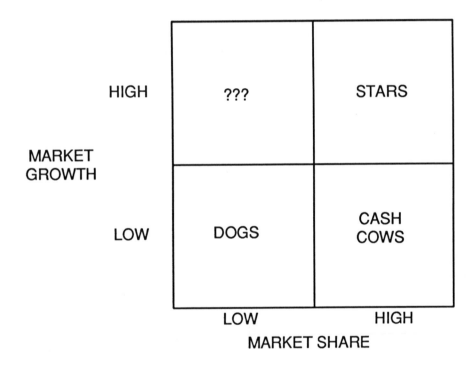

Figure 3.1 Strategic business units plotted on this growth/share matrix will fall in one of four quadrants. Each quadrant has a different value to the company as a whole, described by the names indicated on the graph, and calls for a different strategy.

What is Strategic Planning? 17

a programmed look into what might be called strategic space, and it is possible to take the same principle and apply it to a number of different situations. For example, one could draw a matrix of quality and price and then locate your magazine and your competitors on the matrix. Different places on this matrix will produce different volumes of sale depending on the sensitivity of the market to quality and price, and consequently generate different levels of profit (Figure 3.2).

Similarly, a women's magazine might use a matrix where one of the axes has to do with the quantity of service features (like cooking and cosmetics), as distinct from entertainment, while the other measures the percentage of illustration. It then would be possible to locate several competing magazines on this matrix and, from consumer research, sketch in the areas of reader preference.

There is one kind of matrix that applies perfectly to the publisher whose aim is growth (Figure 3.3). Here, the number of magazines is plotted along the horizontal axis and number of markets along the vertical axis. Any single magazine would normally start in the lower left corner—one magazine serving one market. The opportunity for growth can come in any of three directions. One can go straight up—which means to leave the magazine largely unchanged but extend the sale to new markets. One can go to the right—adding new magazines for the same market. One can go diagonally up to the right—adding new magazines for new markets.

The purpose of these matrices is to assist in the creative development of alternative strategies. They clarify the thinking process and often suggest directions that would not otherwise be considered.

Steps in the Creation of a Strategic Plan

Let's take a quick trip through the process before looking at each step in detail. The first step in the development of a strategy is to set goals. At this stage the goals will be fairly general; later, as the strategy begins to develop, what is realistically achievable will permit you to be more specific.

A publisher sells a product to customers in a competitive environment and so the second step is to study the market. There are three distinct customers for a magazine—the subscriber, the single-copy buyer and the advertiser. What do you know about these customers? What can you find out by research? What information must your publishing instincts provide, and have you clearly labeled what is speculation and what is an objectively determined fact?

The market for a magazine will also include one or more competitors

What is Strategic Planning?

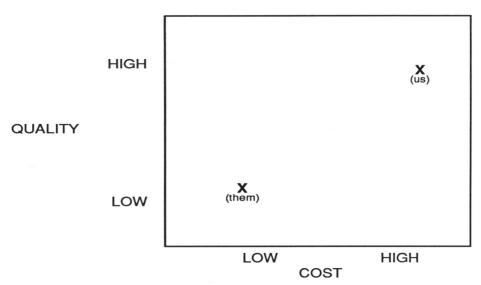

Figure 3.2   A quality/price matrix with two magazines plotted.   Every location on this matrix would have associated with it a volume of sale— higher for the higher quality, lower for the higher price.

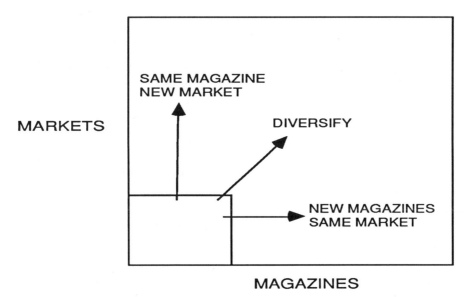

Figure 3.3 A magazines/markets matrix portrays the options a publisher has for growth.   Unlike the previous matrices this one has no quantitative significance but is intended to suggest new ways to think about a company and its strategic alternatives.

What is Strategic Planning?   19 and even the simple definition of who is, or is not, a competitor will have a critical impact on the strategic plan.

Next you will look at your own strengths and weaknesses as a competitor. A magazine's resources include its concept and format, its staff, its image in the minds of the customers and its finances. For each market (subscription, single-copy, advertising) take a hard look at the magazine and its managers in terms of the following questions:

1. Is it tangibly different from the competitors in terms of appearance, content, readership?

2. How is it priced and how important is price to the buyer?

3. How would it be described by readers, by advertisers?

Take a look at your management style (see the quiz in the previous chapter), but also at the company culture as represented by your answers to the following questions:

1. Is there a corporate growth plan with explicit goals and targeted levels of achievement?

2. Does magazine redesign or repositioning come up for regular and repeated consideration no matter how successful?

3. Are new magazine start-ups or acquisitions part of the plan and is there an individual or group assigned to this responsibilty?

4. Does the acquisition or start-up group have a budget and the authority to assign funds?

5. Is there a compensation plan that rewards entrepreneurship and risktaking?

6. Is management willing to accept failure?

7. Does top management provide consistent commitment to the exploration of new ideas in sales approaches, production processes, editorial content?

What is Strategic Planning?

8. Does top management stress long-term profitability as well as short-term returns?

If you know your goals and your resources you have all the external raw data needed to formulate a strategy. The remainder of the strategic planning process is devoted to devising means of applying those resources to achieve the goals.

Now you begin to formulate your first broad strategies. They may later be dismissed out of hand, considered but dismissed, modified, examined in detail or extended and pursued. This is the creative stage. It is the time for the imaginative leap that produces an entirely new format for a magazine or redefines a market in such a way as to clearly indicate the need for another magazine. It has to be a relatively uncritical stage because almost any new idea can be shot down by negative thinking, but you must not be so uncritical as to go off in directions that only waste energy.

Whether the magazine already exists or is still just an idea, strategies will tend to be combinations of three sets of questions:

1. *editorial* and *production* related decisions such as content and format, frequency, number of editorial pages, amount of color, etc.

2. *circulation* decisions such as paid versus controlled, sources of subscriptions, types of offers, choice of newsstand distributor, promotion budgets, ratebase targets; and most importantly, price of subscriptions, renewals, single copies

3. *advertising* decisions such as cost per thousand, promotion levels, ratebase, and the stance or position the magazine and its sales representatives take in the marketplace relative to competitors

Another area of concern that spans all of the three areas relates to personnel and personnel policies. What will you need to pay, or give up in ownership, in order to attract and keep the people you want to assist in creating and producing the magazine?

At the beginning of this stage, the strategies will necessarily be large in scope or scale. They could be as simple as the decision to start a new magazine in a particular field, or to buy an existing magazine in that field and leave it as it is, or to buy an existing magazine in the field and modify it. You could sell a magazine in your stable that has poor prospects, reinvest and redesign a magazine in your stable in order to revive its growth potential, tighten controls and costs on a magazine so as to improve its profits and cashflow, or you could change the positioning of a magazine so as to compete in a new larger (or smaller) market.

Any one, and sometimes all, of the above strategies may have to be considered at the same time. If it is a sale you may end with a pocketful of cash and that can become the minimum performance criterion against which all other strategies will be judged.

As these decisions are made the strategy begins to take enough shape so that you can write the first business plan. Here is where you may use a computer programmed with one of the packaged models that are available (we'll be mentioning them again later), or an original (which we will go into detail about in the next chapter).

Financial analyses and computer models help establish the optimum mix of decisions for a particular strategic plan. They will tell you what resources will be necessary, and what profit or sales goals can be achieved. But they only work within a given strategy; they do not create new strategies. That is a very important limitation and one the publisher usually is more sensitive to than the financial analyst or programmer.

The same analysis must be repeated for each broad strategy so that in the end the publisher can evaluate and compare strategies on equal terms. In effect, you wind up with a set of alternatives that have a predicted return in terms of the original goals, return that should help identify the best strategy and make the choice relatively easy.

To review, you start by setting broad goals for the company and for yourself. Next you look at the markets, both reader and advertiser, and then at the competition. You take a hard look at your own resources and capabilities and come up with one or more approaches that have the most promise. Each approach is analysed in detail and optimized so that you know exactly what the maximum potential is if that plan were followed. Finally, all strategies are compared and a decision made. Note that by the time the decision is made the detailed plan will already have been written. Then it is only a question of following through and tracking progress.

Strategic planning is not always on so rarified a level. In fact, the decisions about starting, stopping or acquiring a new magazine rarely are faced in a publishing career. More frequently the decisions and alternatives are more mundane, but they may be easier for that reason and certainly more amenable to quantitative analysis.

What is Strategic Planning?

Goals

Goals must be general and maleable during the initial stages of the planning process though they will firm up once a particular strategy has been selected. The differences are pointed up by calling the more general statements "open-end goals," as distinguished from more specifically delineated "closed-end goals."

An open-end goal might be, "We want to start a new magazine in the home entertainment field," and the closed-end goal would be, "We expect to achieve a circulation of 200,000 in five years and expect a return of no less than 10 percent on the investment by that time." The open-end goal might be, "We intend to be the leader in our field," but it must be closed with some measure of that "leadership."

Note the closed-end goal has four essential characteristics. It has content, a measure or indicator of some kind, a level of that measure to be reached and a time at which it is expected to be reached. The overall corporate objectives are likely to relate to cashflow, return on investment or equity, and short- or long-term profit; but departmental objectives will ordinarily be expressed in subscription or single-copy sales, renewal rates, advertising pages and advertising dollars.

It is important the publisher be aware that the various goals can be different and sometimes antagonistic. When departmental goals conflict with corporate goals, the corporate goals will always lose out.

For example, a circulation manager has as a goal the acquisition of a certain number of subscriptions to maintain the ratebase. If this manager's performance is only measured by the number of subscribers, it is possible to make the ratebase at exorbitant cost—ultimately losing money for the magazine as a whole.

Or another example, most advertising directors have a number of advertising pages as the performance target; but if a disproportionate number are sold in only one or two issues during the year, and these issues then require additional editorial pages for balance, it is very possible that the extra advertising pages are actually sold at a loss.

In setting goals it is instructive to start with the publisher's own personal objectives. What do you want out of life? Out of work? What kind of professional situation do you prefer—risky or secure? Any venture has a natural life cycle which starts with a slow growth, then has rapid growth, then saturation and decline (Figure 3.4). The entrepreneur is needed during the first half when rapid growth and risk taking are called for.

The caretaker is in charge during the last half when a magazine must be carefully controlled to produce maximum profits—perhaps to fund other new ventures or just to provide a good life for its owners.

Personality differences make managers natural caretakers or entrepreneurs, but time, age and station in life also change managerial styles. It is useful to establish for yourself just exactly what you want out of your professional life.

Next come the magazine owners—either partners or stockholders. If you are the sole owner the question may already have been answered; but if you are the publisher reporting to partners, or to a board of directors, you must be very clear about what they really want. It may be long term profits; it may be slow, steady profit growth; it may be a speculative ride; it may be return on investment or equity; it may be reduction of debt or some sort of tax shelter for other income. It may be liquidity, leaving extra cash around for other investment opportunities or vacations in Europe. It may be sales dollars; it may be circulation. It may even be promotional value for a society or association that results in increased membership or recognition in other magazines or newspapers.

It is important to get at the unspoken desires as well as the obvious ones. For example, magazines are considered risky investments by Wall Street venture capitalists but there is glamor and excitement in being a magazine "angel." If that motive is present it will be very useful for you to know it.

A list of spoken and unspoken goals makes fascinating reading. In a buying or selling situation (acquisition or divestiture, in the current vernacular), this knowledge is more important than almost anything else you will bring to the negotiating table.

Goals have to be a balance of what an organization or individual would like to do and what it can hope to achieve. Thus it is important that goals be reasonable or no one will try. On the other hand, they must be challenging enough to make you stretch.

Markets

In 1977, Lieberman Research Inc. did a study called. "How and Why People Read Magazines," which differed from other syndicated research in that it focused on the buying, as distinct from the reading, of magazines and as such was more directly concerned with the actions of consumers than with their reactions.

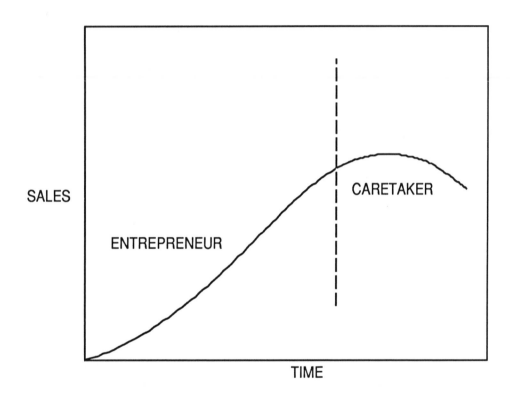

Figure 3.4 A magazine will experience slow initial sales growth in infancy, rapid growth during adolescence, a slow or flat growth during maturity and decline in old age. The entrepreneur is needed during the first half; a caretaker during the second.

Just how do people buy magazines? Lieberman found that there are three distinctly different kinds of buyer. About 26 percent of magazine buyers get their magazines by subscription and only by subscription. Another 26 percent buy their magazines a single copy at a time—at newsstands or supermarkets, for example—and never by subscription. The remaining 48 percent acquire magazines in both ways. They may subscribe to some magazines and buy single copies of others; they may subscribe to a magazine for a year or two, then let their subscriptions expire, then resubscribe at some later time.

Subscriptions are marketed in dozens of different ways—by cards or envelopes bound or blown into the pages of the magazine itself, by direct mail solicitation, by radio and television advertising, by exchange or purchased ads in other magazines or newspapers, by agents selling door to door, by students to other students, by clubs or associations to their members and on and on. Each magazine will find the most economical sources for its subscription sales and presumably mine these to some point of diminishing returns.

The problem with selling subscriptions is in locating and approaching potential customers. Sometimes the individual is easily identified by a prior interest (purchasers of video tape recorders are likely to be interested in a magazine about new videotape releases). Sometimes identifying and communicating with a potential subscriber may be difficult (how would you reach teenage boys and persuade them to get their parents to subscribe to a magazine for them?—not impossible, only difficult). Other problems with subscriptions have to do with bad debt (the people who subscribe on credit and then never pay), low renewal rates, high postage costs and the expectation on the part of the reading public that the subscription copy should cost less than a newsstand copy.

Most single copies are distributed to the market through a channel that goes from national distributor to local wholesalers to individual retailers. For many reasons the system tends to be an inefficient means of getting magazines to the point of purchase and so direct distribution is being explored, particularly by special-interest publications. For example, a home energy magazine could be sold by stores that sell woodburning stoves, or a racketball magazine might go to sports stores and court clubs.

The problem with single-copy sales is that most dealers only accept magazines with full return privileges of the unsold copies. Today the average publisher has to print one hundred copies to sell fifty—hardly an economical way to sell any manufactured product.

The competition is keen. A buyer at a newsstand is bombarded by dozens, even hundreds of other attractively packaged and stimulatingly blurbed covers. And if the retailer is a supermarket the cost and perceived value of a copy is put on the same check-out scale as essentials like milk, butter and eggs.

What sort of person buys your magazine in single copies and how does that person differ from the subscriber? Women tend to buy more single copies than men do; younger people buy more single copies than old ones.

How often do they buy? Over 50 percent of single-copy purchasers buy fewer than four copies a year. Seventy percent of subscribers say they subscribed to their magazine two or more times, though not necessarily sequentially.

How sensitive is the customer to price? Only 16 percent of single-copy purchasers say they will drop out of the market if prices keep going up. Twenty-three percent of subscription purchasers would drop out if prices keep going up.

Is the magazine one of a group that are effectively interchangeable in a buyer's eyes or do the magazines have differences (more about this later).

Finally, you'll be asking a lot of questions about the competition. Who are the direct and indirect competitors for readers? A magazine of entertainment competes directly with television and movies; a city magazine competes with local newspapers; a magazine with fiction competes with mass market paperbacks; a business magazine may compete with a newsletter in the same field. In the last analysis magazines compete with every other lure for the readers' time. Current research indicates that the amazing increase in the ownership of video cassette recorders, and the accessibility of an ever increasing library of tapes, is taking a noticeable percentage of the magazine reader's time and pocketbook.

What about the advertiser? What sort of advertiser would want to use your magazine as a vehicle for the commercial message about his products? Are the advertisers presently in your magazine the most logical ones? Are there others that should be reaching your audience and not doing so? You may want to be a little imaginative here. Why doesn't a manufacturer of sports gloves use space in a photography magazine? Or, should a popular resort hotel advertise in a business magazine?

Who really makes the decision, the advertiser or the advertising agency? What is the basis for their decision? How does price enter into it? With the answers to these questions you can better see how your promotional materials, or the magazine itself, helps or hinders the decision in your favor.

Competition for the advertising dollar means not only other magazines in your field but print advertising in general. It may mean diverting your advertising revenues to television, radio, billboards or direct mail.

In general, the more broadly you think about your competition the larger is the effective market in which you compete and the smaller your market share. If market share has a strong positive effect on profits, as the theorists believe, it may be more profitable to define the market narrowly and aim for dominance—a-big-fish-in-a-little-pool strategy. On the other hand, dominance of a very small market may result in owning a big piece of nothing. Optimizing the size of the market is one of those places where computer modeling can be very helpful.

A best strategy for each of these markets means balancing market share, market growth, distribution patterns, promotion levels, price, and most importantly, what we talk about next, product quality.

Product

On the other side of the equation is the value of the product itself. The ratio of perceived value to price is what competition is all about. If your ratio is higher, the customer buys your magazine; if your ratio is lower, the customer buys a competitor's magazine.

A magazine is a collection of printed pages that have a physical, as well as psychic, value to its buyer. It has weight, size, color and texture that will be compared with other magazines. It has content—stimulation, entertainment, education, information—will be compared to other sources of similar gratification. There is the quality of the printing and the paper, the quality of the writing and the quality of the illustrations.

How do you measure these qualities in any objective way? In fact, the buyer does so every time he or she picks your magazine off the newsstand, sends a check to the subscription department or buys a six- or twelve-time contract for advertising pages. Somewhere along the line you, too, are making a decision about quality and it is far better that the decision be conscious and deliberate rather than forced or accidental.

Do you want your magazine to be best in its field? In the world? How much will that cost? Is better good enough? Does worse have its own campy appeal? Where is the point of diminishing returns on quality? Where does your personal or corporate standard of excellence draw the line?

What is the magazine's purpose and concept? What service or utility does it provide? Is it entertaining, educational, or informative and does it do that job well? If it is informative does it have to be dull (it might, that is not a rhetorical question)? If educational, does it have to look that way or may it be light or funny in its approach and design?

There is a curious fact about most magazine markets. One might normally expect that since they are creative products all would be distinctly different. But in almost every field you will find two or three magazines that are very much alike. Perhaps it is because of the immense size and appetite of the American market for magazines. Perhaps it is simply that there are advertising dollars desperate for a place to go and the second and third magazines in a field provide a pressure relief valve.

There is nothing wrong with the strategy that aims to be the second or third magazine in a field, only that it be pursued as a conscious decision.

When?

There are some who will tell you that full-scale strategic planning is necessary all the time, but that can only be true for publishers large enough to afford the luxury of a chief executive officer or president who is not heavily committed to dealing with day-to-day emergencies. Clearly, strategic planning must precede any new project. The start-up of a new magazine, a divestiture or acquisition, has to be made in the light of a five to ten year horizon. But short of that, when should a publisher formalize the planning process?

There are several events that can trigger a strategic planning study. When a publisher reaches a certain size or complexity and corporate objectives are not automatically known or understood by all department heads, then a reconsideration of the objectives and the strategies necessary to achieve them is a worthwhile endeavor.

Sometimes changes in the environment—the competition, the government, the economy, people's lifestyles, the availability of new educational or entertainment media—must be responded to in a conscious way by the magazine. Recent unpublished studies, for example, indicate that most corporations are underestimating the immense changes in American lifestyles brought about by the women's movement. Almost everywhere you look—food purchase patterns, sexual mores, household creation, child care, all the relationships between men and women—are affected when women take a more active role in managing their lives and families. As women continue to enter the workplace in numbers and redefine their roles closer to those held predominatley by men, their interests and reading habits will more closely parallel those of their male peers. Already we are seeing the negative impact on the circulation of large women's magazines and the positive impact on small business magazines and other special interest magazines.

Similarly, the energy crisis and glut created by the power and then the weakness of OPEC triggered first an inflationary spiral, followed by rollercoaster interest rates and obvious changes in the pattern of automobile purchase and use.

Magazines that are editorially sensitive to such changes, and publishers who are cognizant of the effect of the changes on their markets, will be creating and considering new strategies to put themselves where their markets are going.

Chapter 4

THE COMPUTER AS A TOOL

Strategy is necessarily broad brush. It is usually at the level of keeping, starting, or acquiring a magazine. The question of whether to pursue a particular strategy depends on how close to, or how far beyond, your goals that strategy will take you.

Strategy says, here is an existing or imagined publication with given concept and format. Strategy asks, what is the maximum that can be achieved in this direction? To answer the question you must find the optimum combination of factors such as the subscription price, the cost-per-thousand to the advertiser, which printer to use, whether alternative delivery schemes should be tested, and whether a particular direct-mail campaign should be budgeted or cancelled. At this level, the decisions are quantitatively accessible and they will respond well to computer modeling.

Did I lose you right there? Are you convinced you don't have enough data to make a computer analysis mean anything? You could be right. Remember, however, that the decisions will have to be made whether you have the data or not, and a well-planned computer model has to make the process easier and more accurate than if no modeling were done at all.

Note that I said well-planned. The "garbage-in; garbage-out" warning has often been applied to computers as if it were an original idea, but GIGO is just as true if you use intuition or a stubby pencil and the back of an envelope to make your calculations.

Building a computer model of a magazine forces you to think analytically. If you don't want to do that, forget the model and admit you'd rather make your decisions by instinct and the seat of your pants.

Remember, the computer model will only concern itself with the quantitative aspects of the magazine. There are other decisions to be made at this level such as: Should you change the fulfillment house or printer? Is it time to replace the editor or the advertising director? Is this the best ad campaign the agency can be expected to develop? Should you move to new offices, to New York? Should you fire your secretary, buy a new word processor, attend a seminar, schedule a trip to the West Coast? The computer model won't be very helpful for any of these.

The Accounting Model

For a band of middle-level decisions—ones that are essentially quantitative in nature—you will want to use a model and there are at least two kinds to choose from. The first is what I call a budgeting model. MSI in Stamford, and Policy Development Corporation in San Diego, both offer budget models on a time-sharing basis. Lighthouse Software in New York, and my own company, Sheridan Software in Evanston, Illinois, offer package programs that run on a personal computer (see Appendix C).

All four of these models function like an accounting department with dozens of bookkeepers busily, and accurately, producing financial statements. You type in every detail about your magazine—subscription price, number of pieces mailed, cost-per-thousand pieces mailed, date mailed, response time and quantity, percent credit, percent bad debt, response to renewal notices, conversion percent, renewal percent, etc., etc., etc., and the model grinds out issue-by-issue circulation, cashflow and profit and loss in any one of a dozen or so different reports.

The budget model can be almost as detailed as you like—subscriptions from twenty or thirty different sources, an expense listing for every staff member including when he or she gets a raise, office rental costs, paper and printing costs, photography and editorial costs, even consultants' invoices can all be plugged into the proper slots and will appear on the statements. Thus the model can be used for budgeting and, even better yet, as a wonderfully convincing business plan for venture capitalists or other potential investors because it gives your projections all the authority of a bank statement.

Of course the assumptions that go into the model such as the percentage response to a mailing, or the number of advertising pages you will sell, are yours to make and ultimately to live with. The budget model takes no responsibility for accuracy of the assumptions, only for accuracy in the arithmetic.

Budget models are good for start-up situations because they can tell you that, given your assumptions, maximum cash requirements will fall at a certain time and be of a given amount. This means you can estimate how much money the new magazine needs, and when. You will see how profitable it can be in time, or perhaps what sales level it needs to be profitable at all.

Budget models can also be used as strategy models. If you are reasonably confident of your input data you can run the projections over and over with, for example, a progressive change in response rate to a direct-mail campaign. As you lower the percentage from 4.0 percent to 3.75 percent you see how circulation is affected and the profitability of the mailing.

Or you can lower the number of advertising pages sold in steps and discover exactly how many are needed for break even. This gives you guidepost figures to watch as you actually live out the years. You'll know, for example, that with only 18.5 pages sold in each issue of the second year you'll be in the black, though maybe not yet paying off any of the original investment. Above 18.5 is gravy, below is trouble.

This approach uses a budget model as a strategic tool, and while it is not the most convenient of such tools it is certainly better than nothing. There are two reasons for the inconvenience. First, running budget models over and over takes time and, if a time-sharing system is used, is expensive. Second, you are required to put in the exact, and often far-reaching, consequences of every change.

For example, if you are exploring a change in subscription price you can expect that as the price is increased the subscription response will fall. As the circulation falls you may have to change the rate base guarantee to advertisers. Rate base changes may affect how much space advertisers buy. A change in the number of ad pages may change the look of the magazine to the reader. If you don't increase the number of editorial pages to compensate, the subscriber may be less willing to subscribe or renew. So a simple exploration of subscription price changes may have far-reaching consequences that are very difficult to keep track of in the budget model.

The Strategy Model

Which is why I turned to what other business planners use—a mathematical simulation of the magazine. The strategy model starts with a familiar equation:

$$\text{Profits} = \text{Revenues} - \text{Costs}$$

To find profits we need to be able to forecast our revenues month by month and year by year and our costs over the same periods. Start with the revenue streams and make a list of everything that has an impact on each revenue source. Advertising dollars, for example, are affected by:

1. number of advertising pages sold
2. price per page
3. ratio of color to black-and-white pages
4. rate base
5. competitors' prices
6. state of the economy or of this industry served
7. editorial climate
8. advertising promotion budget
9. number and quality of advertising salespeople
   etc., etc., etc.

In later chapters we will examine in detail every factor that can reasonably be expected to have an impact on the number of advertising dollars, on the number of subscription dollars, and on the number of single-copy sales dollars that flow, or could flow, into our corporate bank account.

We'll look at the three main revenue streams for a magazine and examine the most common factors that affect those streams. We'll look at the costs resulting from changes in circulation or advertising sales and then derive an estimate of profit.

How It Works

Let's look at a strategy model of a hypothetical magazine and see how it works. Assume that on this magazine we sell copies on the newsstand and by subscription and we also sell advertising pages. Total income from these sources is reduced by all the usual expenses—manufacturing, editorial staff and purchases, promotion dollars spent for subscriptions, for newsstand sales and for advertising, staff salaries for all these departments, administrative staff salaries and overhead, fulfillment, shipping, postage, etc. Some of these are fixed expenses—staff, overhead and editorial are not easy to change drastically or rapidly. Some are directly related to the number of copies printed. But all can be estimated and projected.

There is a difference between the kind of information you can forecast with reasonable assurance and that which is dependent on your ability to predict consumer behavior. The subscription manager will give us more (and more accurate) detail about subscriber response than any other sales division of the company, but how do newsstand sales respond to changing draw (the number of copies distributed)? To promotion effort? To the number of editorial pages? To the weather? Well, you simplify as much as possible and eliminate the unlikely, then you may turn a statistician loose on the historical data to see if cause-and-effect relationships can be found (see Chapter 8 on single-copy sales for an example of this analysis).

Similarly, for advertising pages sold, ask what really determines how many pages of advertising appear in your magazine each month or each year? Is it the rate base? The size of the sales force? Promotion dollars? You will make informed guesses and hold aside the factors you aren't sure of or want to explore later.

When all the numbers and relationships have been collected and built into a model it can be run to produce a table something like Table 4.1.

The publisher in this case had limited the analysis to just three decisions that had to be made for the coming year. The decisions were: Should the cover price remain $1 or be raised to $1.25 since manufacturing costs were going to increase about 10 percent next year? (We can assume that subscription price would automatically go up in proportion.) Should the newsstand draw be held at the current 150,000 copies or should it be raised or lowered? Should the subscription acquisition budget be increased from the current $400,000 level?

The table makes a profit prediction for every possible combination of the three variables. At the intersection of each cover price, draw, and subscripton acquisition budget there is a predicted profit for next year. A quick scan over the table indicates that maximum profits are $1,969,000 at a cover price of $1.25, a draw of 150,000, and a subscription acquisition budget of $800,000. Note that this is more than three times the $667,000 profit which would be earned if cover price, draw, and subscription acquisition budget were left at $1.00 cover, 150,000 draw, and $600,000 subscription acquisition budget!

Look at the top half of this table (the $1.00 cover price section) as if it were a contour map with mountains and valleys represented by the profits. There is a maximum profit at 150,000 draw and $800,000 subscription acquisition budget, of $1,704,000. The model that produced this table is telling us that profits can first be more than doubled by spending more to acquire more subscriptions, which permits a very profitable increase in the rate base. Profits can be further increased by raising the cover price to $1.25.

Now you must be asking all the right questions. How did the model decide on how circulation sales were affected by price? By draw? By how many subscriptions were brought in at each level of acquisition budget? What was the total circulation reached for each of these sets of decisions?

What about advertising?

These are exactly the questions that must be answered when the model is "built." In this case, we started with all the standard budget information about this magazine plus three critical relationships—an estimate of how newsstand sale changes with draw at each of the two price levels, and how the number of advertising pages would be affected by the rate base. Given this same data you could use pencil, paper and a hand calculator to find the maximum profit points and the strategy to reach them. It's just that it would take time and your calculations would be very prone to error.

You couldn't do it in your head—and if you are setting your strategy for next year and don't go through this sort of analysis you are, in effect, relying on intuition. You are saying that you can find the best strategy by guesswork or "feel," and maybe you can. Certainly there are many examples in publishing history when publishers seem to have made exactly the right decisions given far more complicated situations.

But we'll never know how much profit they could have made, will we?

NEXT YEAR'S PROFITS

Cover	Draw	Subscription Acquisition Budget			
		$400,000	$600,000	$800,000	$1,000,000
$1.00	50,000	-14,000	232,000	930,000	718,000
1.00	150,000	469,000	667,000	1,704,000	1,558,000
1.00	250,000	763,000	1,113,000	1,687,000	1,069,000
1.00	350,000	1,126,000	1,649,000	1,531,000	1,008,000
$1.25	50,000	14,000	302,000	1,195,000	991,000
1.25	150,000	536,000	726,000	1,969,000	1,664,000
1.25	250,000	812,000	1,268,000	1,741,000	1,114,000
1.25	350,000	1,257,000	1,257,000	1,694,000	1,034,000

Table 4.1 Profits are forecast for every combination of cover price, draw, and subscription acquisition budget.

Chapter 5

ADVERTISING

Advertising is usually the largest and therefore the most important revenue stream for a magazine. Our purpose at this stage is not necessarily to maximize the income from this source but to determine what factors influence the revenues. Some of the factors will be under the publisher's control and some will not. Factors not under the publisher's control are the "givens" of a situaton. If we know the givens and their impact, the factors that are controlled by the publisher can then be tuned to produce best performance by whatever criteria were previously established.

Under the pressures of managing a magazine from day to day, it is sometimes easy to forget that the driving force in any business is the customer, who is neglected only at great risk. The advertising buyer is a specialized kind of customer, but a customer nonetheless. The questions that follow identify the many decision makers involved in the sale of a single advertising page. Each has several motives, conscious and unconscious, that influence the decision—motives that will have to be considered fairly early in the strategic plan.

Who makes the purchase decision?

A number of different individuals have functional titles or positions that give them power over the decison to use, or not to use, your magazine in an advertising schedule—the account executive, the media analysts, the creative directors. There are the advertiser's own executives such as the product manager, the advertising director, the marketing director, and an entire hierarchy of top management to whom they report.

There are also the unseen influences—the spouses, friends and colleagues working for other agencies or with similar functions in other divisions of the company. There are the columnists and reporters who write for newspapers, newsletters, or magazines read by the advertiser or agency. All contribute to an impression of your magazine that has an impact on sales. It is this impression that publishers hope to influence when they buy space in the *New York Times, Advertising Age,* or the other magazines for the media, when they prepare rate cards or promotion pieces, and when they send their sales representatives out to make calls. It is the human and qualitative part of the selling equation.

On a more objective level, you must do a full-scale market analysis to understand your customers and their motivations. First, you must be able to define the market quite specifically. Is it defined by a leader in the field, by demographics, special interest, SIC classification, individuals or product types? How much money is being spent by advertisers to reach these readers? Is there enough to support the magazines that serve it? Is there a possibility of interesting new advertisers in the current or potential reading audience, or of increasing the investment now being made by existing advertisers by describing the audience in a different way?

As you have defined it, do you really want to be in this market?

Is the market segmentable? Is it growing or declining?

Specifically, who are the advertisers by company name and by category—liquor or tobacco, mail-order book or record clubs, perfume or toiletries, fashions, automobiles, insurance, airline companies. For trade magazines the federal Standard Industrial Classification (SIC) system may be useful because it will then be possible to make correlations between reported profits in these categories and the number of advertising pages or dollars carried by your magazine and its competitors. Make a list of the categories that run in your magazine as well as ones that might, but don't. We'll be referring to it again later.

Who is the customer for the products or services being advertised and what are the buying patterns of that customer? Is it a one-time purchase or a product that is bought repeatedly? How is the product or service actually sold to the customer? How is it distributed?

It is important to track how you share this advertising market with your competitors. There are services that provide such data customized to your specific group of magazines or for more general groups. But if it is a small group of three to five magazines, you can set up a simple computer spreadsheet which accumulates data in page counts and/or dollar estimates by magazine and by category (Table 5.1). Most computer spreadsheets today will also provide graphing capability so you can track performance trends (Figure 5.1).

As part of the market analysis you will want to examine the structure of this market. What is the frequency of advertising placement? Statisticians use something they call a histogram, which in this case is simply a count of the number of pages that run, say, 12 times, 11 times, 10 times, 9 times, etc. This can be an important determinant of what your publishing

12 months thru>	1/87	2/87	3/87	4/87	5/87	6/87
Magazine A						
Fashions	72.0	74.6	76.8	81.6	80.2	84.9
Food & Drink	28.7	33.7	35.7	40.6	38.6	38.0
Electronics	40.6	43.6	38.7	39.9	42.8	38.9
Total A	141.3	151.9	151.2	162.1	161.6	161.8
Magazine B						
Fashions	88.9	85.8	89.0	91.4	87.3	89.0
Food & Drink	100.3	102.8	110.1	98.7	99.0	105.3
Electronics	20.2	29.5	30.7	27.9	29.9	32.5
Total B	209.4	218.1	229.8	218.0	216.2	226.8
Magazine C						
Fashions	55.6	45.8	53.5	48.8	52.5	49.7
Food & Drink	49.9	48.6	53.5	52.2	51.6	53.8
Electronics	12.2	15.5	15.1	13.8	12.2	16.5
Total C	117.7	109.9	122.1	114.8	116.3	120.0
All Magazines						
Fashions	216.5	206.2	219.3	221.8	220.0	223.6
Food & Drink	178.9	185.1	199.3	191.5	189.2	197.1
Electronics	73.0	88.6	84.5	81.6	84.9	87.9
Total A+B+C	468.4	479.9	503.1	494.9	494.1	508.6
Magazine A						
Fashions	33.3%	36.2%	35.0%	36.8%	36.5%	38.0%
Food & Drink	16.0%	18.2%	17.9%	21.2%	20.4%	19.3%
Electronics	55.6%	49.2%	45.8%	48.9%	50.4%	44.3%
Total A	30.2%	31.7%	30.1%	32.8%	32.7%	31.8%
Magazine B						
Fashions	41.1%	41.6%	40.6%	41.2%	39.7%	39.8%
Food & Drink	56.1%	55.5%	55.2%	51.5%	52.3%	53.4%
Electronics	27.7%	33.3%	36.3%	34.2%	35.2%	37.0%
Total B	44.7%	45.4%	45.7%	44.0%	43.8%	44.6%
Magazine C						
Fashions	25.7%	22.2%	24.4%	22.0%	23.9%	22.2%
Food & Drink	27.9%	26.3%	26.8%	27.3%	27.3%	27.3%
Electronics	16.7%	17.5%	17.9%	16.9%	14.4%	18.8%
Total C	25.1%	22.9%	24.3%	23.2%	23.5%	23.6%

Table 5.1 A section of a spreadsheet used to accumulate page counts on three magazines in each of three categories. Advertising pages for each issue are added month by month and then accumulated in the moving twelve month total shown here. Market shares are calculated by category and then graphed to show trends. Here Magazine A is increasing its share of fashion advertising at the expense of magazine C.

Advertising

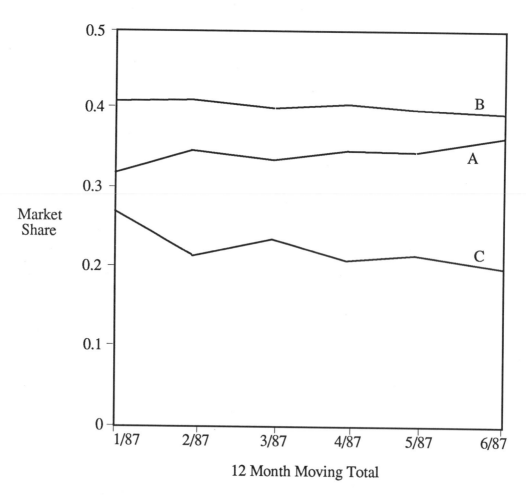

Figure 5.1   Market shares of fashion advertising in three magazines have drifted slightly over the course of this graph.   Magazine A is increasing its share at the expense of magazine C.   The graph was created by the spreadsheet program from data in Table 5.1

Advertising

frequency can afford to be. If you are publishing nine or ten times a year and all your advertisers are taking six time schedules or less, you would probably lose very little space by reducing your publishing frequency to bimonthly and readers might not notice—at a considerable reduction in manufacturing and postage costs.

The structure also includes the size, color and placement of advertising. Are most of the advertisements full page, four-color? Do the competitors get all the large display ads and you get the small mail order stuff? If so why? Note that it isn't necessarily bad. You can make a lot of profits out of small space and get good and loyal readership as well. I only insist that it be a conscious decision—recognition of the way things are and an attempt to make use of the facts.

The advertising analysis should take a hard look at advertising profitability as well. To this end I recommend a very simple spreadsheet based on exactly the same structure as the rate card. A typical rate card looks something like Table 5.2.

The same structure can be used to review a magazine's advertising sales. In Table 5.3 the number of pages carried during the last twelve months replaces the price per page.

By multiplying the numbers in Table 5.2 by the numbers in Table 5.3, you take the pages times the page rate and get the gross revenues earned by each frequency of insertion and ad size. A few keystrokes, therefore, can produce Table 5.4.

Table 5.4 is a contour map of where your gross advertising sales are coming from. It is dependent on the kind of advertising market you are serving, but it will also be modified by the kind of magazine you are producing editorially and in the make up of its readership. Again, it is easy to jump to the conclusion that more color and larger insertion sizes are automatically better. That is a value judgement not necessarily borne out by the facts.

The next logical step is to accumulate costs relating to each cell in this table. Paper, printing and binding are almost totally dependent on the size of the space—a quarter-page ad costs one quarter of a full page to manufacture. But other costs related to the selling of the space may be dependent on the total revenues (commissions) or on the manner of selling (phone or personal calls). Admittedly, it is arbitrary, but some such allocation of costs can be made and subtracted from the revenues to produce a profit contribution (Table 5.5).

Now we have a contour map of profits. Clearly, the discount structure in the rate card,which provides reduced costs for the 6, 9, and 12 times b/w

ADVERTISING RATECARD

B/W	1 Time	3 Time	6 Time	9 Time	12 Time
1 Page	1500.00	1350.00	1125.00	975.00	900.00
2/3 Page	1050.00	945.00	787.50	682.50	630.00
1/2 Page	900.00	810.00	675.00	585.00	540.00
1/3 Page	600.00	540.00	450.00	390.00	360.00
1/4 Page	450.00	405.00	337.50	292.50	270.00
1/6 Page	300.00	270.00	225.00	195.00	180.00

4/C	1 Time	3 Time	6 Time	9 Time	12 Time
1 Page	1950.00	1755.00	1462.50	1267.50	1170.00
2/3 Page	1365.00	1228.50	1023.75	887.25	819.00
1/2 Page	1170.00	1053.00	877.50	760.50	702.00
1/3 Page	780.00	702.00	585.00	507.00	468.00
1/4 Page	585.00	526.50	438.75	380.25	351.00
1/6 Page	390.00	351.00	292.50	253.50	234.00

Table 5.2   A typical advertising ratecard shows the cost per page for insertion orders by freqeuncy, size and coloration.

ADVERTISING PAGES

B/W	1 Time	3 Time	6 Time	9 Time	12 Time
1 Page	50.00	45.00	37.50	32.50	30.00
2/3 Page	40.67	36.60	30.50	26.44	24.40
1/2 Page	30.50	27.45	22.88	19.83	18.30
1/3 Page	29.33	26.40	22.00	19.06	17.60
1/4 Page	13.00	11.70	9.75	8.45	7.80
1/6 Page	18.17	16.35	13.63	11.81	10.90

4/C	1 Time	3 Time	6 Time	9 Time	12 Time
1 Page	65.00	58.50	48.75	42.25	39.00
2/3 Page	45.50	40.95	34.13	29.58	27.30
1/2 Page	39.00	35.10	29.25	25.35	23.40
1/3 Page	26.00	23.40	19.50	16.90	15.60
1/4 Page	19.50	17.55	14.63	12.68	11.70
1/6 Page	13.00	11.70	9.75	8.45	7.80

Table 5.3 Each cell of this spreadsheet carries the number of pages sold in that size, frequency, and coloration.

Advertising

GROSS REVENUES

B/W	1 Time	3 Time	6 Time	9 Time	12 Time
1 Page	$75,000	$60,750	$42,188	$31,688	$27,000
2/3 Page	$42,704	$34,590	$24,021	$18,042	$15,373
1/2 Page	$27,450	$22,235	$15,441	$11,598	$9,882
1/3 Page	$17,598	$14,254	$9,899	$7,435	$6,335
1/4 Page	$5,850	$4,739	$3,291	$2,472	$2,106
1/6 Page	$5,451	$4,415	$3,066	$2,303	$1,962

4/C	1 Time	3 Time	6 Time	9 Time	12 Time
1 Page	$126,750	$102,668	$71,297	$53,552	$45,630
2/3 Page	$62,108	$50,307	$34,935	$26,240	$22,359
1/2 Page	$45,630	$36,960	$25,667	$19,279	$16,427
1/3 Page	$20,280	$16,427	$11,408	$8,568	$7,301
1/4 Page	$11,408	$9,240	$6,417	$4,820	$4,107
1/6 Page	$5,070	$4,107	$2,852	$2,142	$1,825

Table 5.4 Gross revenues are calculated by multiplying the page rate by the number of pages.

NET REVENUES

B/W	1 Time	3 Time	6 Time	9 Time	12 Time
1 Page	$8,750	$3,488	($2,578)	($5,403)	($6,450)
2/3 Page	$6,067	$2,962	($654)	($2,371)	($3,022)
1/2 Page	$5,643	$3,472	$886	($392)	($897)
1/3 Page	$3,617	$2,226	$568	($251)	($575)
1/4 Page	$1,203	$740	$189	($83)	($191)
1/6 Page	$1,121	$690	$176	($78)	($178)

4/C	1 Time	3 Time	6 Time	9 Time	12 Time
1 Page	$30,388	$19,934	$7,343	$1,009	($1,540)
2/3 Page	$16,103	$10,860	$4,508	$1,283	($27)
1/2 Page	$14,060	$9,984	$4,983	$2,391	$1,317
1/3 Page	$6,249	$4,437	$2,215	$1,063	$585
1/4 Page	$3,515	$2,496	$1,246	$598	$329
1/6 Page	$1,562	$1,109	$554	$266	$146

Table 5.5 Costs are subtracted from revenues to produce a profit contribution which varies dramatically over the range of frequencies and space size.

Advertising

buyers, are actually costing the magazine money. If this is intentional as a loss leader to bring in these desirable pages, that's fine. But if it comes as a surprise to the publisher, critical reconsideration of the rate card structure is very much in order. Either the overall rates should be increased or the discount made much less severe.

Why do they buy?

If it is a product or service being advertised the facile answer is—sell the product or service. But we won't stop there. Each of the influencers identified by the "who" question will have at least three motives—a personal as well as two or more professional motives operating when a decision is being made.

This is where great sales presentations are made because whether subtly or openly, you must address the "why" when you are selling a campaign.

Let's skip the deeper swamps of psychological motivation. Simply put, the advertiser wants to tell potential customers about a product, service or company. If it is a product the message may be price, quality or features. It may be the sizzle—not the steak—that does the selling job. It may be implied that the product will make the owner sexier, more beautiful or more powerful. You need to know how the advertiser is selling the product and how the messages work in the atmosphere created by your magazine.

Less obvious motivations are also important. When an advertiser's competitor is in your magazine there is considerable reason for him to be there. Agencies have an easier time recommending a magazine when it appears to be hot and growing rapidly. To turn around a magazine that is skidding requires overcoming a negative impression in the advertising community that may have nothing to do with how many readers love you.

Several of these "why" factors are quantitative and we'll be examining them in detail later. They include: the impact of the rate base (the minimum number of buyers the publisher guarantees will see each issue); the advertising page cost-per-thousand readers within specific demographic groups such as ages 18 to 34, or females, or households with incomes over a certain level; the magazine's own advertising promotion budget or sales budget; the state of the economy—and so on.

In sum, the combination of the "who" and the "why" will tell you almost everything you need to know about the salability of the magazine as an advertising medium. You might also give passing thought to the "why not?" question—why does this category of advertisers not buy the magazine, why do media analysts not recommend it?

What will change in the future, and when?

Near future depends a lot on near past. The advertising space you carry may depend on last year's promotion efforts, the success or failure of a particular advertiser's campaign, or the personality of a new advertising director or sales representative.

Looking into the more distant future means considering lifestyle changes of the advertiser's customers and your readers. You should be able to identify which are the growing and which are the faltering advertising categories, companies and agencies. If a large percentage of your advertisers are in fading industries it may be time to consider a change, or at least a repositioning, of your magazine to be of interest to a new group of potential advertisers.

How does the economy affect advertising sales in general and your category of magazine in particular? It has been conventional wisdom in the magazine business that magazine advertising rises and falls with the economy, but the results are delayed by six months to a year. I have never seen reliable correlations with any of the standard economic indicators. Unemployment statistics and gross national product don't move in swings as wide as advertising pages, and housing starts and disposable income are relatively unrelated to advertising. But it turns out that corporate profits are the key. Figure 5.2 shows that advertising in national magazines going to the consumer public closely parallels corporate profits.

The two lines are remarkably similar and, even more interesting, the advertising pages do lag reported profits by a year. When you think about it, this is a very logical relationship. When corporate profits are down the company pulls in its horns and reduces spending in the easiest way—advertising budgets. But it takes a little time for this to be seen in actual pages at the magazine. Similarly, when profits are up the company feels a little more bullish and opens the purse strings to advertising.

We argue in vain that the time to build market share is when times are tough and competitors are being tightfisted. It is interesting to note that we are guilty of the same tactics—when our own magazine revenues decline we reduce sales and promotion expenses in a desperate attempt to hold on to near-term profits at the expense of long-term gains.

Not all magazines serve national markets, so if profits are to be the forecasting tool you must pay particular attention to profits reported by the industry you serve. Some industries are counterrecessionary. You can expect that advertising in magazines serving these industries will be counterrecessionary as well.

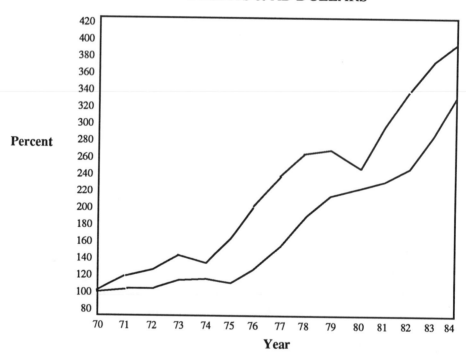

PROFITS & AD DOLLARS

Figure 5.2 Annual advertising page counts for a group of large national magazines closely follows corporate profits reported by the Department of Commerce, but lags by approximately one year.

Advertising

Who are the competitors?

They can be thought of in a series of concentric circles. Closest in the series are the direct magazine competitors whose editorial and advertising appeal is similar to yours. Then come other magazines or newspapers in which your customers spend advertising dollars to extend their voice to other audiences. Then there are the other places where advertisers spend promotional dollars—in direct mail, radio or television, sales staff and sales literature, conferences and exhibits, hospitality suites or educational seminars. Even training courses or public relations staffs may cut into an advertising budget and ultimately your revenues.

The longer your list of competitors, the larger the potential market in which you are selling. This has good and bad aspects: The larger the total market the more there is for you to go after; however, there is evidence that company profits are directly correlated with market share, that is, the companies that have larger market shares tend to have larger profits both in percent of sales and in absolute quantities. But many corporate strategists expect that better profits will result from concentrating sales efforts on more narrowly defined markets.

What do they offer?

Each sales medium has advantages, and within each medium the competitors are different—different in what they are and different in the way they sell themselves. Each is regarded differently by the advertising agency or company, and you may find it a useful research exercise to ask your customers for their frank opinions of the differences between you and your competitors.

You cannot make a meaningful plan without knowing how customers and competitors regard themselves and the other companies serving the same market. To the advertiser a magazine is first, a pipeline, a vehicle which carries a message to a reading audience; and second, an editorial atmosphere that will color the message. Each magazine has a different audience: How does it actually differ demographically and psycho-graphically? How does that magazine's sales staff say it differs? Does their pitch better fit the purchase motives of the buyer than yours? Is your sales approach well fitted to the goals you settled on earlier?

Is the competition changing?

Both in terms of who competes in this market and how they compete, you should ask if the competition is different now than it was in the past and will it be even more different in the future? When is all of this going to happen?

These questions shouldn't be answered only qualitatively. Competitors can be measured in terms of numbers of pages, or dollars of sales. If you have tracked market share, as was suggested earlier, you will have a good sense of the trends by magazine and by category of advertiser.

Make a table of data for your own magazine and each direct competitor, listing the advertising pages and dollars sold year by year, advertising pages by category, by proportion of color to black-and-white, by proportion of full page to part page, rate base, cost-per-thousand circulation, size of sales staff and advertising promotion. Perhaps ratios will be useful, such as promotion spent per advertising page or per dollar of advertising sales, advertising revenues per sales person, advertising pages per sales person, editorial pages per advertising page.

We are looking for cause-and-effect relationships. Why does one category of advertiser prefer this magazine and another prefer a different one? Do most of the numbers group themselves within a narrow range or are there seemingly random differences among the competitors? Is the magazine with the largest market share known to be the one with the maximum profits? Are there specific things a competitor is doing that seem to account for the success?

Our intention is to discover and consciously examine every factor that has an effect on the number of advertising pages sold next year and on to the planning horizon. Some of the factors will be strictly qualitative, coming as answers to questions we have asked. For example, when *Sports Illustrated* started to speak of itself as "the third newsweekly," it put itself in a different market and one that would appeal to a larger group of advertisers. Or when *Fortune* became biweekly after many years as a monthly, it changed its image and potential advertising base. Later, you may attempt to quantify the impact of all these factors, but there are a few that are obviously and naturally quantitative. We'll spend a little time now looking at these and deciding how to deal with them.

Cost per thousand circulation (CPM)

The cost per thousand is a measure an advertiser uses to gage the efficiency of an advertising medium. It is one of the few factors that permit comparison, albeit a limited one, of such different media as television, magazines and newspapers.

There are many CPMs, even for a single magazine. There is the four-color one-page CPM, which is the cost of a single insertion of a four-color page divided by the rate base in thousands. Or the CPM may be a black-and-white one-page CPM—the cost of a black-and-white page divided by the rate base in thousands. It may be narrowed to a single characteristic of a reading audience, such as the four-color CPM of personnel directors who read a particular business magazine, or the four-color CPM of readers in a defined zip code. For simplicity we will consider the one-page black-and-white cost per thousand as representative of a magazine's overall rate structure, because it is from this keystone number that the entire ratecard is usually built.

Our question is, how does the CPM affect the number of advertising pages sold if everything else is held constant? This is a very important limitation. We don't want to confuse the issue by allowing any of the other factors to change while we consider the first.

When examining factors quantitatively it is usually helpful first to look at the extremes of a range—a CPM of zero, or at a level ten times that of competitors. Once you have the extremes of a cause-and-effect relationship it is usually easy to sketch in the way the relationship progresses between the extremes.

Response to CPM levels is similar to the response any consumer makes to the price of a product. At the very low prices there is a limit established by the size of the market—the number of advertisers interested in reaching your audience. So a CPM near zero will generate some maximum number of advertising pages.

At the high end of CPM there will be a few diehard advertisers reluctant to stop buying space no matter how expensive the space is, until finally, at some very high price, you do lose everyone. In between, we can expect first a slow fall-off of sales (in pages) as the CPM is raised, and then a more precipitous drop as the price moves into, and past, the competitive range.

The CPM elasticity curve will, therefore, be shaped something like that shown in Figure 5.3. What we need to do for our model is to "fit" a curve of this shape to specific data about our magazine. For example, suppose the

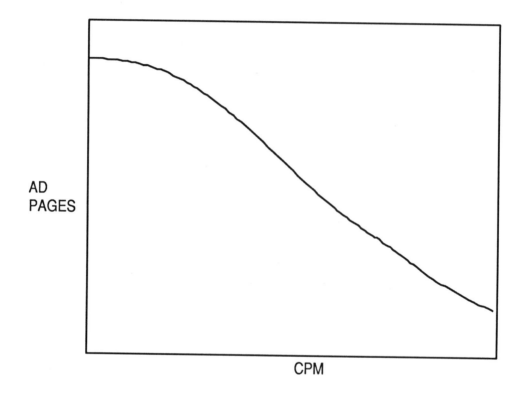

Figure 5.3 As advertising cost per thousand (CPM) increases the number of advertising pages sold is likely to decline in a typical elasticity curve which rounds slowly to approach zero pages at very high CPMs.

CPM for the coming year has been set at $25.00 and the magazine is expected to carry 1,000 pages of advertising. That gives us one "point," or pair of values for our curve. You set up a graph with coordinates of CPM along the X axis, and number of advertising pages along the Y axis. Mark the point on the graph that indicates the intersection of $25.00 CPM and 1,000 pages of advertising. You can now imagine that the curve in Figure 5.3 is pushed down, or to the right, so that it traces through the plotted point.

We will also want two more points to fit our curve more exactly to our data. Now you must consult the advertising director, space salespeople, your own intuition based on your assessment of the market, the number of complaints you have had about your advertising prices and a crystal ball. You must ask yourself and your "cabinet" of senior staff members what would happen to the number of advertising pages sold if the CPM were raised to $30.

Initially, you may get a lot of resistance from advertising space salespeople to the very thought of so large an increase in CPM. Or you will get comments such as, "That would be disastrous!" or, "We wouldn't sell a single page!" But be persistent, because without this estimate of how CPM affects the number of advertising pages we are left with unquantified feelings of discomfort with a given price level, and it is precisely the transformation of such feelings into quantified data that is our goal in model building.

Remember, too, that we are not saying that the CPM will be moved up to $30 or $35. It is much too early to know where our maximum profits will fall. But to find that optimum CPM we need an estimate of how serious a loss in pages will result from prices at these levels. If the advertising director says you will lose 200 pages of space at the $30 price, and if you agree that that is a fair assessment, fine.

As a parenthetical note, you must be pushing prices against the resistance of advertisers or you will never reach optimum profits. In other words, if you aren't hearing a few complaints about your prices you can be sure you are underpriced—assuming maximizing profits is the objective. As a further illustration of this fact, suppose we have a magazine with 100,000 rate base, $25 CPM, and sell 1,000 pages of advertising. Suppose that if the CPM were raised to $30, the advertising director predicts a loss of 200 pages of advertising. Which would be more profitable, the $25 CPM or the $30 CPM?

Note that the total revenues in both instances are fairly close. At the $25 CPM and 100,000 rate base, the price per page is $2,500 and total revenue is 1000 pages times $2,500, or $2.5 million. At the $30 CPM the price per page is $3,000, the total revenue is 800 pages times $3,000, or $2.4 million. But a magazine that carries 200 fewer pages is bound to be cheaper to print, bind and mail, and the savings in manufacturing cost will probably compensate for the $100,000 loss in gross revenues. Thus, it is likely that the higher CPM will produce more profits despite the fewer total advertising pages.

Getting your advertising director to see this and to understand that the driving force is profits, not pages, can be an illuminating experience for you both. You want your advertising director to have the same goal you have. Ideally, commissions and bonuses are also structured to produce the proper incentive.

Advertiser reaction to price will depend on what competitors do when you make your change. If it is anticipated that you will lose 200 pages with a CPM going from $25 to $30, and the competitors make no change in their prices, then if competitors make proportionate changes in their prices you won't look quite so far out of line and you will probably lose less. Thus, two curves may be drawn depending on what strategy the competitors use in response to your price change.

Advertiser reaction will also change with time; that is, the initial reaction to a price increase may follow the curve exactly, but as the advertiser becomes accustomed to the new price, and as inflation changes prices of other magazines and competing media, the impact may disappear and you will find the advertiser buying at the same rate as before the change.

Curve fitting

This process of finding the equation of a curve that goes through two or more specific data points is called "curve fitting." The basic character of the relationship between the two factors is determined by a mathematical form. The equation is made specific to given points by values calculated for constants or "coefficients."

The equation form I use for price elasticities is that of the "normal" curve—so named because it represents a statistical relationship often found in nature, such as the distribution of men's heights about the mean (Figure 5.4). Mathematically the equation is written:

$$\text{AD PAGES} = a/\exp((\text{CPM}-c)^2/b)$$

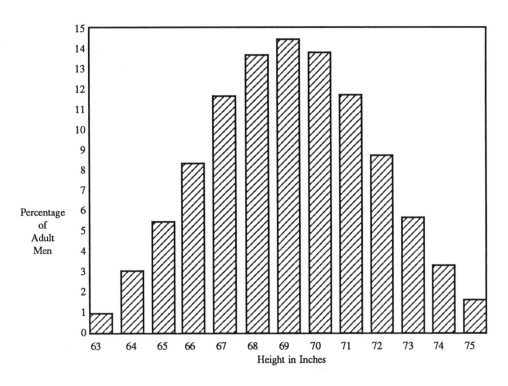

Figure 5.4 The normal curve is the probability distribution of an event such as the percentage of men who fall within various height ranges.

Advertising

We are using computer notation for this equation where "/" means divide; "^" means raise to the following power; "exp" means raise the constant 2.71828 to the power in parentheses immediately following, and "a," "b," and "c" are constant coefficients.

The exact coefficients to shape this curve to trace through three given points can be found using fairly simple mathematics or, more easily still, using a curve fitting program.

The equation for the following data:

CPM	No. Ad Pages
25.00	1000
30.00	800
35.00	615

is approximately:

$$\text{AD PAGES} = 1{,}700/\exp((\text{CPM} - 0.5)\char94 2/1{,}250)$$

Thus the coefficients are: a = 1,700; b = 1,250; c = 0.5

Note that by adjusting the values of these three coefficients, a wide range points can be fitted so long as the Y values (ad pages) move down while the X values (price) move up.

See Appendix A for program listings that can be entered into any computer with a BASIC language interpreter to fit curves to your data. See Appendix C for information on how to buy a compiled and packaged program for this purpose.

Rate base

In a paid-circulation magazine the rate base or guarantee, is the minimum number of readers who have paid to receive the magazine. In a controlled- circulation magazine the rate base is the minimum number of readers who have been, or are expected to be, qualified by a signed statement stating their titles and companies, and that they wish to continue receiving the publication.

Usually the rate base is set a small amount below the average of six months or a year's issues, so that if a single issue drops below the rate base no penalty is involved, though an advertiser in that issue is likely to feel cheated. Most major magazines have their rate base audited and certified by the Audit Bureau of Circulations (ABC) for consumer magazines, or The Business Publishers' Audit (BPA) for business or trade magazines, both of which have strict rules about who counts as a bona fide reader and who does not.

A magazine without single-copy sales is in a good position to know precisely how many copies will be delivered over the coming budget year. If there are substantial single-copy sales through newsstands, supermarkets, etc., the number of copies of any issue sold may differ enough to pull the total issue count below the rate base.

In any case, our question is, how does rate base alone affect the number of advertising pages sold? Again, let's think about the extremes. At the lowest levels of rate base a magazine is really too small to be of interest to many advertisers. It simply doesn't expose enough people to the message to be worth bothering about. This is particularly true for the large national advertisers seeking mass audiences who have extremely wide-ranging advertising campaigns and will buy space in almost any national magazine and many regional magazines—but only if the circulation is above 200,000.

As the rate base rises above the minimum levels, therefore, the magazine becomes more and more a factor in the marketplace and attracts new categories and amounts of space. As the rate base continues to rise into the hundreds of thousands and millions, it reaches a level where the raw cost of a page (remember, we are holding the CPM constant in this analysis, so a higher rate base produces proportionately higher page rates) goes so high as to begin to discourage the smaller advertisers. Eventually, as with any price-sensitive market, the magazine page costs are so high as to eliminate all but the very largest advertisers—some of the large women's magazines, plus *TV Guide, and Reader's Digest* are good examples of magazines whose circulations are near or over ten million and whose page rates average close to one hundred thousand dollars.

The curve shape of advertising pages versus rate base therefore is going to look like a mountain—the number of advertising pages rises from a very low value at low rate bases, to a maximum, and then declines. It is important to realize that maximum profits are not achieved at the rate base that produces maximum page sales—the top of the mountain. If the CPM and the manufacturing cost per page are properly related, maximum profits are going to be achieved at a higher rate base when page sales are beginning

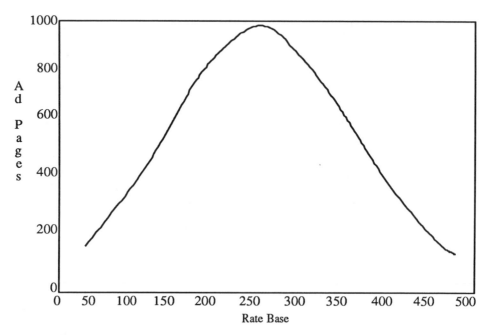

Figure 5.5 As the ratebase grows the magazine becomes of more interest to a larger market of advertisers and so the ad pages will increase. But higher ratebases mean higher pagerates and eventually the pages become too expensive except for the large national advertisers so page counts start to decrease.

to fall, but not as quickly as the rate base (and price per page) are increasing.

Different markets put the peak and the steeper slopes of this mountain at different rate bases. If a smooth curve is anticipated for this market the normal curve may be used as the generic shape (Figure 5.5).

The normal curve for the following data:

Rate base	No. Ad Pages
90,000	900
150,000	1200
200,000	1050

would take these coefficients:

$$\text{AD PAGES} = 1{,}200/\exp((RB - 155)^2/15{,}000)$$

But the normal curve is very smooth and perfectly symmetrical which may not be a good representation for your magazine. A more generalized equation form is provided by the polynomial equation which looks like this:

$$\text{AD PAGES} = a + b * RB + c * RB^2 + d * RB^3 + \ldots$$

Here, "*" is the computer symbol for multiplication; "^" means raise to the following power; "RB" is the rate base; and "a," "b," "c," and "d," are coefficients. The dots at the end of this equation indicate that you may add still higher powers of rate base to get a better fit, but note that if there are four coefficients you will need four sets of data. If there are five, you will need five sets of data, etc.

Suppose your data was similar to the table above with the addition of one point at a rate base of 100,000:

Rate base	No. Ad Pages
90,000	900
100,000	975
150,000	1,200
200,000	1,050

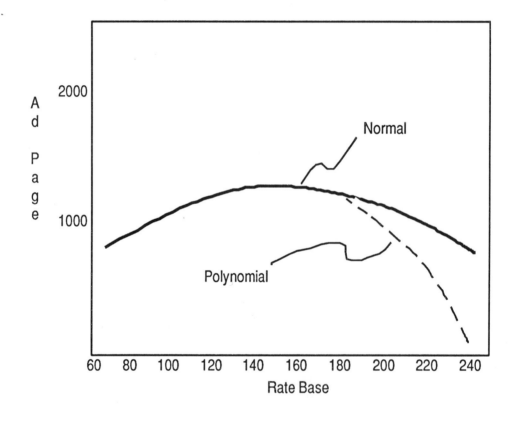

Figure 5.6 A normal curve applied to rate base data tops out at 1200 pages when the rate base is 150,000. Here two curves are shown — one fitted with a normal curve; the other with a polynomial.

Advertising

The polynomial fitted to this data would be:

AD PAGES = 82 + 8.5 * RB + .027 * RB^2 + .00023 * RB^3

You can see the two curves drawn in Figure 5.6. Over the range of given data the curves are almost identical. Where they separate is beyond the 200,000 rate base level when the normal curve is much flatter (over 600 pages at 260,000 rate base) and will never reach zero, while the polynomial plunges to 135 pages at 250,000 rate base and 0 pages by 260,000 rate base.

So the polynomial form can match any set of data you provide, though it may have to go through some strange contortions to do so. The disadvantage is that beyond the range of entered data the polynomial can sweep up or down to totally unrealistic extremes.

Marketing and Sales Promotion

There are basically three different kinds of sales costs to be considered. The simplest is the fee taken by a sales representative. Usually it is a fixed percentage of the net advertising revenue and therefore cannot itself be expected to raise or lower the number of advertising pages sold. However, the amount of the percentage may be assumed to function as an incentive and one could draw a curve, or at least make a qualitative note, to the effect that a higher percentage paid to the sales representative may increase the number of advertising pages sold.

The second areas of sales cost is for advertising staff salaries, expense accounts, office space, secretarial assistance, fringe benefits, etc. It is a worthwhile exercise to calculate the sales per staff member by category or territory. A very small staff must impose limits on the number of pages sold, conversely a large staff spends a lot of time talking to itself. In true point-of-diminishing returns fashion, each incremental salesperson produces a smaller and smaller increment in advertising income.

Promotion effort is the third kind of sales cost. Media advertising, hospitality suites and conventions, media kits, brochures and rate cards, all follow a similar point-of-diminishing returns curve in their impact on advertising pages sold. Assume last year's budget was halfway up this curve. An increment of a number of dollars of promotional effort will produce a certain number of pages of additional advertising. A second increment in promotion of the same amount will produce another increment in space sold, but the space increment gets smaller and smaller for each increment in promotion.

At the very low levels of promotion the curve may take one of several shapes. It can be argued that even if the promotion level is zero, the magazine will still sell some pages because the advertising market has some experience with the magazine and its capabilities as a sales medium. In that case, the curve curves to the left and intersects the left axis above zero. One might also decide that the first few dollars of promotion expense are for writing or preparation costs of sales literature, and that there is some minimum expenditure that must be made before even the first additional advertising page is sold.

The most general form of the equation of this curve is one that is found very frequently in nature:

$$\text{AD PAGES} = a + b * (1 - 1/\exp(\text{MARKETING}/c))^d$$

Here, "*" is multiplication, "^" is an exponent, "exp" is the constant 2.71828 to be raised to the power in parentheses, and "a," "b," "c," and "d" are constants that shape the curve to fit your specific data. We will need four sets of data points to fit this curve, though one can be the number of ad pages sold when the marketing is zero.

Let's say the sales promotion budget was $100,000 last year and the magazine carried 1,000 pages of advertising. The advertising director wants a budget of $125,000 this year. How does the publisher respond? The obvious question is, what do we get for the additional $25,000? The advertising director says, "maybe 25 pages." We now have two points on the curve.

We need two more pairs of data. One pair might be the number of ad pages that would be sold if the promotion budget were reduced to zero. Let's say they agree that the advertisers would buy at least 500 pages even if no money were spent on advertising promotion. The advertising director might also estimate that they would buy 1,040 pages if the promotion budget were increased to $150,000.

Ad Prom	Ad Pages
$ 0	500
100,000	1000
125,000	1025
150,000	1040

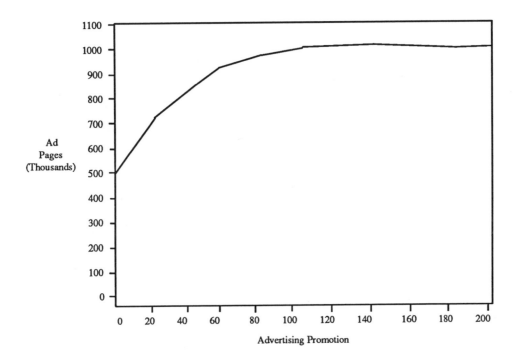

Figure 5.7 The diminishing returns curve fitted to advertising promotion data provided.

Advertising

The equation of the curve that would be fitted to these data is shown in Figure 5.7.

$$\text{AD PAGES} = 500 + 562 * (1 - 1/\exp(\text{SALES PROM}/50))^{0.82}$$

Where is the best place to be on a curve of this shape? You can't be sure at this point in the analysis. Not until all the various relationships are combined in the total strategic model will we be able to make that decision with any degree of accuracy. However, in this case you may want to try a quick estimate. Note that for an additional $25,000 in advertising promotion the advertising director expects to sell 25 more pages. Is the profit generated from the sale of the 25 pages more than the $25,000 it cost to sell them? If it is, then it pays to make the investment. If it is not, you may want to consider reducing the budget.

The profit generated by 25 additional pages of advertising may not be easy to calculate. Are they four-color or black-and-white pages? What are the discounts applied to these pages? What are the actual sales costs, commissions, etc? What does it cost in paper and printing to add these pages to our magazines? Were the editors required to add editorial pages in the issues in which the ads appeared? What is the cost of these additional editorial pages in paper, printing, contributor expenses, editorial salaries and overhead?

You may be surprised to discover that the net income doesn't cover the promotion expense, and that if editorial pages have to be added you are actually losing money on each additional advertising page sold! This can happen but is often overlooked because the editorial pages and production costs appear on a separate accounting statement.

This is likely to happen only when the magazine attracts a large number of advertising pages in certain issues—December for the holiday selling season, or September when people come back from vacations. These fat issues require an increase in editorial pages that may effectively double the paper and printing cost attributable to the extra advertising pages. Losses may be experienced when the additional advertising pages come from advertisers who buy large schedules and any increase in their schedules is with pages that earn still deeper discounts.

One solution is to raise all rates so that the advertiser pays for the cost not only of the page the advertisement is printed on, but the facing editorial material as well, or to make sure that the high frequency discounts are not so deep as to make the page unprofitable. Another option is to raise rates generally and then offer discounts to advertisers who use the less popular issues—July or August, for example.

Frequency

It is amazing how often publishers forget that the frequency of a publication is not set in concrete but may be changed if that will improve profits. Let us first look at frequency from a readership standpoint, then from its impact on advertising, and finally as an economic decision.

The natural frequency of readership for news-oriented magazines and newsletters is weekly—slower than the newspapers, but frequent enough not to be easily dated by passing events.

It is my conviction that the natural frequency of readership for special interest magazines and newsletters is fortnightly. Research indicates that most readers will have spent as much time with a magazine as they are going to within two weeks of receipt or purchase. If it is a magazine of particular interest, the reader will be ready for another issue every two weeks. This explains how two or more monthlies can acquire large and often highly duplicated audiences covering the same material. Readers are eager for more information and a second magazine is welcomed.

It may seem a contradiction, but it is true that the reader who responds to a subscription offer is rarely sensitive to the number of issues to be received in a year. She will be more concerned about the size of the check she has to write than the cost per copy. Thus, $19.95 for a one-year, six-issue subscription is going to be a much easier sale than $39.95 for a one-year, twelve-issue subscription.

And advertising will not always support a high frequency. The publisher must look hard at the way the advertising is distributed by frequency of insertion. The analysis done for rate card construction (see Table 5.3 and the discussion earlier in this chapter) will serve very well for decisions about frequency.

How many twelve-time contracts does the magazine carry? How many 24, 36, 52? Would an advertiser now in every issue of a monthly want to be in every issue of a biweekly or weekly? Are there enough such additional advertising pages to pay for the cost of creating, printing, and mailing the additional copies?

There are many monthly magazines on the market today that would be much more profitable if they were published six or eight times a year. The sacrifice at lower frequencies is in reader loyalty—it is hard to develop a reading habit on a bimonthly frequency. Renewal rates may be a little lower, but not so low as to make the six-time frequency a loser.

So the economics tend to prefer lower frequencies unless there is clear evidence that the editorial concept demands more frequent publication and that the advertiser will support it.

Factors Review

The list of factors that influence advertising sales can be extended almost indefinitely, but every magazine will be more or less responsive to the following:

External Factors:

1. state of the economy
2. profits experienced by the industry served
3. competitors' prices
4. competitors' rate bases
5. competitors' promotion
6. syndicated research findings

Internal Factors:

1. editorial image
2. cost per thousand
3. rate base
4. size and competence of sales staff
5. incentives to sales staff
6. discount structure
7. sales position or stance
8. size and competence of sales promotion campaign
9. frequency
10. quality of printing, paper, editorial content

Chapter 6

SUBSCRIPTIONS

Newsletters and certain specialized magazines depend entirely on subscriptions for their income. For many other magazines, subscription income is at the least a second important revenue source after advertising. So we will certainly want to know as much about the subscriber as we did about the advertiser; however, while the advertising buyer is relatively easy to describe and locate, the subscriber may be difficult to locate in a large population of potential readers.

For example, what psychographic or demographic characteristics differentiate the buyer of a high fidelity magazine except that he or she buys a subscription to the magazine? Or, what mailing lists would be most appropriate for a subscription to *Games* magazine that is full of pencil and paper challenges to the reader? The ideal reader could have any level of education, could be a blue-collar worker or a professional, could live in an upscale neighborhood or a slum. To find the universe of subscribers to such a magazine you might seek customers of adult games manufacturers, but these manufacturers don't sell direct to consumers and their retailers usually don't maintain mailing lists for rental. You might explore the catalog houses if they would be willing to select out the purchasers of adult games. The only other alternative is to go for a broad sweep of potential readers such as one of the large magazine sales agencies, but the response rate is likely to be relatively low.

Yet, the description of the reader, or at least a clearly definable interest of the reader, is essential if you intend to sell the subscription and then turn around and sell the reading time of the acquired audience to the advertiser. After all, that is the essential strategy as seen from the point of view of the advertising director, and often of the publisher and shareholder—to entice a reader to spend time with a publication so that they may, in turn, sell that time and attention to the advertiser.

Lest this sound too exploitive of the reader let me quickly add that the advertising messages are often a very important, and sometimes the sole, reason a reader subscribes. Being informed of what is newly available in fashions, electronic products or tools is, if you will forgive the pun, of consuming interest to readers of *Vogue*, *Popular Electronics*, or *Popular Science*.

A good definition of the reader is also essential to the proper creation of an editorial concept. If the editor can't describe who the reader is in a brief and easily understood way, the editorial product will be vague, wandering, inconsistent, incapable of winning reader loyalty or, at the bottom line, subscription renewals. So the questions we used for defining the advertising customer have their parallel here.

Who is the subscriber?

The question will have to be answered statistically and in demographic or psychographic terms—by sex, age group, family income, education, profession, geographical area of residence or employment, organization membership, lifestyle, marital status, parental status, and buying habits, such as whether or not the subscriber owns a home, car, camera, lawnmower, etc.

Syndicated research organizations like Simmons Market Research Bureau or Target Group Index do annual market surveys of magazine audiences to measure all these characteristics, as well as hobbies, leisure-time activities, reading preferences and television viewing. These buying habits provide a psychographic profile that can be cross-tabulated with the demographic descriptions and will assist the publisher in accurately targeting a subscription promotion effort.

For example, if the magazine is about soap operas, its audience will be made up largely of people with similar demographic profiles—married females in the middle age groups, probably without advanced degrees—who watch television. The demographics are well defined as is one of their preferred leisure-time activities. If the magazine is about cooking, on the other hand, the demographics are broader since the subject is of interest to both sexes, a large age range, people of all education levels and geographical locations. The publisher of a food magazine will have to research the audience and in that way hopefully discover unexpected characteristics that distinguish this group of readers. He may find that people who subscribe to a food magazine are more interested in travel than the general population, or there may be a higher percentage of retired couples in its audience.

A matrix of audience demographics versus specialized interests will produce a map that can be extremely helpful in identifying approaches and appeals that can be used to sell subscriptions.

Why do they subscribe?

The reader has to receive a value in return for the subscription payment. For many magazines the value is obvious—entertainment, education, or information. For some magazines the value is not so obvious. On a coffee table, *The Atlantic Monthly* may suggest to guests that their host reads highly intellectual subjects. A doctor may subscribe to magazines for an office waiting room that have little to do with the interests of the doctor or the patients, but which are appropriate for people seeking a distraction from worry or boredom.

For the most part, however, entertainment, education, or information are the prime motivators and it is the editorial content which largely establishes the value. Magazine design and concept are central to strategy and worthy of a textbook of their own; here we can only call attention to the important aspects.

Concept: Can you write a description of the editorial concept in twenty-five words or less so that a sales promotion writer, an advertising space salesman, or a receptionist can understand and communicate it to an interested outsider? The editor needs a clear vision of the concept and must have the conviction and strength of personality to reproduce the vision issue after issue with a staff that is, by its very creative nature, frail, unreliable, recalcitrant and given to working at cross purposes.

Cover: Is the logotype (the magazine name) easy to read and recognize? Is a subhead or underline necessary to make the concept or its target audience immediately understandable? Does the cover illustration attract the reader and pertain directly to the subject matter? Is it a strong, simple image? If not, the readers are going to have trouble finding it among all the other covers vying for attention on the newsstand. Are the cover blurbs appealing to the specific target reader and do they honestly tell what each article is about?

Contents: Is the page intended as another sales tool, or is it an index to the contents for a quick overview of the entire magazine and for later referral? Either is acceptable; it is only necessary that the function be

Departments and columns: Are they automatically included because of tradition or is there a genuine need for each in this magazine? For example, a magazine that doesn't generate a dialog between reader and editor needs no letters column; a newsmagazine needs no coming-next-month column.

Features: Are the subjects and approach in line with the overall editorial content? Are there enough different articles to provide the necessary variety so that at least one article will be read with interest by every subscriber? Are article lengths appropriate to the subject matter and to the time the reader anticipates spending with the magazine or with the article? Is the illustration genuinely related to the subject, or is it included simply to lighten the visual load? Is the headline accurate as well as interesting? Is the subhead an additional incentive to read? Do the lead paragraphs grab the reader and make him want to read on? Does a reader finish an article with the sense of having spent time valuably or enjoyably?

Typography and layout: How the headline, deck and illustration are handled control the reader's eyes and can make or break an article. Does the art director lay out a spread as an entire frame rather than a collection of different pieces that have to be squeezed together on the pages? Is the designer sensitive to pacing—the flow of visual experience from spread to spread as the reader moves through the magazine? The reader must experience variety yet have the reassurance of familiarity. Is the body type legible and of adequate size for the age and reading skill of the target audience? Are headline typefaces appropriate to the subject and do they reinforce the content?

Is the market changing?

Is a competitor breathing down the back of your neck? Is he providing a magazine as good as yours? Is the leader in your field fat, happy, dumb, and vulnerable? Is this market so tempting that another publisher is sure to follow your lead? Can you set up barriers to entry by getting a lock on readers or advertisers, such as a unique personality for the magazine as a whole or of its writers. Can you develop a special distribution system, such as an exclusive relationship with a group or association that sponsors your magazine?

Should you be shifting emphasis to respond to changes in the lifestyles of readers? The traditional women's magazines, for example, were suddenly faced with the fact that women were leaving home to be full-time housewives and mothers. Their interests changed, their shopping patterns changed and their reading habits changed.

Is the subscriber in a different place than he or she was, either physically or psychologically? Should you change your magazine or the way it is sold to the subscriber? Check the idea lists published in direct-marketing books, newsletters and magazines, and see which of them would be appropriate for you to adopt. Computers and high-speed communications are changing the ways people buy things. Increasingly, people are ordering and buying all sorts of products by mail. That means more direct-marketing competition for subscription sales from other magazines, book publishers, videodisc publishers, record companies and catalog houses. Modern communications will open new channels of sales, but the competition for the reader's time—if only to read the selling message—is going to be fierce.

A magazine is as likely to experience obsolescence as any other product. However, it has an advantage over most manufactured products in that it can move quickly to align itself with changing interests of the marketplace. It can, if its editors will make, or let, it happen. We all know magazines that did not change and disappeared when the world went by. We know others that moved quickly to line themselves up with the flow, or even started the flow in a new direction when a brilliant and creative editor had the vision, the power, and the opportunity.

The point is that audiences change, and that this represents both a threat and an opportunity to which the publisher and editors must be sensitive. We have seen entire new categories of magazines explode in recent years—city magazines, for example, or computer magazines, when there had been none before. Everyone associated with the publishing business has one or more ideas for a new magazine floating around somewhere in his head. If you can't start that new magazine, it doesn't mean you can't change the one you have.

The timing of change is as important as the change itself. To be too far ahead of your time is as much a disaster as to be behind, and proper timing is a magical mixture of hard-nosed business sense and creative inspiration.

Who are the competitors and what do they offer?

We're talking here about competition for the subscriber's money and time. As in any market description, you can define it narrowly or broadly. Narrowly, you may think of your magazine as competing only with other magazines serving the same fare. More broadly, you may be competing with other magazines of a different nature but also selling subscriptions to similar readers. More broadly, still, you are competing with newspapers, television, movies or participatory sports for the reader's time and attention.

Make a list of competitors in their various categories and then think about what they offer their readers.

It may be difficult to be objective in your answer to this question and so some independent market research may be in order. Interviews with subscribers often produce so large a range of opinion that you can find anything you already believe in their responses; but when the market researcher also goes to the competitor and asks for their opinions, you may be forced to face some unpleasant truths.

How well do you and your competitors answer the needs and interests of the subscribers? We're talking about content, appearance and service. Content and appearance were reviewed above on editorial matters. Add the advertising and you have the full-packaged product.

By service we mean the way the magazine treats is customers. A subscriber expects some delays in starting a new subscription, but not inordinate ones. Billing should be courteous and efficient and the business office should honestly fulfill whatever commitments were made. Renewals should be efficiently and honestly handled. Nothing in this says you can't be clever, or humorous, or sincere in attempting to stimulate renewals. But horrendous stories are the rule rather than the exception when it comes to complaint handling in the subscription fulfillment operation. Make sure you occasionally do your own spot check of how the subscriber feels, and don't always accept as gospel the statistics reported by the fulfillment house.

Paid versus Controlled

Before we get into a consideration of subscription sources we should consider the question of paid versus controlled circulation. Controlled circulation simply means that the publisher decides who will receive the magazine and for how long a time. The Business Publications Audit checks controlled circulation magazines as well as paid. The BPA has its own rules of what constitutes a bona fide controlled subscriber. Normally, a validation procedure is required which gives the subscriber the opportunity to acknowledge receipt of the magazine and to say that he or she wishes to continue to receive it. This validation procedure is not unlike a billing or renewal operation except, of course, the magazine is free. Controlled circulation can be derived from almost all of the sources described below.

The Audit Bureau of Circulations (ABC) checks paid consumer magazines and functions in a similar way to confirm that a publisher's circulation is genuine.

Renewals

The first time a new subscriber comes up for renewal it is considered a conversion. After that it is called a renewal. Whether conversion or renewal, next to white mail (which costs the publisher nothing—see below) this is the least expensive subscription you can sell. In operation you inform the reader that the subscription will soon expire and some percentage of subscribers will renew—from as low as 25 or 30 percent to as high as 90 percent.

The renewal series is a sequence of notices sent to the subscriber, usually starting some months before the subscription expires and on through three or four months after expiration. Make sure you review yours frequently, that the price and offers are up-to-date, that the printing quality is up to par, that the series is mailed on the scheduled dates. Since the renewal series is often used repeatedly for many years, it can easily be neglected. Renewal percentages may start to sink and you will be scratching around for editorial reasons when they can be totally unrelated to the editorial product.

Telephone solicitation of renewals has become increasingly popular and economical since people often find it difficult to reject a personal call for a product they know and have been receiving for a while.

Bind-in and blow-in cards

A magazine should be its own best salesman. Despite the distaste most people feel for a card that drops into their laps when they open a magazine, it has proved to be an extremely effective and relatively inexpensive way to sell subscriptions. Cards in subscription copies sell almost as well as cards in newsstand copies, so don't automatically limit them to newsstand copies. However, this will vary from magazine to magazine depending on where the subscription copies go and how many pass-along readers a subscription copy may have. If bad debt is a problem (people who order a subscription on credit and never pay), consider cash-with-order sales with a bind-in or blow-in envelope, or only accept subscriptions billed through bank credit cards. At Christmas season, cards or envelopes may be used to sell gift subscriptions, but we will consider these as a separate source, called donor subscriptions.

White Mail

The term refers to unsolicited, over-the-transom subscription orders. Other than producing an excellent magazine there isn't much one can do to generate white mail. It is acquisition at zero cost.

Direct Mail

Probably the source of the largest number of subscriptions for magazines, direct mail means sending a letter, brochure, business reply card or envelope all put together in a carefully designed "package." It is the quickest way to test a new magazine idea because you don't actually have to have an issue on press before sending out a subscription offer. Note, however, that there are legal restrictions on how much time there may be between the original offer and delivery of the first issue to a subscriber.

Direct mail is another of those subjects that is too large to cover in detail here. There are several good books as well as magazines devoted to the subject. Price or premium offers, charter subscriptions and introductory offers, sweepstakes and prizes, no-obligation offers and dozens of other possibilities are available to the creative and imaginative subscription manager. Direct mail also makes testing easy and reliable. One can test prices, selling copy, different lists of names, time of the year, special offers, different terms (such as two-or three-year subscriptions), etc.

Donor

If the magazine has any appeal as a gift this is an excellent way to develop two or more subscription sales from each customer. You start by making special mailings to the existing subscription list to encourage subscribers to give the magazine to friends or family—and incidentally to renew their own subscription at the same time. Similar offers are made on blow-in cards. Over the years you will develop a separate list of names of donors that will be a fertile universe for magazine sales.

Subscription Agencies

There are several national subscription agencies that make regular mailings to millions of potential subscribers offering dozens of different magazines. The agency pays the publisher only a small percentage of the subscription price but is responsible for billing the subscriber and getting the payment and, in theory, at least, leaves the renewal to the publisher. The only problem is that agency mailings are made frequently, so many people who subscribe through an agency simple resubscribe the next year and ignore the publisher's renewal notices. Hence, agency-sold subscriptions have a poor renewal performance for the publisher unless the renewals series is started very early in the subscription term.

College

Certain subscription agencies have student representation at colleges and universities and sometimes high schools around the country. These agencies sell your subscriptions at student rates and perhaps special terms—a nine-month subscription to match the school year, for example.

Television and Radio Promotion

City magazines can make good use of local radio and television commercials to sell the magazine—either as a subscription or off the newsstand. National magazines have to be of general interest to make this an economic source, since network time and 800 telephone numbers and order takers may make for a very high acquisition expense. Bank credit cards at least eliminate the bad-debt problem.

Supermarket and Store Pockets

You've seen them on the bulletin boards in supermarkets or bus cards—a stack of order forms in a metal or plastic container and a notice or placard behind it.

Groups and Associations

Often a magazine that is in some way related to a club or association membership can be sold in conjunction with the membership dues. The association gives the publisher a list of names and addresses of paid-up members and they are added to the subscription list. The club gets a lower rate on the subscriptions and the publisher gets a number of subscribers at minimum cost.

Bulk Sales

Certain magazines may sell to groups of readers. We mentioned groups and associations above, but you should also consider whether a club or

Subscriptions

company might be interested in buying a number of copies to distribute to members or customers as a good will gesture.

Advertising

You can buy space in newspapers or other magazines to sell your subscription but, you may also be able to barter space in your magazine for space in the other. The deal is usually made based on relative page rates.

Telephone Solicitation

Increasingly, direct marketing firms are using telephone calls to potential buyers with a salesperson making the pitch and taking the order. Usually this is an expensive source and only pays for a high-ticket item, but more and more we have seen local newspapers use the technique because they can identify particular neighborhoods by the telephone exchange.

Door-to-door

"I'm working my way through college," is the foot-in-the-door cliche, but it still works. The salesperson usually offers a selection of magazines and depends on personal appeal to make the sale.

Conferences and Shows

A magazine in a field where potential subscribers attend shows or conferences can do well with a booth that calls attention to the magazines just when the reader is thinking about the subject.

Arrears

While not really a source of new subscriptions, we must recognize that a publisher can boost circulation during a difficult period by serving arrears—extending subscriptions beyond expiration for up to three months, according to auditing rules. This is a free subscription and is only justified if the advertising covers the cost.

Complimentary Subscriptions

Almost certainly the advertising director will have a customer and prospect list that should be served with a free subscription. The "comp" list should be reviewed periodically and purged of old or outdated names.

What determines how many subscriptions are on the list?

Each of the sources mentioned above, as well as others mined by special-interest magazines, responds to its own specific influencing factors. We will look at the most important factors and how they modify the total of subscription sales.

Subscription Price

A consumer magazine providing entertainment is likely to find that the response from almost any of the sources is sharply reduced as the price is increased. A subscription to such a magazine is a luxury, and people have sharply defined limits as to how free they will be in treating themselves.

But a magazine of interest to the very rich will find almost no price sensitivity because the magazine is so small a part of the subscriber's income that it is negligible. Also, a magazine that goes to business executives which will be paid for by a company rather than by the executive personally will find much less resistance to price increases.

The typical economist's graph, called the *elasticity* of the market, of quantity sold versus price, is a straight line (Figure 6.1). The equation of this line is in the form:

$$SUBS = a - b * PRICE$$

Where "a" is the number of subscriptions that can be given away (when the price equals zero) and "b" is the slope of the line, "*" is the symbol for multiplication.

Lacking any other data about an audience this is as good a first guess as any. But as price increases, the quantity sold continues straight down and across the zero line and then becomes negative, which would imply that you are paying people to accept subscriptions.

A more realistic shape is in the form we used to show how advertising cost per thousand influences the number of advertising pages. Here, a maximum number of subscriptions will be sold at very low prices. As price is increased the unit sale drops, at first slowly, then more rapidly as the price goes beyond the range of competing products. Finally, response flattens and approaches zero gradually when even the most loyal subscribers slowly drop out (Figure 6.2).

The equation of this curve is in the form:

$$SUBS = a/exp((PRICE - c)^2/b)$$

Where "a," "b," and "c" are constant coefficients that determine the exact shape of the curve, "exp" is the constant 2.71828 raised to the power of the following parenthesis. "^" means raise to the power; "/" is the symbol for division.

In the search for the most realistic curve, we found that curious things can happen in the marketplace. We have seen magazines cautiously raise subscription price and actually sell more subscriptions rather than fewer! The reason for this is that people's buying preferences separate them into nodes. Some people always buy the luxury model, and given any kind of choice they will prefer to spend more for something, rather than less. Others always buy the economy model.

The double-humped curve shown in Figure 6.3 recognizes this tendency; if a magazine happens to be priced in the valley and raises price, the sale will actually increase.

The equation of this curve is the sum of two of the exponentials.

$$SUBS = a/exp((SALE - c)^2/b) + d/exp((SALE - f)^2/e)$$

It is difficult to derive this equation for a specific magazine because the six coefficients will require no fewer than six data points.

The transient nature of these curves is even more pronounced than what we spoke of earlier in relation to advertising CPM. The subscriber probably won't remember what he paid for his subscription last year, and so price increases that remain within the competitive range of other magazines of the same kind will, if anything, depress response only for relatively short periods of time.

The effect of inflation and of subscriber's changing sensitivity to price is to shift the curve to the right as time passes, indicating that customers soon become accustomed to higher prices.

Promotion Effort

While price is an across-the-board sort of factor that will have an impact, and probably a similar impact, on almost any of the subscription

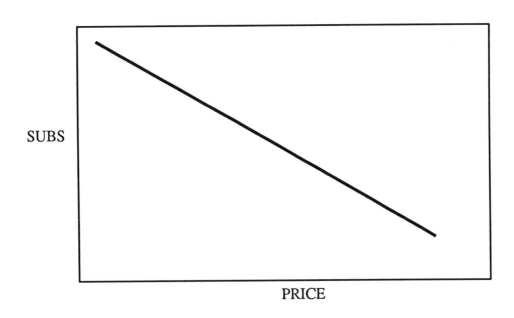

Figure 6.1 The typical economist's elasticity is a straight line indicating that each increment of price produces a proportional reduction in unit sales.

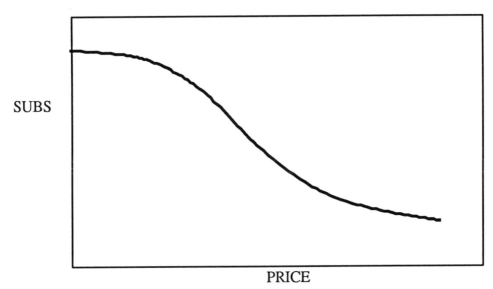

Figure 6.2 A more realistic elasticity uses the normal curve which rolls over at the very low prices and curves more gently toward the X axis at the very high prices.

Subscriptions   79

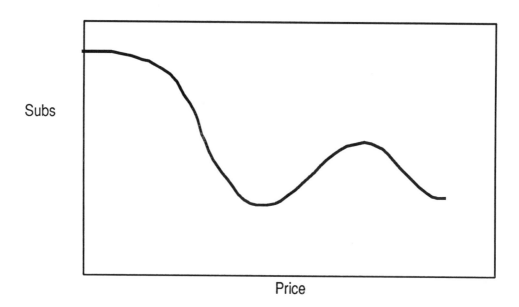

Subs

Price

Figure 6.3   Some markets may have two or more "nodes" or peaks, indicating that the consuming market has some members who always want the high-priced luxury model while others will always prefer the economy model. In this market the worst place to be is in the middle.

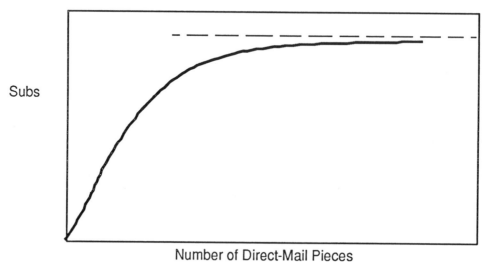

Subs

Number of Direct-Mail Pieces

Figure 6.4   Subscribers respond to subscription promotion in much the same way that advertisers respond to advertising promotion. However, in this case no promotion produces no subscribers, then each additional increment in promotion produces a slightly smaller increment in the number of subscriptions.

Subscriptions

sources, the investment made to acquire subscriptions will produce a substantially different return depending on the source. In addition, subscription response will be dependent on the amount of effort. At lower levels of promotion investment, renewals and direct-mail effort will produce subscriptions almost in direct proportion to the number of pieces or renewal notices put in the mail. However, there is a point of diminishing returns that begins to take hold as the direct-mail efforts are sent to less and less well-targeted lists, or as the fifth, tenth, or twentieth renewal notice goes to the same expire. Ultimately, any further effort produces no additional subscriptions so the curve is asymptotic to a horizontal line (shown dashed in Figure 6.4).

The equation of this curve is in the form:

$$SUBS = a + b * (1 - 1/exp(PIECES/c))^d$$

Where "a," "b," "c," and "d" are constant coefficients, "exp" is 2.71828, "*" is multiplication, "^" is exponentiation. "PIECES" is the number of pieces, or renewal notices, put in the mail.

Certain subscription sources require a minimum expenditure just to get started. Advertisements have to be written and designed, television commercials have to be produced, even before the first one is placed in a magazine or on the air. This initial investment may have the effect of slightly flattening the beginning of the curve. Normally this is too small an effect to be worth it to modify the equation.

For a complete and detailed model of the magazine, each source will have to be examined separately with both the price and promotional effort influencing the number of subscriptions produced. However, for most magazines, and given that the curves are at best estimates of what will actually happen over the full range of factors, many, if not all, of the sources can be lumped into one or two equations with the control variables limited to one subscription price and a total promotion effort (in dollars).

The subscription director should be able to rank every source of subscriptions and, if necessary, within each source to rank them into a table which, in abbreviated form, might look something like Table 6.1. The publisher or subscription manager need only go down the list as far as is necessary to acquire the desired number of subscriptions. Note, that when you graph this table, the result is a series of straight lines that approximate the diminishing returns curve (see Figure 6.5).

SUBSCRIPTION SOURCES BY COST PER SUBSCRIPTION

Source	Max Inv	No. Subs	$/Sub	Cum Inv	Cum Subs
White mail	0	2,000	$0.00	0	2,000
Renewals	110,000	98,000	1.12	110,000	100,000
Blow-in cards	40,000	16,400	2.44	150,000	116,400
Dir mail to donor list	485,000	52,000	9.33	635,000	168,400
Dir mail to rented list #1	240,000	20,000	12.00	875,000	188,400
Dir mail to rented lists #2	700,000	40,000	17.50	1,575,000	228,400
Television	300,000	12,500	24.00	1,875,000	240,900

Table 6.1. Each source is listed in ranked order with the maximum investment possible to that source and the number of subscriptions that could be acquired. The investment and number of subs are accumulated in the last two columns.

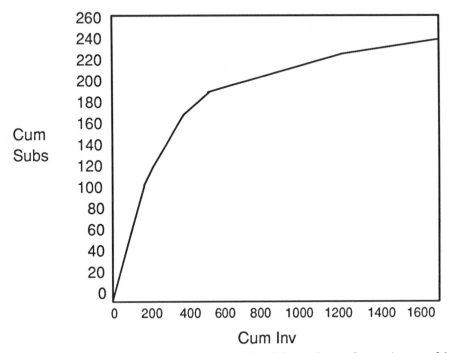

Figure 6.5. The cumulated data from Table 6.1 are here shown in graphical form. Each entry in the table appears as a straight line showing the incremental cost and number of subscriptions acquired. The graph approaches the shape of the diminishing returns curve

Subscriptions

Renewals—A note for the modeler

Before we leave the subject of subscriptions, a few words are in order regarding the way renewals are handled by the computer model. Chances are the renewal notice series has already been optimized by the subscription manager, that is, the content of the various notices is set and the number of notices has been checked out to be the most economical. Either on a source-by-source basis, or broken out as first-time renewers (conversions) and second and later renewals, the subscription manager should be able to provide an estimate of renewal percent as a function of price.

This gives you all the information you need to derive the number of subscription conversions and renewals in later years, as a function of the number of new subscriptions acquired this year. It's a straightforward, if messy, data-handling job because of the different lengths of subscription.

Consider a single source of subscriptions—say a direct-mail effort made in January. This produces one-, two-, and three-year subscriptions that start in January, February, March, maybe even April, depending on how long subscribers take to respond. The one-year subscribers come up for conversion in January, February, March and April of the next year. The two-year subscribers in the same four months a year later, and the three-year subscribers in the same four months a year later, still.

Do all of these renew at the same percentage? Even assuming they do, some are going to switch from one-to two-or three-year subscriptions. Some are going to be late in renewing and may have to be restored. Thus, the one direct-mail effort made in January creates a whole tree of subscribers and renewers that explodes and spreads throughout the future issues. It is easy to make critical modeling errors in this calculation, so the algorithm should be as simple and rigorous as possible. It will cut the complexity down dramatically if only one-, or one- and three-year subscriptions need to be dealt with; if the response to the initial mailing can be limited to one month; if all longer term subscribers renew for the same terms; and so on.

Chapter 7

SINGLE-COPY SALES

Postage costs have been taking an ever-increasing percentage of the expense of acquiring and delivering subscription copies. As a result, many publishers are looking enviously at their newsstand brothers and wondering whether that might not be a more profitable way to reach the reading public.

In the seventies single-copy sales were very strong for all titles and particularly for the category of men's magazines called "sophisticates." But the introduction of videocassette players and prerecorded tapes at reasonable prices, and the greater freedom of expression permitted to television and tape programming, has dramatically changed purchase and entertainment habits. Single-copy sales for almost all magazines is now lower and likely to remain so for the foreseeable future.

Let's look down a list of best-selling single-copy magazines and see if there is anything to be learned.

At the top is *TV Guide* with some nine million copies (50 percent of its circulation) in supermarket and newsstand sales each week. Then come *Family Circle* and *Woman's Day* with no subscriptions, a relatively low cover price, and around seven million each in supermarket sales. Next are the *National Enquirer* and the *Star* with four million going out through the checkout counters. Close behind is *Penthouse* with about three million, then what I suppose should be called the "woman's sophisticate," *Cosmopolitan* at around two and a half million. *Playboy* circulation is next with a newsstand sale under two million.

People is around one and a half million, and then the women's magazines are grouped in the one half to one million range—*Good Housekeeping, Glamour, Ladies' Home Journal, Redbook, Vogue, Mademoiselle, Seventeen. Reader's Digest* is just under a million as well.

Except for *Penthouse* and *Playboy* (which are not sold in supermarkets), most of the big single-copy sellers are purchased by women in supermarkets. Ten years ago only *Family Circle* and *Woman's Day* were selling any substantial number of copies in supermarkets. The news weeklies occasionally got rack space near the checkout counters, but there were no supermarket departments full of magazines and paperbacks as there are today. Obviously publishers (and supermarket managers) heard a clear answer to our first question.

Who is the customer?

For most of these magazines the customer is a woman in a shopping frame of mind. A dollar or two for a magazine disappears in the household food budget when it is tossed on top of the grocery cart. Part of the reason single-copy sales are weakening is that the woman now shares the shopping chores with her husband or male roommate who is not in the market for a women's magazine and who won't find *Playboy* or *Penthouse* at the checkout counter and might not buy it if he could. Further, the woman is no longer a housewife but is working nine-to-six at a career. When she gets home she is tired and has less time and interest in magazines than she did when she was at home full time.

Knowing who your customer is will clearly direct you to other places where your magazine should be displayed. *Rolling Stone* is careful to distribute the magazine in music stores. *Popular Photography* aims at camera stores. Airport newsstands get, and sell, tall stacks of *Penthouse*. This relationship of sales location and magazine is critical to success in single-copy sales and should be thought through carefully and creatively because, as we shall see, the path to profitable single-copy sales is fraught with danger.

Why does the customer buy?

Much of the discussion in the chapter on subscriptions applies as well here. Magazine content—the editorial concept and how it is embodied—makes most of the difference, but now the cover moves up to the number one spot in importance. I have seen research indicating that when a magazine buyer approaches the magazine rack the customer often does not know which magazine he or she is going to buy. He may know the type of magazine—food, or photography, or fishing—but not the specific title.

What tips the decision in favor of one magazine over another has absorbed editors and art directors for years. We have accumulated a fund of conventional wisdom in our industry. A large percentage of it is wrong, of course, but it is at least comforting. We also have a no-man's land of conventional ignorance which editors, publishers and circulation managers preserve with the obsessiveness of religious zealots.

Nobody knows, they will tell you, which covers sell better than others, or why; which cover lines are really best (given reasonably legible, catchy ones); what the impact of display is (more is better, of course, but there are always exceptions because sexy is better and sexy may result in less display); and what effect that extra subscription sale has on the potential newsstand sale.

Maybe newsstand managers don't trust their experience because so often when they make predictions they are proved wrong, but there are other ways to attack the problem. Statisticians have become very adept at finding cause-and-effect relationships between sets of data. Suppose you have a list of the monthly sales dollars for a given breakfast cereal over a period of a year and the advertising dollars spent during the same period, the price that was charged, the price of competing products, the quality of the product, its newness, and a whole raft of other factors that can be presumed to have an impact on sales. The statistician performs some mathematical magic called a "step-wise multiple regression analysis" and soon will tell you which of the variables have a statistically measurable effect on sales and to what extent.

Several studies of single-copy sales have been made over the years using this technique. The first was done on *Playboy*. At the time of this study *Playboy* was selling close to three and a half million copies on the newsstand for most months. It also sold over two million subscriptions. These are numbers so large that they must offer enough statistical mass to be amenable to mathematical analysis, and that analysis would have to teach us something—if only that the conventional ignorance was right after all.

The study started with a list of all the variables thought likely to influence the number of copies sold during any one month. It was a long list, it is true, but finite:

> Cover picture
> Cover blurbs
> Appeal of contents of a particular issue
> Cover price
> Number, price, quality of competitors on same newsstand
> Economic climate
> Season
> Promotional efforts
> Number of days on sale
> Number of subscribers
> Number of copies distributed (draw)
> Number of full-cover displays

When you look at the list you may be tempted to throw up your hands and say: The conventional ignorance is right, it is impossible to handle all of these. Magazines move in mysterious ways; they are unknown and unknowable and we may as well rejoice in the mystery.

But the statisticians aren't so pessimistic. Many of the items on the list are quantifiable, at least insofar as past history is concerned: the publisher knows how many copies of the magazine were sold, how many the competitors sold and the prices. Unemployment figures were used as a measure of the economic climate. Figures on promotional expenditures were available, the number of days on sale were known, etc.

The qualitative factors provided an interesting challenge to the judgment. A group of editors and art directors were asked to estimate, on a scale of one to ten, the appeal of the covers, cover blurbs, and the content of individual issues.

It was a tedious but not difficult job to assemble a table of data which provided, for a number of issues, a value for each of the factors thought to have an impact on newsstand sales. The data was plugged into one of the readily available regression programs that will run on a microcomputer. The results at least gave us a start at answering the question: Why does the *Playboy* reader buy *Playboy*? And ultimately, why does any newsstand buyer choose a copy of one magazine over another?

Many of the listed factors were rejected because their influence was too small to be isolated from the random "noise." They were swamped by the impact of the other factors. It was surprising, however, to find that the promotional effort had no discernible impact on sale. Now all logic tells you that radio or television commercials have to have some effect. No matter how bad the commercial may be, someone is reminded that there is a new issue on the newsstand and the next day, or that evening, the individual goes out and buys a copy. It is just that there weren't enough such reminders, or else other influences were so much more powerful that the small effect of the television commercial could not be separated out. Clearly it was necessary to spend a lot more, or none at all.

On the other hand, the state of the economy in the form of the percentage of unemployed men aged 18 to 34 turned out to be very important as a factor, as was the number of subscribers receiving copies that month.

To be specific, the analysis said that subscriptions, draw, male unemployment, competitors' sales, number of days on sale, and a qualitative index of cover excellence, were important factors in the monthly newsstand sale, and the analysis even went so far as to make an estimate of how many additional copies were lost or gained for each unit change in the causal factor.

We'll be talking about some of these again later on. The thing I want to leave with you at this stage of the discussion is that there are techniques for studying cause-and-effect relationships like the qualitative and quantitative factors that influence single-copy sale. With more and more small computers in the hands of statisticians and programmers, these techniques become accessible and useful in a way they have never been before.

What will change?

The customer will change, is always changing. See this same discussion in Chapter 6, Subscriptions. Single-copy sales differ, however, in that the magazine is out where it can be seen, touched, scanned or read before purchase so the reaction is more immediate, more point-of-purchase. The magazine marketplace moved from the newsstand to the supermarket and specialty stores in recent years, and then magazines started losing place to videocassettes. Magazines won't be replaced by video because they offer information in a form that video can't duplicate, but the entertainment and the story- telling that magazines and soft cover books provided is now more accessible on the tube. Who will be the benefactors next time? Can you arrange to be in the flow when the new traffic pattern establishes itself?

If you're all alone in a category of magazines you can be certain others will be coming soon. If you're in a crowd and finding the going rough you can be certain others are hurting, too, and someone is likely to fold.

If you find a formula for cover photographs that works, watch how quickly the others copy you. If you have an idea hooked to a current event someone else is sure to be struck by the same thought. Like Alice, you'll have to run, and run fast, just to stay even. That's okay. That's the excitement, the challenge, and the satisfaction of being in a creative and competitive business. When it gets too tiring appoint yourself Chairman of the Board, or become a consultant.

Who are the competitors?

The immediate competitors are easy to find—they are sitting right there next to your magazine. Hundreds of titles are sent to the newsstand every month now, and the number is growing. You compete with magazines like your own, of course, but you also compete with magazines very different from yours that happen to be near yours and attract the wandering eye. And you compete with other demands on the reader's time, attention and pocketbook.

What do the competitors offer?

Don't look at your cover as it is framed for display by your art director. Strip away the white border and put it among dozens of other magazine covers and see how it stands up in that mass of color and words, all clamoring for attention.

Spend an hour or two watching at a large newsstand where you hope to sell magazines. See how the customers move along the racks, what they pick up and what they pass over, how much time they spend with magazines like yours, what they seem to be looking for. Note how the decision to buy is made—you can read it in their faces.

Draw

The average nationally distributed magazine sells about 50 percent of the draw (the number of copies distributed). That's hardly wonderful since the publisher pays for twice as much printing and paper as is sold. On the other hand the publisher doesn't dare reduce the draw because, as the national distributor will be quick to point out, he's going to lose sales if he does so.

On the surface it makes no sense that the number of copies distributed should have a progressive effect on the number of copies sold— particularly when magazines on average sell considerably fewer copies than they distribute. What other business is like that? If the average newsstand receives 20 copies of a magazine and sells 10 of them, then one should be able to distribute 15 copies to each newsstand and still sell 10, which would raise the percentage of sale from 50 percent to 67 percent and make a much happier profit statement for the publisher.

But it doesn't work that way, and there is only one explanation (outside of the inefficiency of the distribution system) that seems to have any logic at all. While it is true that an average newsstand may receive 20 copies and sell 10, averages really aren't relevant. Some of the newsstands will sell only 5 copies in a particular month and some will sell all 20. If you reduce the distribution to 15 across the board you will definitely lose sales from some dealers and you won't know which ones until it is too late. Next month the situation will reverse itself and the dealer who sold 5 copies will sell 18—but only if you give him 20.

It is this random factor which suggests that at least some waste is necessary. Remember the impulsive nature of the newsstand purchase; if the magazine isn't there the reader probably won't go to another newsstand to find one. Instead, he'll probably buy a competitor's magazine and you will have lost a sale.

For the publisher, an average sale of 50 percent is awful enough but there is still worse news. If the overall average is 50 percent, the publisher is selling many copies at a far lower ratio—the last few copies of a draw aren't selling at anywhere near the gross 50 percent figure. We all know that is so when we think about it, but it is incredible how rarely we think about it.

Just exactly how does draw affect sale? Take as an example a magazine that sells 60,000 newsstand copies per month. To sell this 60,000 copies per month the publisher has discovered through trial and error that he must distribute 120,000 copies.

Clearly, if he were to distribute only 10,000 copies he'd sell them all. If he distributed 20,000 copies he'd still probably sell almost all of them. But as additional increments of draw are distributed the increments of sale don't keep up. What I have described here is the law of diminishing returns. It is our by now familiar curve adapted to the two special characteristics of magazine sales. The first is that at very low draws, the sale equals the draw. This is a 100 percent sale line which moves up at an angle of 45 degrees to the two axes.

At the upper right of this curve is a saturation ceiling which says that if you keep on increasing your draw you will eventually come to the point where not a single additional copy will be sold. The 50 percent sale line—where, as we have mentioned above, most magazines now operate—intersects the curve at a point very close to saturation and that's bad news, as we'll soon see (Figure 7.1).

The equation of this curve is in the form:

$$SALE = a * (1 - 1/exp(DRAW/b))$$

Where "a" and "b" are constant coefficients that fit the diminishing returns curve to the specific magazine and its market; "exp" is the constant 2.71828 raised to the power of the following parentheses; "*" is multiplication.

There are some important lessons to be learned from this curve. Remember that the gross percentage of sale for a magazine is the sale divided by the draw. However, the marginal percentage of sale—the increment in sale divided by an increment in draw—is always a lot lower

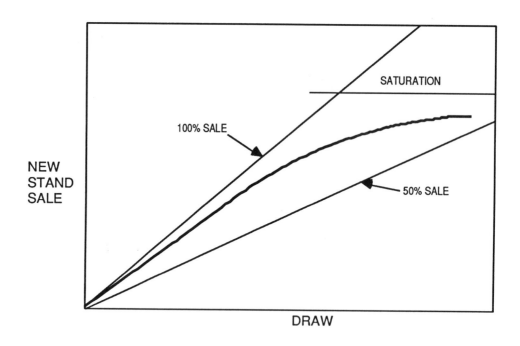

Figure 7.1 The diminishing returns curve fitted to the draw/sale relationship. Near zero draw the curve moves up at a 45 degree angle for 100 percent sale. At very high levels of draw the curve approaches saturation.

Single-Copy Sales

DRAW

Sale	1	2	3	4	5	6	7	8	9	10	11	12	13	14	15	16	17	18
0.2	1	-	-	-	-	-	-	-	-	-	-	-	-	-	-	-	-	-
0.4	11	1	-	-	-	-	-	-	-	-	-	-	-	-	-	-	-	-
0.6	33	4	1	-	-	-	-	-	-	-	-	-	-	-	-	-	-	-
0.8	63	11	2	1	-	-	-	-	-	-	-	-	-	-	-	-	-	-
1.0	-	20	6	1	1	-	-	-	-	-	-	-	-	-	-	-	-	-
1.2	-	33	11	4	1	1	-	-	-	-	-	-	-	-	-	-	-	-
1.4	-	47	17	8	3	1	1	-	-	-	-	-	-	-	-	-	-	-
1.6	-	63	24	11	5	2	1	1	-	-	-	-	-	-	-	-	-	-
1.8	-	81	33	15	8	4	2	1	1	-	-	-	-	-	-	-	-	-
2.0	-	-	42	20	11	6	3	1	1	1	-	-	-	-	-	-	-	-
2.2	-	-	52	26	14	9	5	3	1	1	1	-	-	-	-	-	-	-
2.4	-	-	63	33	18	11	7	4	2	1	1	1	-	-	-	-	-	-
2.6	-	-	75	40	22	14	9	6	3	2	1	1	1	-	-	-	-	-
2.8	-	-	-	47	27	17	11	8	5	3	2	1	1	1	-	-	-	-
3.0	-	-	-	54	33	20	13	9	6	4	2	1	1	1	1	-	-	-
3.2	-	-	-	63	38	24	16	11	8	5	4	2	1	1	1	1	-	-
3.4	-	-	-	72	44	28	18	13	10	7	5	3	2	1	1	1	1	-
3.6	-	-	-	81	50	33	22	15	11	8	6	4	3	2	1	1	1	1
3.8	-	-	-	-	56	37	25	17	13	10	7	5	4	2	2	1	1	1
4.0	-	-	-	-	63	42	29	20	15	11	9	6	5	3	2	1	1	1
4.2	-	-	-	-	70	47	33	23	17	13	10	8	6	4	3	2	1	1
4.4	-	-	-	-	78	52	37	26	19	14	11	9	7	5	4	3	2	1
4.6	-	-	-	-	-	57	41	29	21	16	12	10	8	6	5	3	2	2
4.8	-	-	-	-	-	63	45	33	24	18	14	11	9	7	5	4	3	2
5.0	-	-	-	-	-	69	49	36	27	20	15	12	10	8	6	5	4	3
5.5	-	-	-	-	-	-	60	45	34	26	20	16	13	11	9	7	6	4
6.0	-	-	-	-	-	-	73	54	42	33	25	20	16	13	11	9	8	6
6.5	-	-	-	-	-	-	-	65	50	40	32	25	20	16	14	12	10	8
7.0	-	-	-	-	-	-	-	77	59	47	38	31	25	20	17	14	12	10
7.5	-	-	-	-	-	-	-	-	69	54	44	36	30	24	20	17	15	12
8.0	-	-	-	-	-	-	-	-	79	63	51	42	35	29	24	20	17	15
8.5	-	-	-	-	-	-	-	-	-	72	58	48	40	34	28	24	20	17
9.0	-	-	-	-	-	-	-	-	-	81	66	54	46	39	33	28	23	20
9.5	-	-	-	-	-	-	-	-	-	-	75	61	51	44	37	32	27	23
10.0	-	-	-	-	-	-	-	-	-	-	-	69	57	49	42	36	31	27
11.0	-	-	-	-	-	-	-	-	-	-	-	-	71	60	52	45	39	34
12.0	-	-	-	-	-	-	-	-	-	-	-	-	-	73	63	54	48	42
13.0	-	-	-	-	-	-	-	-	-	-	-	-	-	-	75	65	57	50
14.0	-	-	-	-	-	-	-	-	-	-	-	-	-	-	-	77	67	59
15.0	-	-	-	-	-	-	-	-	-	-	-	-	-	-	-	-	78	69
16.0	-	-	-	-	-	-	-	-	-	-	-	-	-	-	-	-	-	79
17.0	-	-	-	-	-	-	-	-	-	-	-	-	-	-	-	-	-	-

Table 7.1. Percent sale of the last few issues at given gross sale and draw

Single-Copy Sales

| Pcnt | Percent increase in draw | | | | | | | | | | |
Sale	0	5	10	15	20	25	30	35	40	45	50
20	0.7	0.6	0.5	0.5	0.4	0.4	0.3	0.3	0.3	0.3	0.2
25	1.4	1.3	1.2	1.1	1.0	0.9	0.8	0.8	0.7	0.6	0.6
30	4.1	3.8	3.5	3.3	3.0	2.8	2.6	2.5	2.3	2.2	2.0
35	7.6	7.1	6.7	6.3	5.9	5.6	5.3	5.0	4.7	4.5	4.3
40	11.1	10.5	10.0	9.4	9.0	8.5	8.1	7.7	7.4	7.0	6.7
45	15.0	14.3	13.7	13.1	12.5	12.0	11.5	11.0	10.5	10.1	9.7
50	20.0	19.2	18.5	17.8	17.1	16.5	15.9	15.3	14.7	14.2	13.7
55	26.1	25.2	24.4	23.6	22.9	22.2	21.5	20.8	20.2	19.6	19.0
60	32.8	31.9	31.1	30.2	29.4	28.7	27.9	27.2	26.5	25.8	25.2
65	39.8	38.8	38.0	37.1	36.3	35.5	34.7	34.0	33.2	32.5	31.8
70	46.7	45.9	45.0	44.2	43.4	42.6	41.8	41.0	40.3	39.6	38.9
75	54.3	53.4	52.6	51.8	51.1	50.3	49.6	48.8	48.1	47.4	46.7
80	62.8	62.1	61.4	60.7	60.0	59.3	58.6	58.0	57.3	56.7	56.1
85	72.1	71.5	71.0	70.4	69.8	69.3	68.7	68.2	67.6	67.1	66.6
90	80.8	80.4	80.0	79.6	79.1	78.7	78.3	77.9	77.5	77.1	76.7

Table 7.2. Enter this table with the present percent sale (first column on the left) and the contemplated percent increase in draw (first row). The table gives you the calculated percentage that the increase in draw can be expected to sell.

Single-Copy Sales

than the gross percentage of sale. Yet it is this marginal percentage that determines whether or not you make a profit from an increase in draw.

Table 7.1 gives you the bad news. Take as an example a magazine selling 60,000 copies on a draw of 120,000 copies. Move across the columns until you get to "12," representing 120,000 copies. Now move down the rows until the column intersects the row led by a "6," representing 60,000 sale. The intersection of the chosen row and column has a "20" in it. That means this publisher is selling only 20 of the last 100 copies (20 percent)—a long way from the overall gross sales percentage of 50 percent (60,000 sale on 120,000 draw).

In another example, if the publisher's gross sales percentage is 40 percent, the marginal percentage is only 11 percent! He has to distribute nine additional copies to sell only one!

Table 7.2 looks at the same relationship in a slightly different way. Table 7.1 listed the marginal percentage of sales at given gross draw and sales values. It only applies to a very small range of draw above and below the given values. If you really want to hype the sales by adding, say, 10 percent or more to the draw, you must work with Table 7.2. Here you enter the table with your present gross sales percentage at the left column and then work your way across to the column which lists the increase in draw that you are contemplating.

Suppose the present sale is 50 percent (60,000 sale on 120,000 draw) and the distributor says he needs another 30,000 copies to give you full national distribution. The present gross percentage of sale is 50 percent, the increase in draw of 30,000 copies on the present 120,000 copies is 25 percent. Enter the table at the 50 percent row and move across the columns to 25 percent increase in draw. The intersection reads 16.5, meaning you can expect to sell only 16.5 percent of the additional 30,000 copies!

It sounds disastrous and clearly not a recommended strategy, but we won't know for sure that it is until we have completed the analysis of the magazine as a whole because the impact of this decision has a way to go until it gets to the bottom line, which is what we are interested in.

Price

The effect of single-copy price on sale is a typical elasticity similar to the effect of subscription price on sale. The equation of this curve (Figure 7.2) is:

$$SALE = a/\exp((PRICE-c)^2/b)$$

Where "a," "b," and "c" are constant coefficients; "exp" raises the constant 2.71828 to the power in the parentheses.

It is important to remember that, as with subscriptions, the reaction to price increases is tempered by time. That is, a price change in January may well produce the drop off in sales called for by this curve, but by April or May, and certainly by September, the increase will have been absorbed and possibly forgotten by some of the customers and the sale may have climbed back to its former location on the graph.

The impact of a price change is therefore an ephemeral thing which may be slowed or speeded by inflation, the state of the economy, and what the competitors do with their prices.

The Economy

There are so many economic indicators to choose among that it may be difficult to select one that is relevant, but the subject matter of the magazine will help. As we saw above, the percentage of unemployed males aged 18 to 34 was used in the *Playboy* analysis, and reports of corporate profits were used to predict advertising in large national magazines. Automotive sales and gasoline prices would probably be correlated with sales of an automotive magazine. Film prices and sales might be keyed to a photography magazine's sales. Tourism might be proportional to a travel magazine's sales. It's worth a mental browse through the kinds of economic data that are available to see which would be most appropriate for your magazine, and then collect and plot it alongside your single-copy sales figures. If the zigs and zags in the graphs are at all synchronized you've got a lock on how the world out there affects you at the newsstand.

Season

Some magazine sales are seasonal, some are not. There are fancy computer programs to find out if yours is, but here is a simple way to check it out.

Take the average single-copy sale for the last few calendar years of publication. Now divide each month's sale by the average for that year. You will have a number for each month's sales that moves above and below 1.0.

Figure 7.2 Elasticity of single-copy sales at the newsstand is a typical downward sloping curve best matched by the equation for a normal curve.

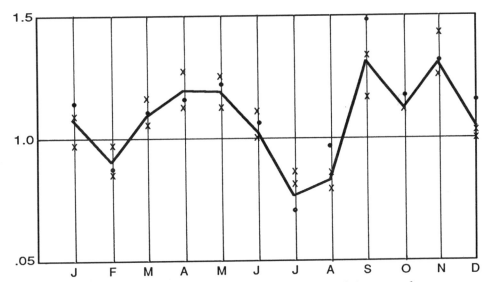

Figure 7.3 Seasonality charts the ratio of sales of each issue to the average for that year. Seasonality appears when the plotted points move in a band above and below the center line.

Single-Copy Sales

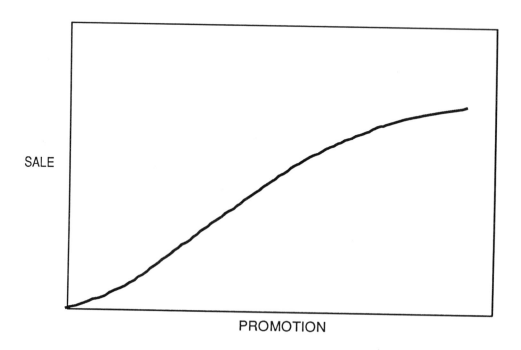

SALE

PROMOTION

Figure 7.4   Single-copy promotion impact starts slowly, then rises more rapidly as more and more potential readers are informed about the existence of the magazine. Eventually additional increments of promotion have little or no effect on sales.

Single-Copy Sales

Make a graph like that of Figure 7.3 with the horizontal axis running across the middle of the graph and divided into twelve months. The vertical axis should have 1.0 at this center line and go from about 0.5 at the bottom to 1.5 at the top.

Now plot each set of twelve numbers with a different color or symbol and identify each by its year. If the points fall all over the page with no discernible pattern, you have no seasonality in your sales. If the points all seem to stay within a band that moves above and below the centerline, you do have seasonality to contend with. Draw a line more or less through the center of the band and read the values of the line for each month.

Thus, if the central line is around 1.3 in September and 0.8 in July you can expect that in September you will, in general, sell 30 percent more copies than the year-long average, and in July 20 percent fewer. If any issue sale departs in a substantial way from these averages, you can be sure that something else is going on—some other factor is having an effect on sales.

Promotion

Newsstand promotion consists of point-of-purchase cards and racks, billboards and bus or subway signs, newspaper advertising, radio and television commercials and the like. One would also have to include entertainment for wholesalers and retailers in this category, although the effect on individual issue sales is less direct.

The Retail Display Allowance is a promotional expenditure as well but it, too, may not have a readily discernible effect on sales. The Retail Display Allowance is an extra incentive paid by the publisher directly to retailers for keeping the issue on sale throughout the on-sale period and giving the magazine some special form of display—such as full-cover and racked close to the cash register. The allowance is ordinarily around 10 percent of the retail price of the copies sold. Outside of the yes-or-no decision as to whether the allowance is offered or not, it is not a factor that would enter a computer model as a control factor.

If the number of full-cover displays does vary substantially over the course of the strategic plan, some recognition of that should be built into the model using a curve and equation as suggested here.

Those parts of the promotional budget that have a direct impact on newsstand sales probably take a curve shape like that in Figure 7.4. The slow start of this curve is caused by the initial investment in creative production that precedes any purchase of air time or billboard space. After that, each increment of investment presumably reaches more potential buyers until a point of diminishing returns brings the curve to the horizontal.

The equation of this curve is in the form:

$$SALES = a + b * (1 - 1/\exp(PROM - c))^{\wedge}d$$

Where "a," "b," "c," and "d" are constant coefficients that fit the curve to the data; "exp" is the value 2.71828 raised to the parenthetical power; "*" is the symbol for multiplication.

Days on Sale

Monthly magazines are normally distributed to the newsstand in the United States on specific days of the week and this may mean an on-sale period that varies by as much as five days from the shortest "month" to the longest.

It is reasonable to expect that an issue on sale for 33 days will sell more copies than one that had been on sale for 28 days, but how much more? The data is difficult to dig out since individual newsstands don't pay much attention to specific magazines, particularly toward the end of their on-sale periods when the stack has shrunk down and what remains is dog-eared, shopworn, and possibly relegated to a back room. In the *Playboy* study mentioned above it was possible to measure this effect and it was determined that the last few days were selling something like 0.2 percent of the draw per day. You might think this negligible, but it amounted to around 10,000 copies a day nationwide and so was well worth knowing about and possibly even planning for in terms of larger draws for those issues known to have longer on-sale months.

Because it is so small a percentage, days on sale may be neglected in the models of most magazines. When the single-copy sale approaches the million mark it is probably adequate to include a strict linear relationship of 0.1 or 0.2 percent of the draw, added or subtracted for each day above or below 30.

Number of Subscriptions Served

Here's another influence for which data should be easily acquired and normally is not. It is reasonable to suppose that the new subscriber sold this month was probably a newsstand purchaser who will not buy a copy on the newsstand this month.

Magazine readers tend to fall into one of three categories. About 25 percent are newsstand buyers. They will only buy their copies on the newsstand and never subscribe. About 25 percent are subscribers. They never pass a newsstand, or at least never buy a magazine from one, but they sit at home and write checks for subscriptions a year or more at a time. The remaining 50 percent are both newsstand buyers and subscribers at one time or another. They flow into and out of subscription lists as their interests and their financial resources change.

So, to begin with, the "swing" buyer only represents half the total audience for a magazine. Market research intended to discover just how many new subscribers would have bought a newsstand copy indicates that a magazine that sells about an equal number of subscriptions and newsstand copies will lose about one newsstand sale for every four subscribers.

For modeling purposes it would be best to have specific research discover what percentage of subscribers would buy a newsstand copy if they had not previously subscribed. In the absence of hard data it is probably advisable to use a factor that depends only on new subscribers acquired in the month in question. Take about 25 percent of these as a cost to the newsstand sales as a first approximation.

Cover and Contents

We mentioned the cover and contents of particular issues earlier but did not attempt to quantify the impact for modeling purposes. The poll of editors and art directors is well worth the effort—if only to discover who differs from whom and by how much. If you can then run a regression along with the other factors, you will discover which of your staff seem to best reflect the tastes of the audience and at least some sense of what kinds of covers do well and what kinds do poorly.

Lucky or unlucky, juxtapositions of news events and articles are always possible and may even be planned for when the editors think forward in their scheduling.

Other Factors

Since a single-copy purchase is often made on impulse one can think of many other factors that might affect the market. The number of weekends or holidays in the on-sale period, severe weather, transit strikes, newspaper strikes, a major television series or a popular movie or book that appeals to the same audience can have a strong positive or a negative effect on sales for a particular issue.

Chapter 8

OTHER INCOME

One of the wonderful things about a magazine is that it is not just a magazine. Unlike many businesses, a publication has personality, individuality, gender. It can be a parent to its readers, a big brother or sister, a friend, a lover, a confidante, a political opponent or ally, a teacher, a colleague, financial advisor, clown, bedside storyteller.

And so while the magazine may remain the primary source of revenues, there are sure to be related services or products that can create revenue as well. Some are offered by the publisher, others are sold to the reader by outside companies and use the publication as the vehicle, while still others merely use the publication as the means of identifying and locating the audience. As an example of the latter, renting the subscription list to direct-mail marketers takes little or no investment on the part of the publisher yet can be a very substantial source of income.

List Rental

From the tax accountant's viewpoint the subscription list is a liability—you owe the subscribers the remainder of their subscriptions. But in reality a subscription list is definitely an asset. Even if you were to go bankrupt and stop publication, the unfulfilled subscription "liability" would be welcomed by other publishers to the point of their paying you for the privilege of serving your readers the rest of their subscriptions with their magazines.

Within two or three months of start-up most publishers will be approached by direct-mail houses who want to make mailings to the subscription list and, depending on the quality and rarity of the list, the publisher can charge from $35 to $90 for every thousand names each time a mailer uses the list. The expenses associated with marketing a list are minimal and a publisher can expect to clear 60 to 75 percent of sales in net profits.

The list-rental business is a specialization all its own. There are brokers, list managers, bonded lettershops, and all manner of consultants. In addition, the business is highly dependent on the state of the economy and on the season. Mailers can show that certain times of the year are far better than others for specific products. So if your time is limited and this is truly a side income for your publication, it is probably wise to put the list in the hands of a list management specialist and let them worry about marketing it—for a percentage.

As far as strategic planning is concerned, list rental is another powerful incentive to sell subscriptions. It brings in an income per subscription which you should be able to estimate and add to total magazine revenues. Normally it would be calculated as a certain number of net dollars per thousand subscribers a month or per year.

Other Publications

A magazine is an ephemeral thing, but the editorial material may not be. Having paid for the material once and written it off as an expense associated with a particular issue now in the past, the publisher may republish the same material and get additional income either in the form of single reprints of articles or special reports or in one-shots, flats, or books.

When second publication is a possibility it should be planned for at the time of purchase of the original material from the contributor. The new copyright law makes it necessary for a magazine publisher specifically to contract for the acquisition of second rights if second publication is anticipated.

A one-shot is usually a soft cover book on a single subject, often of current but passing interest. If you had published a series of articles in the magazine on earthquakes and volcanoes, you might have had a writer add some connective tissue for the series, introduced it with a new chapter or two, rounded it out with some conclusions, reset it in pocketbook size, and produced a very salable book for newsstands and bookstores at the time when Mt. St. Helens erupted.

Flats are usually magazine size and are in soft cover. A magazine publisher gathers together all the travel articles published in the last two years, for example, and simply reprints them with an introduction of some kind. Again, these go to bookstores as well as newsstands.

The only problem is in getting display. There are so many magazines sold at the newsstand these days that persuading the wholesaler or retailer to take on another—particularly one that has no particular topicality—may be difficult unless it is a sure seller.

The alternative is to put the material between hard covers and sell it exclusively through bookstores. Basically, this is not a profitable business. The authors will usually get a percentage of the standard book royalties for this second use of the material unless it was an all-rights purchase, and the economics of hardcover book publishing are not all that attractive. But the material will make it pretty obvious if there is something worthwhile to be done here.

General-interest book clubs have fallen out of favor recently, but the special-interest club with books specifically associated with a subject related to the magazine has everything going for it—not the least of which is the promotion-at-cost that can be carried in the pages of the magazine.

Foreign Publication

If any language is an international language it is English, which gives our magazines a larger market than just the United States. One way to make these international sales is to distribute additional copies to Canada, Mexico, or overseas. It is necessary to make sure that additional sales in foreign countries are profitable on the basis of the cover price alone, since these readers will most likely be of little interest to the advertiser and so add nothing to the rate base.

There are distributors who specialize in foreign sales and it may be well worth contracting with one to send your magazine overseas. Another possibility is to enter into a royalty arrangement with a foreign publisher. You make your editorial material available to them, and possibly your magazine name, in return for a percentage of sales. The foreign publisher knows the market and has a distribution system and editorial and production staff in place. They select appropriate material from what you have already published, translate it into their language, add material of strictly local interest, and sell their own advertising. Again, make sure you have bought the right to republish the editorial material in these foreign editions at the time of the original purchase agreement.

Conferences and Seminars

Having established the magazine's expertise in a particular area, it is an easy step to sponsoring seminars and conferences for the audience. Speakers are drawn from the field—often people who already contribute regularly to the magazine—and will lead these sessions at the cost of their expenses, if any. They get desirable personal publicity; you get a professional teaching staff. The seminars are promoted at minimum expense in the magazine itself and perhaps with additional mailings to lists of subscribers, expires, and prospects.

It happens very often, and may seem like the tail wagging the dog, that the conference produces more profit than the magazine. However, one must never forget the essential contribution the magazine makes in originally opening the lines of communication to readers in an industry or profession, and in maintaining the authority of the editors and contributors.

Shows

Often associated with the seminars or conferences, shows and exhibits give the advertisers and other suppliers to the industry an opportunity for face-to-face communication with the audience. Shows have become a big business all their own with millions of dollars being spent by exhibitors, and even more millions by attendees.

Products

A magazine with a personality and trademark can offer a whole range of related products to its readers—from tee shirts to jewelry, from games to do-it-yourself kits. The products are designed and manufactured by suppliers to the specifications of the publisher at a preset price, and are sold by the publisher in direct-marketing advertising in the magazine or by direct mail to subscriber and prospect lists.

Clubs and Associations

If the character of the magazine is such as to suggest that readers might like to get together and exchange ideas or expertise at intervals, it makes sense for the magazine to be the sponsor. If the association is to enjoy nonprofit status a true arms-length relationship must be maintained between magazine and club, but a mutually helpful relationship is still possible.

We are speaking here of the magazine spawning the club or association, but more often the opposite is true—the credit-card company starts a magazine related to travel, or a professional association starts a periodical to publish technical papers. The flow of funds between association and magazine can then be exceedingly complex, but promotional or scientific motives probably outweigh profits in the strategic decision making.

A Note for Strategists

Each of the additional sources of revenue mentioned above, as well as the many others found by ingenious publishers, adds a new dimension to the decisions made about the magazine. For example, the list available for rental is enlarged by a subscription promotion effort, or the editors might be persuaded to publish additional articles in a series in anticipation of a book.

It is not impossible to build other income sources into a magazine model, but ordinarily it is wise to wait until a model of the magazine alone has been written and tested. More computer models have been scrapped because the designers tried to do too much rather than because they tried to do too little. Unless the other income has a clear and direct relationship to the magazine circulation or advertising, and the costs are also easily determined, it is best to consider them as bonuses for a well-run magazine and not try to modify magazine decisions in anticipation of other income.

There are instances when this is not true, as when shows or conferences are so profitable as to far outweigh the magazine as a contributor to the corporate bottom line. The strategist may then prefer to consider the other income strategies before the magazine—or set an objective other than profit for the magazine, i.e. promotional values in building attendance.

Chapter 9

COSTS

We are now half way through the right side of the profit equation:

Profits = Revenues - Costs

Revenues result from the three basic streams—advertising, subscriptions, and single-copy sales—and from an all-other category which is important but ancillary to the basic thrust of this book about magazine strategies.

Now we must look at the cost side of the profit equation. From a strategist's point of view this is the easier half because, for example, while the response of a list of prospects to a direct-mail effort is at least somewhat unpredictable, the costs associated with making the mailing are entirely determinable. And so it is with almost all expense items. Once a strategy has been decided on, the costs associated with that strategy are usually a straightforward calculation.

So this part of the analysis is essentially an accounting process but obviously just as important to accurate planning as the first half. And just because it is mechanical accounting don't suppose that it is less prone to error. The surprises that lurk around the corner of a misplaced decimal point, or a bleary reading of those little blue numbers on a calculator at midnight, can blow the best-made strategies as easily as the wildest optimism of a space salesman.

Each of the revenue streams has several direct costs attached to it, and we'll consider them first.

Advertising

Selling effort requires money as well as other resources (often including a large part of the publisher's own time). The sales staff has a payroll of salespeople and a support staff of secretaries and administrative help to process the advertising as it comes in, to see that the insertion order is correct and correctly placed in the magazine, to answer the phone, to make appointments and travel arrangements. The advertiser must be billed promptly, payment acknowledged and complaints handled politely and efficiently.

If you use outside advertising sales representatives to sell space there may be jurisdictional disputes to be arbitrated about territories or advertisers. Sales reps will handle some of their own paperwork and promotion, but if they represent other magazines as well as yours, you'll want to make sure you're getting your fair share of attention.

Associated with any payroll is an overhead in fringe benefits, personnel record keeping, travel and entertainment expense, telephone, office furniture, typewriters and copying machines, and other occupation costs.

A good estimate of fringe benefits is 20 percent of the payroll. Travel and entertainment can be plugged in on a per-person basis. Telephone, office equipment, furniture, rent, and the like will be included as an administrative cost to be discussed later.

As a rule of thumb, the total of all direct advertising sales expenses should rarely exceed 15 percent of the net advertising billing, and preferably should be under 10 percent. Most representatives will happily sell pages in your magazine for a 20 percent commission, so your own internal costs of doing the same thing should be substantially lower. The exception to this guideline is when the publisher intentionally overspends for sales staff as part of a market-building strategy. For a limited period of time (perhaps a year or two) the sales costs may go well above the normal, but if sales don't improve and thereafter reduce this percentage to the 10 to 15 percent range, then the strategy has failed and should be abandoned.

Advertising promotion is one of the factors discussed earlier as a factor influencing the advertising revenue stream. It includes the cost of the rate card and other promotional materials, discounts on the CPM or other deals offered to bring in a difficult agency or advertiser. It is the space purchased in the *New York Times* or *Advertising Age*, hospitality suites at trade shows where advertisers promote their products, promotional gifts to media directors or advertising managers, the cost of the ABC or BPA audit and the cost of researching readers (including syndicated research) to prove to the advertiser that the magazine is indeed read by who you say it is.

Advertising promotion is a decision variable in most magazine models. It is a valve the publisher turns on or off, based on the belief that it sells more advertising pages. Thus, for the modelmaker, the advertising promotion budget may take any one of a range of values and the strategist will be looking for the value which, with optimum values for the other control factors, maximizes profits, or whatever the measured objective.

Depending on the class of service, there may be a postal surcharge for that portion of the magazine which carries advertising. Magazines do get reduced postal rates, but these rates apply only to the editorial portion of the magazine; the advertising portion is charged at normal rates. The difference may be too small to attempt to separate out and charge against advertising, but it is a cost that will affect the bottom line and should not be neglected.

Subscriptions

The subscription manager and staff can be nonexistent (the publisher takes on the function), or as large as several dozen people with director, manager, writers, artists, photographers, designers, paste-up and statisticians. Salaries make up the bulk of this expense with the usual fringe benefits.

Each subscription source adds special costs associated with the effort:

Renewal percentages may differ drastically from source to source and between first-time conversion and later renewals. The renewal series of five to ten letters requires reproduction, printing, paper, stuffing postage out and in. Renewal cost may be calculated on a cost-per-renewal basis, but is probably more accurately figured as an average cost-per-expiration so that change in the percentage return can be handled directly without a tedious recalculation of its effect on the cost-per-renewal received.

Bind-in cards and envelopes have printing, paper and binding charges. If the preproduction costs are contracted for by outside services they are easy to isolate and assign to this effort. If the work is done in-house, the allocation of time and overhead may be more difficult.

Direct-mail efforts have the fixed preproduction cost, and then a variable cost depending on the size of the mailing. The variable cost includes list-rental charges, postage out, return postage and manufacturing cost of materials.

Donor mailings differ from direct-mail only in that the publisher may acquire multiple subscriptions from a single subscriber. The response statistics are slightly different and the costs spread over a larger base.

Agency-sold subscriptions may involve no out-of-pocket cost at all to the publisher who simply indicates how many subscriptions he is willing to accept and at what price. The agency is responsible for acquiring the subscription and collecting the subscription price. The publisher receives a small percentage of the subscription price and a list of names to be served with copies of the magazine. Other arrangements, however, as with college agencies, may set a fixed discount per subscription to the agent and leave all collection responsibility to the publisher. The number of agency-sold subscriptions is, within limits, a decision of the publisher. The model should have the ability to test a range of subscriptions from this source and to track the results for three to five years because renewals, and renewals on renewals, can often make up for the losses incurred during the first year.

Television and radio promotion have the fixed production costs and then the purchased time. Subscriptions are received by telephone with 800 numbers and credit cards. Answering services have set fees per call and the credit-card company charges a percentage of the subscription.

All other sources are handled in similar ways—usually a fixed cost for some sort of preparation of materials, then a variable cost which produces a number of subscriptions related to the size of the investment. The shape of the curve and the exact form of the equation were given in Chapter 6.

Other costs attributable to subscription acquisition and service are fulfillment and postage. Fulfillment usually is handled by an outside service with the computer equipment and experience to handle this function. The charges include a fee for entering the new subscription, and an additional fee for maintaining the name on the list and delivering labels to the printer each issue.

If the number of subscriptions is more than a few thousand or so, it pays to go to a fulfillment house since this is a complex and messy business—both labor and capital intensive. A full-service fulfillment house will provide:

Caging in which the envelopes are opened, and checks or cash
      set aside for deposit in a bank account
Entry of the new or renewed subscription into the computer
Purging of expires

Providing a List of Expires to a lettershop for mailing the
   renewal series
Correcting Errors and handling complaints
Printing Mailing Labels each issue
Reports of all relevant statistics

Postage charges are based on weight for the class of mail usually applied to magazines. As postage charges go up, publishers are more and more frequently exploring methods to reduce the costs or adopt entirely new delivery systems. These include trucking large bundles of magazines to post offices around the country and then breaking the bundles there for local delivery, zip-coding bundles, printing in several locations to reduce shipping costs, and so-called "alternative" means of delivery in which privately owned services deliver magazines to homes or offices.

We mentioned above the postal surcharge for advertising pages. For modeling purposes it may be convenient to lump all postal charges, rather than try to assign part to the advertising cost and another to subscription fulfillment.

Single-copy Costs

In-house circulation department staff and overhead costs are payroll, fringe benefits, etc. In addition, the larger newsstand magazines may support a staff of route men and women who regularly check newsstands and supermarkets to dress up the display and make sure an adequate number of magazines is always available.

Single-copy promotion expenses include the retail display allowance, racks for the magazines and other point-of-purchase materials, radio or television production and time charges and, of course, the critical decision of draw that is essentially a single-copy cost although it appears as a production expense on the operating statement.

Editorial

A small magazine or a newsletter may have an editorial staff as small as one person. A large weekly newsmagazine may have hundreds located all over the world. There are three main functions necessary in the creation of a magazine:

Text departments generate the words that will be published and are responsible for the accuracy of the type in content, grammar, spelling, etc. Newsmagazines have large editorial staffs because they are almost 100 percent staff written. Correspondents and researchers generate raw text which is shaped and edited by writers in the editorial offices. Several iterations of approval and rewrite are applied to the text before it goes to the typesetter, and proofreading, and final page fitting may call for resetting and reproofing. We'll hold actual typesetting expenses for later discussion under the production category, although with the increased use of word processing equipment and "desktop publishing", this function is becoming more and more an editorial responsibility.

When the magazine publishes contributed material, the editors are responsible for commissioning the text or reading and editing over-the-transom contributions. They buy what they feel is publishable and the purchases are an additional cost of the editorial function. Purchase terms are an important legal matter since they will determine whether the publisher has the right to republish the material in books or other forms, andmentioned in Chapter 8.

Art departments are responsible for laying out the text and illustrative material as it appears on the pages, determining size and type of illustration, specifying typefaces and particularly headlines, decks, captions and other display type since these usually differ from that used in the body of the text. Art directors and designers commission art and photography where appropriate, and purchase the contribution.

In-house photography departments are a feature of many magazines. Photographers require special studio space and equipment, as well as staffs of assistants who acquire props, interview models, choose appropriate clothes, makeup models faces and hair, prepare food. Picture laboratories process the film; photographic editors select the specific pictures and recommend their sequence and relative size to the designers.

Photography is often purchased from free-lance photographers or from photo libraries. Free-lancers get expenses plus a fee for the assignments; libraries get a fee for one-time use of the photographs.

Total editorial costs can be figured as the sum of staff costs and editorial purchases, and either, or both, of these categories is predicated in some way on the number of editorial pages. Presumably, as the number of editorial pages goes up, the editorial staff size will have to be larger and/or the purchases will have to rise.

Usually, the number of editorial pages is in some way related to the number of advertising pages. A typical relationship might be as shown in Figure 9.1.

Every magazine has its own formula for figuring the number of editorial pages. Sometimes it is a fixed number regardless of the number of advertising pages. Sometimes it is a percentage of the number of advertising pages. More often it is a combination of the two, with a set minimum number of editorial pages that increases when the advertising goes above some trigger number. On an issue-by-issue basis, the number of editorial pages will seem to make uneven jumps as advertising climbs because magazine pages grow in minimum form increments of 4, 8, or even 16 pages.

For the flat part of the graph at the lower left the equation is:

EDIT PAGES = minimum

The equation of the slanted part of this line is in the form:

EDIT PAGES = AD PAGES/a - a

Here "a" is the percentage of advertising in the magazine.

Knowing the number of advertising pages and the formula, one can calculate the number of editorial pages. Knowing the number of editorial pages and the ratios of editorial purchase and staff cost per editorial page, one can calculate the total editorial cost. There will be considerable variation in these ratios from magazine to magazine, but the ratios should represent some measure of the editorial quality—the higher the ratios of purchase and staff cost per page, the higher one expects the quality of material being purchased—and it is a publisher's strategic decision as to how high the quality must be to achieve the set goals.

We cannot leave the subject of editorial costs without some mention of editorial inventory. This is the material purchased but not yet published, and it may be as small as one or two issue's contents, to as large as six or more. Every magazine has at least one issue in the works at all times.

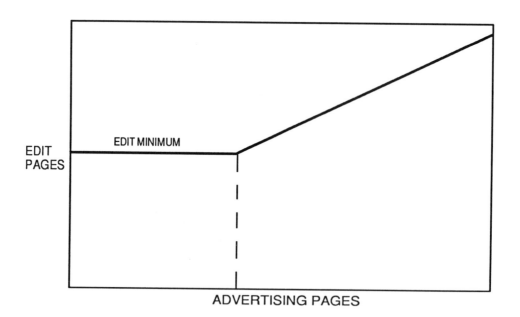

Figure 9.1 Editorial pages are based first on the minimum necessary to cover the topic in each issue. However, the publisher will also establish a desired ad/editorial ratio. When the number of advertising pages sold exceeds this ratio, editorial pages must be added to maintain it.

Costs

Most accumulate some material in advance for upcoming issues, or to be published in the appropriate season. In theory, it is all usable; in fact, some becomes dated, some is purchased in error, some is always replaced by something new thatis better and, the editors are eager to see in print. So some part of the editorial inventory is an investment that simply must be made and will never be used. In a start-up situation, this is a temporary drain on resources that is part of the cost of publishing a magazine. In an on-going situation, inventory build-up or replacement is only required when a significant change in the number of editorial pages is anticpated or a new editor takes charge.

Production Costs

On the payroll side there will be a production manager, an advertising production manager (who handles placement of the ads in the magazine), and assistants and secretaries consistent with the size of the production staff.

Far more important are the costs of typesetting, platemaking, paper, printing, binding and shipping. In most publications these costs can add up to as much as half the total expenditures.

Editorial typesetting costs can be plugged into the model as a factor times the number of editorial pages. Separations, if more than one color will be printed, and platemaking in general, are also proportional to editorial pages unless the publisher gives the editors a budget of so many dollars to spend on engravings of all kinds, and requires that they stay within those limits.

All other production costs are proportional to the total number of pages printed during one print run. Here is the way this is calculated: Under editorial costs we suggested a formula that might be used to establish the number of editorial pages. Once you have editorial pages and advertising pages, it is an easy matter to calculate total pages:

$$\text{Total Pages} = \text{Edit Pages} + \text{Ad Pages} + \text{House Ads}$$

House Ads are pages used to sell subscriptions, other company publications or products, and also as filler to make the total number of pages add up to an economical number and size of printed forms.

Next we need the print order—the number of copies printed per issue.

$$\text{Print Order} = \text{Paid Subs} + \text{Controlled Subs} +$$
$$\text{Unpaid Subs} + \text{Draw} + \text{Comp Copies} + \text{Office Copies}$$

Paid Subs are those for which a subscription payment has been, or is expected to be, received. Controlled Subs are those distributed to readers free. Unpaid Subs are an estimate of the number of new subscribers who will never pay (called the bad debt). Comp Copies are complimentary copies sent to advertisers, advertising prospects, contributors, and newspapers or magazines for promotional purposes. Office Copies are used in the offices or retained for archival purchases, as when the contents are to be republished in some other form.

The product of the total pages and the print order is a measure of the amount of printing actually being done.

$$MP = Total\ Pages * Print\ Order/1000$$

Here MP is simply a convenient abbreviation for "thousands of pages." The total number of pages printed during one issue run is divided by a thousand to bring the number down to a more manageable size. Thus, if your magazine was 164 pages (including covers) last August, and your print order was 500,000 copies, you printed 82,000,000 pages, or 82,000 MP.

Paper or printing costs are calculated from the MP with a convenient number called the CMP, meaning "cost per thousand pages." There is a CMP for paper and CMP for printing, and this is a far easier way to enter production costs into the strategic model than to try to program the printer's contract which will depend on the number of forms, their size, the number of color pages, and finally the print order.

Binding charges are also related to the number of pages and the number of issues in a complicated way, but they are a small part of the total production cost and may be conveniently included in the CMP for printing.

Shipping to wholesalers, or directly to single-copy sales outlets, is a charge that can also be based on the CMP since it is directly related to the weight of magazines being moved.

Administrative Costs

The publisher heads the payroll of the administrative staff that includes the business manager, personnel, finance and accounting, legal, and any other staff departments not directly responsible for the production or sales of the magazine. In general, the larger the payroll in the line departments, the larger the payroll will be in these staff departments. One could almost set a ratio—one unit of staff payroll for every two units of line payroll, or something similar.

Other administrative costs include housekeeping (rent, electricity, heat, telephone), or those which are simple costs of being in business (insurance, taxes, interest, depreciation), plus certain outside services that may replace internal departments in small companies (outside legal or accounting help, pension management, business consultants).

Average Percentages

The Magazine Publishers Association (MPA) does a survey every two years and accumulates financial data on between 150 and 200 magazines. The data is divided among categories of magazine by circulation and advertising revenues (Tables 9.1 and 9.2). These percentages change somewhat from year to year and must be compared with caution to specific individual publications.

According to this survey, magazines in the $1 to 4 million advertising revenue range have trouble making a profit. In these magazines advertising, postage, and administrative expenses are just high enough to eat up any potential profits. The under $1 million category of magazines are essentially subscription supported, and they have less problem with turning that into a profit despite the much higher circulation costs.

On the circulation breakout it is better to be very small—under 250,000—or over 500,000. The category between 750,000 and 1,000,000 offers the best prospects for profitability.

Time and Inflation

We mentioned earlier that a buyer's initial negative reaction to price change tends to disappear with time. That's a positive as far as the publisher is concerned. We must now note that, given our inflationary economy and the expectation that the trend will not change dramatically in the foreseeable future, some provision must be made in all of the above costs for price escalation. Not all costs will climb at the rate of the cost of living, as published by the Bureau of Labor Statistics, but many may. It is wise to include some form of increase in any strategic or tactical thinking.

Any factor or cost figure that is subject to inflationary pressures will follow a standard compound-interest formula:

$$\text{FUTURE COST} = \text{PRESENT COST} * (1.0 + \text{infl})^t$$

Annual Net Advertising Revenues in Millions

	< 1	1 - 2	2 - 4	4 - 10	10 - 20	> 20	NonProf
Ad Revenues	14	36	45	43	47	54	30
Sub Revenues	73	40	41	42	24	29	67
S/C Revenues	13	24	14	15	29	17	3
Total Rev	100	100	100	100	100	100	100
Adv Expenses	4	10	14	12	10	9	8
Circ Expenses	41	31	31	31	31	25	27
Editorial	7	9	9	7	7	9	9
Production	18	27	27	26	28	31	26
Distribution	6	7	8	8	7	7	8
Postage	5	6	6	5	2	3	6
Gen & Adm	12	13	9	8	6	5	9
Total Exp	94	103	105	98	91	88	92
Oper Prof	6	-3	-5	2	9	12	8

Table 9.1 Percentages of revenues and major cost elements of consumer magazines grouped by the total advertising billed. (Data from MPA.)

Circulation Category in Thousands

	< 250	250-500	500-750	750-1000	1000-2000	>2000	Wkly/Bi
Ad Revenues	56	49	55	49	44	45	56
Sub Revenues	27	33	32	37	47	27	29
S/C Revenues	17	18	13	14	9	28	15
Total Rev	100	100	100	100	100	100	100
Adv Expenses	15	14	14	12	10	6	9
Circ Expenses	24	31	24	26	30	25	27
Editorial	10	9	9	6	5	5	11
Production	25	27	27	27	27	39	26
Distribution	5	6	7	8	9	7	7
Postage	2	3	5	3	5	3	2
Gen & Adm	11	10	7	8	7	4	6
Total Exp	93	100	95	89	93	88	89
Oper Prof	7	0	5	11	7	12	11

Table 9.2 Percentages of revenues and major cost elements of consumer magazines grouped by the circulation category. (Data from MPS.)

Costs

Where "t" is the number of years and inflation over these years is "infl." The cost item may be salaries, rent, production— anything subject to a regular or predictable inflation in price. This formula assumes an average inflationary rate over the years—probably untrue, but a reasonable estimate of an average inflationary rate is as good as any forecast that might take into account and changes during the span of the projection.

Chapter 10

AT THE MARGIN

We have gone to great lengths so far to show that a magazine is best analyzed in terms of factors which the mathematician calls variables. You want to know how profits are affected if you raise or lower a price, a newsstand draw or a subscription effort. In business terminology, this is analysis at the margin, and if you automatically think in terms of margin when considering a change in strategy, the answers are surprisingly easy to find and understand.

The questions to ask in any margin analysis are: What would happen if we changed this factor by a small amount? How much would we gain or lose at the bottom line?

Let's take an example—a magazine with three revenue streams— and see how margin analysis will forecast the results. We'll simplify the income sources by assuming that:

1. Subscription revenue depends solely on subscription promotion (we won't concern ourselves with price changes or other factors right now).

2. Newsstand sales depend solely on draw.

3. Advertising gross depends on rate base (which, in turn, is dependent on subscription plus newsstand sales), and promotion effort.

The key statistics about the magazine are given in Table 10.1.

The magazine is printed on a thin newsprint stock and carries very little color. Revenues from advertising are $934,000, and from circulation almost $1,850,000, for a total of $2,784,000. Profits are $333,100. By today's standards this magazine is doing very well.

Subscriptions

The subscription manager has been bringing in the necessary 50,000 new subscriptions every year at an average net paid cost of close to $7.50 each. You can add more subscriptions, but the cost per additional subscription will be higher.

Subscription Promotion	Number of New Subscriptions
$300,000	41,200
400,000	53,000
500,000	64,000
600,000	74,000

The graph of these four points is shown in Figure 10.1.

Renewals cost $2 each, on average, so total subscription acquisition costs are $374,000, plus $100,000, or a total of $474,000.

Newsstand

Let's review our reasoning as to how draw affects newsstand sale. It is logical to suppose that, if you put out only 100 copies of a magazine at the ten best retail outlets, you will sell all 100 copies. If you put out 200 at the twenty best outlets, you'll sell 200 copies. Therefore, at the lowest end of the draw, you can expect to sell everything you distribute. The graph of sale versus draw starts up at a 45 degree angle to the graph coordinates.

At the other extreme, even if you were to distribute a huge number of copies, the chances are you'd only be able to sell some limited number. In this example, the publisher estimates that the total number of people who would have any interest in his magazine is 250,000. With pass-along taking its toll, the most he could ever expect to sell, with total saturation, is 125,000 copies. Therefore, even if the publisher were to distribute half a million copies or more, something close to 125,000 would be sold. The line at the right end of the graph is a flat horizontal—any increase in draw produces no further change in sale.

Between the two extremes, an effective draw produces a smooth curve that rises rapidly at first, and then reaches saturation and approaches the maximum sales as an asymptote. We have all the information necessary to sketch in the actual curve of this magazine's newsstand response (Figure 10.2).

At The Margin

Frequency. . . . . . . .Monthly	Advertising CPM. . . . . . .$9 net
Subscription Price $9.50	Ratebase 200,000
Number of Subs (1-yr). .100.000	Number of Ad Pages/Year. . . . 519
New Sub Promotion. . . $374,000	Paper and Printing/1000pp. . $2.50
Renewal Rate 50%	Fulfillment and Postage. $.15/copy
Cover Price. $1.50	Editorial Pages. 60/issue
Newsstand Draw 200,000	Editorial cost/year. . . .$400,000
Newsstand Sale 100,000	Advertising sales costs. .$200,000
	Administrative Costs . . .$300,000

Table 10.1 The key statistics about a monthly magazine

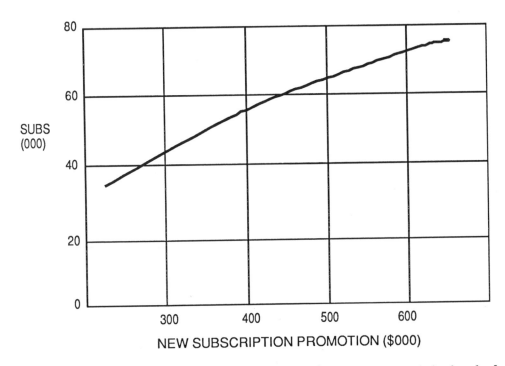

Figure 10.1. A curve fitted to the number of subscriptions and the level of subscription promotion.

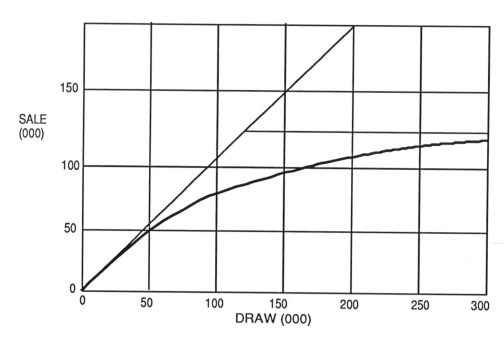

Figure 10.2. Sale versus Draw of the Magazine starts at a 45 degree angle up from zero and approaches 125,000 copies at saturation

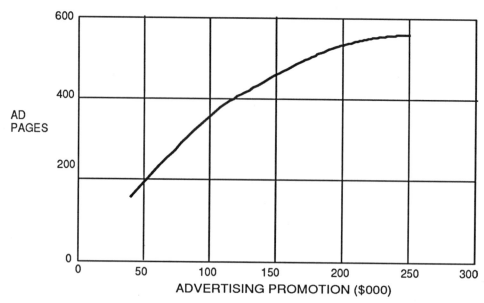

Figure 10.3. Advertising promotion has an impact on the number of advertising pages. This is a diminishing returns curve based on the data provided by the advertising director.

At The Margin

Draw	Sale
150,000	87,350
200,000	99,750
250,000	108,100
300,000	113,650

Advertising

Last year the advertising department sold 519 pages at $1,800 per page. Salaries of the advertising director and the sales staff, plus their promotion expenses, added up to $200,000. The advertising director runs a tight ship. She says that if you hope to sell another 50 pages, she would have to add 50 percent in staff and promotional effort. There is a saturation that takes place here, and it is already in sight according to the person who should know. This gives us the data we need to sketch in a curve that looks about right (Figure 10.3). In detail:

Advertising Promotion	Advertising Pages
$150,000	466
200,000	519
250,000	551
300,000	570

Choose a Strategy

You have been appointed chief strategist for this publisher. You would like to find out whether one can increase profits by a better combination of budgets for subscription promotion, newsstand draw, and advertising sales effort. Which combination is the winner? Choose one value from each of the following columns:

Subscription Promotion	Newsstand Draw	Advertising SalesEffort
$300,000	150,000	$150,000
400,000	200,000	200,000
500,000	250,000	250,000
600,000	300,000	300,000

The profits from all combinations of the above budgets will be found on the following pages. Before looking there, however, check the reasoning that will take you to the right answer. Remember, in any margin analysis we should ask ourselves, "What would happen if we changed this factor by a small amount?"

Subscriptions

If we add 1,000 subscriptions to our list by increasing promotional mailings, how much would those subscriptions net us?

1. Income from 1,000 new subscriptions would be $9,500.

2. Income from a rate base now 1,000 larger would be $9 for each of 519 advertising pages, or $4,671.

3. Cost to acquire 1,000 subscriptions would be approximately ($400,000 - 300,000)/(53,000 - 41,200), which is $8.47 per subscription, or $8,470 for 1,000 subscriptions.

4. Cost to manufacture 1,000 additional copies for 12 issues would be 1,239 pages * $2.50 per thousand. Fulfillment and postage is $.15 * 12 months * 1,000 subscribers. So the total for manufacturing and distribution is $4,898.

Total income, therefore, is $14,170; total cost is $13,368. Clearly, it pays to increase the investment in subscriptions, because the income exceeds the cost. It would be worth your while to look even further than $400,000 in subscription effort.

Newsstand Sales

In the newsstand sales area, if we sell an additional 1,000 copies a year, what would be the income and what would be the cost?

1. The income would be a net of $.75 * 12 * 1,000, or $9,000.

2. The income from the increase in the rate base is the same as for subscriptions, or $9 x 519 ad pages, or $4,671.

3. Manufacturing cost depends on the number of copies distributed, and

to figure that we need the percent of sale of the additional copies. For 50,000 more copies distributed above the present 200,000, the sales percentage is:

$$(108,100 - 99,750)/(250,000 - 200,000) = .167 \text{ or } 16.7\%$$

Therefore, to sell 1,000 more copies every month you would have to distribute 6,000. The manufacturing cost of 6,000 copies times a yearly total of 1,239 pages, is 6,000 * 1,239 * $250/1,000, or $18,585.

Total income, however, is only $13,671, so it makes no sense at all to increase the draw. When you investigate the strategy of reducing the draw, you find that the disastrous effect of the low percentage of sale at higher draws is now not so overwhelming.

1. The percentage of sale of 50,000 fewer copies distributed below 200,000 is (200,000 - 150,000)/(99,750 - 87,350), or 24.8 percent.

2. This means that to reduce the sale by 1,000 copies, one would reduce the draw by 4,032 copies.

3. The savings in not printing 4,032 copies is $12,489, which is less than the $13,671 in income we would lose by reduced rate base and newsstand income. It looks as if the 200,000 draw is just about right.

Advertising

If the advertising department were to sell another 10 pages by virtue of extra sales promotion effort, what would be the net income and what would be the cost?

1. The income would be $1,800 x 10 pages, or $18,000.

2. The cost would be the promotion effort which the advertising director estimated is $50,000 for 32 pages (551 - 519), or $1,562 per page, and $15,620 for 10 pages.

3. Manufacturing cost for 10 pages in 200,000 copies would be $2.50/1000 * 10 * 200,000, or $5,000. Total cost, therefore, is $20,620, which is $2,620 more than the income. Obviously we won't try for more advertising pages through sales promotion.

Newsstand draw: 150,000 copies

Subs	Sale	Ratebase	Ad prom	Ad pages	Tot Rev	Profits
91,215	87,351	178,566	150,000	466	2,401,806	305,178
91,215	87,351	178,566	200,000	519	2,486,463	308,069
91,215	87,351	178,566	250,000	551	2,537,810	290,149
91,215	87,351	178,566	300,000	570	2,568,953	259,606

Newsstand draw: 200,000 copies

Subs	Sale	Ratebase	Ad prom	Ad pages	Tot Rev	Profits
91,215	99,763	190,978	150,000	466	2,565,586	320,693
91,215	99,763	190,978	200,000	519	2,656,128	322,884
91,215	99,763	190,978	250,000	551	1,711,044	304,539
91,215	99,763	190,978	300,000	570	2,744,352	273,739

Newsstand draw: 250,000 copies

Subs	Sale	Ratebase	Ad prom	Ad pages	Tot Rev	Profits
91,215	108,083	199,299	150,000	466	2,675,372	282,213
91,215	108,083	199,299	200,000	519	2,769,857	281,764
91,215	108,083	199,299	250,000	551	2,827,166	261,818
91,215	108,083	199,299	300,000	570	2,861,926	230,046

Newsstand draw: 300,000 copies

Subs	Sale	Ratebase	Ad prom	Ad pages	Tot Rev	Profits
91,215	113,660	204,876	150,000	466	2,748,963	207,539
91,215	113,660	204,876	200,000	519	2,846,093	203,149
91,215	113,660	204,876	250,000	551	2,905,005	180,813
91,215	113,660	204,876	300,000	570	2,940,737	147,592

Table 10.2 New subscription promotion: $300.000

At The Margin

Newsstand draw: 150,000 copies

Subs	Sale	Ratebase	Ad prom	Ad pages	Tot Rev	Profits
1C2,972	87,351	190,322	150,000	466	2,562,809	314,391
1C2,972	87,351	190,322	200,000	519	2,653,039	321,307
1C2,972	87,351	190,322	250,000	551	2,707,767	305,829
1C2,972	87,351	190,322	300,000	570	2,940,,737	276.767

Newsstand draw: 200,000 copies

Subs	Sale	Ratebase	Ad prom	Ad pages	Tot Rev	Profits
1C2,972	99,763	202,735	150,000	466	2,726,589	329,906
1C2,972	99,763	202,735	200,000	519	2,822,704	336,122
102,972	99,763	202,735	250,000	551	2,881,001	320,219
1C2,972	99,763	202,735	300,000	570	2,916,359	290,900

Newsstand draw: 250,000 copies

Subs	Sale	Ratebase	Ad prom	Ad pages	Tot Rev	Profits
1C2,972	108,083	211,055	150,000	466	2,836,374	291,426
1C2,972	108.083	211,055	200,000	519	2,936,434	295,002
1C2,972	108.083	211,055	250,000	551	2,997,123	277,498
1C2,972	108.083	211,055	300,000	570	3,033,933	246,207

Newsstand draw: 300,000 copies

Subs	Sale	Ratebase	Ad prom	Ad pages	Tot Rev	Profits
1C2,972	113,660	216,632	150,000	466	2,909,966	216,752
1C2,972	113,660	216,632	200,000	519	3,012,669	216,388
1C2,972	113,660	216,632	250,000	551	3,074,962	196,493
1C2,972	113,660	216,632	300,000	570	3,112,745	164,753

Table 10.3. New subscription promotion: $400,000

Newsstand draw: 150,000 copies

Subs	Sale	Ratebase	Ad prom	Ad pages	Tot Rev	Profits
113,858	87,351	201,208	150,000	466	2,711,891	315,518
113,858	87,351	201,208	200,000	519	2,807,282	326,162
113,858	87,351	201,208	250,000	551	2,865,140	312,944
113,858	87,351	201,208	300,000	570	2,900,233	285,253

Newsstand draw: 200,000 copies

Subs	Sale	Ratebase	Ad prom	Ad pages	Tot Rev	Profits
113,858	99,763	213,620	150,000	466	2,875,671	331,033
113,858	99,763	213,620	200,000	519	2,976,947	340,977
113,858	99,763	213,620	250,000	551	3,038,374	327,334
113,858	99,763	213,620	300,000	570	3,075,631	299,386

Newsstand draw: 250,000 copies

Subs	Sale	Ratebase	Ad prom	Ad pages	Tot Rev	Profits
113,858	108,083	221,941	150,000	466	2,985,457	292,553
113,858	108,083	221,941	200,000	519	3,090,677	299,857
113,858	108,083	221,941	250,000	551	3,154,496	284,613
113,858	108,083	221,941	300,000	570	3,193,205	255,693

Newsstand draw: 300,000 copies

Subs	Sale	Ratebase	Ad prom	Ad pages	Tot Rev	Profits
113,858	113,660	227,518	150,000	466	3,059,048	217,879
113,858	113,660	227,518	200,000	519	3,166,912	221.242
113,858	113,660	227,518	250,000	551	3,232,335	203,608
113,858	113,660	227,518	300,000	570	3,272,017	173,239

Table 10.4 New subscription promotion: $500,000.

At The Margin

Newsstand draw: 150,000 copies

Subs	Sale	Ratebase	Ad prom	Ad pages	Tot Rev	Profits
123,937	87,351	211,288	150,000	466	2,849,936	309,158
123,937	87,351	211,288	200,000	519	2,950,106	323,253
123,937	87,351	211,188	250,000	551	3,010,862	312,128
123,937	87,351	211,288	300,000	570	3,047,712	285,707

Newsstand draw: 200,000 copies

Subs	Sale	Ratebase	Ad prom	Ad pages	Tot Rev	Profits
123,937	99,763	223,700	150,000	466	3,013,716	324,673
123,937	99,763	223,700	200,000	519	3,119,770	338,068
123,937	99,763	223,700	250,000	551	3,184,096	326,518
123,937	99,763	223,700	300,000	570	3,223,111	299,840

Newsstand draw: 250,000 copies

Subs	Sale	Ratebase	Ad prom	Ad pages	Tot Rev	Profits
123,937	108,083	232,020	150,000	466	3,123,501	286,193
123,937	108,083	232,020	200,000	519	3,233,500	296,947
123,937	108,083	232,020	250,000	551	3,300,218	283,797
123,937	108,083	232,020	300,000	570	3,340,684	256,147

Newsstand draw: 300,000 copies

Subs	Sale	Ratebase	Ad prom	Ad pages	Tot Rev	Profits
123,937	113,660	237,598	150,000	466	3,197,092	211,519
123,937	113,660	237,598	200,000	519	3,309,736	218,333
123,937	113,660	237,598	250,000	551	3,378,057	202,792
123,937	113,660	237,598	300,000	570	3,419,496	173,693

Table 10.5. New subscription promotion: $600,000.

At The Margin

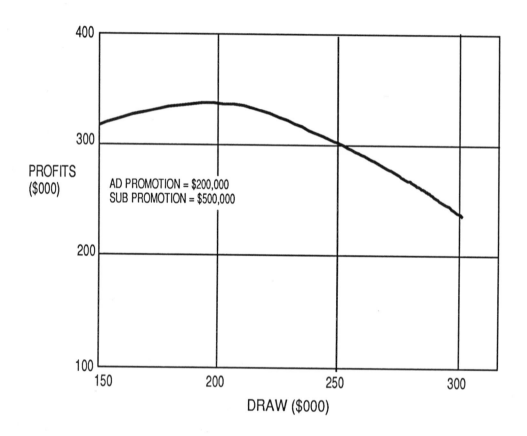

Figure 10.4. Profit sensitivity to changes in draw with advertising promotion set at $200,000 and subscription promotion at $500,000. Maximum profits appear at a draw of 200,000 copies.

At The Margin

You can also work the same analysis in reverse. Assume 10 fewer advertising pages at a reduction in sales effort and manufacturing cost to see if it would pay to reduce the sales effort. Remember, the margin analysis works both ways, up and down. Take a look at Table 10.2 and see how well you did.

How Did you Do?

Look closely at the tabled results on the previous pages. The tables show where the best profits would be—no change in newsstand draw or ad promotion; some increase in sub promotion. We had little to change in this case because the magazine was being run very close to its maximum profit potential. An increase in the subscription effort would raise the net a few thousand dollars, but in reality you probably couldn't set a rate base to the exact circulation achieved. This is particularly true for a magazine that depends on newsstand circulation which is bound to vary considerably from month to month.

It is interesting to see that profits are most sensitive to changes in the newsstand draw. Figure 10.4 is a graph of profits versus draw, as taken from the tables. Note that because of the advertising contribution, one can still make a profit on newsstand sales at as low as 25 percent of the draw. It is an outrage, of course, to consider throwing away three-quarters of what one prints, but is that different in any important way from sending a promotion mailing that costs $9 or more for each $9.50 in subscription income received?

Chapter 11

SPREADSHEET AND MODEL DESIGN

Marginal analysis is a good method for small changes of one or two factors. It can be cumbersome and misleading if the strategist wishes to explore more extreme changes of a number of factors. To do this we must create a more elaborate model, either with a spreadsheet program or with a program tailored to the specific magazine.

To review our method, the first step is to decide on the objective—growth, publicity, profit, whatever—and the method of measuring achievement. For growth, is circulation the measure of achievement over the next five years? Is it the number of advertising pages? For publicity, is it a number of inches in newspaper quotes? Is it recognition of the magazine name by a percentage of the general population? For profits, is it dollars this year? A total over the next five years? A present value of the future profit flow?

Whatever the objective, it should be stated clearly and in quantitative terms so that, at the start, everyone knows what it is and can begin thinking about how they can help achieve it. One of the biggest problems facing corporate organizations today is that individuals and individual departments usually have objectives that differ from, and even conflict with, the objectives of the company as a whole. They don't realize this because they are not apprised of top management thinking and, in most cases, do not know how their department can directly contribute to the achievement of corporate objectives.

This is not reprehensible, or even surprising. We already know how difficult it is for a publisher to see the impact of a single budgetary decision on the bottom line, so why should we expect a department head—with a narrower viewpoint, less data, and vaguely stated objectives—to be a better, and more unselfish, strategist than the publisher?

Left to himself, a subscription manager measures success by the number and acquisition cost of the subscribers—not magazine profits. A newsstand manager measures success by the percentage, or absolute sale of a magazine. An editor measures success by the number of letters readers write, or the circulation growth, or the renewal rate. An advertising director measures success by advertising pages sold, or gross billings. All of these have very complex relationships with what the publisher is most concerned about—profits—and they may even be negatively related! Uncontrolled circulation growth often means decreased profits and possible bankruptcy. Additional advertising pages can eat into profits if editorial pages have to be added. Therefore, the more department heads who are involved with the strategic and tactical decision making, the better they will be able to cooperate to achieve the publisher's objectives and to be rewarded accordingly.

Having settled on objectives, the publisher now must decide on a strategic plan. This may be as large as: Should a new magazine be attempted? Should there be a change in frequency or a major editorial concept shift? The strategic plan is a broad-brush outline that responds to changes in the economy, in the competitive environment, to an opportunity in the marketplace brought about by a technological or social shift. It grows out of the questions we asked in Chapter 3.

The publisher then wants to determine how close to the previously set objectives each strategic plan can take him. To achieve that he builds the strategic model. The model helps tune the publisher's control factors. The publisher will make a list of which factors are really under his control, and which are not. For example, the environment is not; it will be included in the model in inflation of costs, or a more or less difficult advertising sell, but it is not a control factor. Neither are many of the costs associated with publishing the magazine, although they may vary as a result of control factor decisions. Neither are the shapes of the response curves described in Chapters 5, 6, and 7. The shapes of the response curves are not under the publisher's control; the place on the curve that the publisher chooses to occupy, however, is.

Many control factors are optimized individually with a "best" of some kind—the best advertising campaign the agency can dream up, the best editor you can hire for a reasonable salary, choice of the best advertising representative in the field. But a goodly number are of the water-valve variety we spoke of earlier, such as cover and subscription prices, advertising CPM, subscription promotion budget, advertising promotion budget, draw, single-copy promotion budget, editorial staff size and purchase budget, number of editorial pages and amount of color. The best values for these can be found only when all are considered at once, and that is impossible to do analytically except with a computer model.

In making this selection of control factors we don't want the list to get too long. Each added factor creates a new dimension in the field of possible solutions. If there is only one control factor, the field of possible solutions is just the set of all values of that factor. If there are two factors,

Spreadsheet and Model Design

all combinations of the two factors are possible solutions. If there are three factors, the range of possible solutions is every combination of all three factors.

I have found that it is a rare business that has more than six true control factors; even when I built a model with six, I found that only two were critical. Of course we couldn't know that when we started, but if you're doubtful about including a factor in an already large set, you will probably be safe to leave it out.

The rest of the material to be presented in this chapter will assist the modelmaker to assemble the data and relationships we have been discussing into a functioning program that accurately represents the magazine as a strategic entity, and will display the tactical options open to its publisher.

The Spreadsheet Model

The simplest strategy model can be written on any one of a number of spreadsheet programs available. The spreadsheet consists of a series of columns and rows, and the intersection of each row and column is called a cell. The power of the program lies in the fact that data in any cell can be derived as a result of an equation involving data from other cells. We described an advertising rate card application in Chapter 5. Now let's see a spreadsheet designed to function as a strategy model of a magazine.

Table 11.1 starts with the three decision variables judged to be critical in this magazine. These are the number of controlled subscriptions, the advertising cost per thousand, and the advertising promotion budget.

The three factors are identified as decision variables that the publisher will have to make. The most important line in the spreadsheet is the calculation of the number of advertising pages. The equation entered here uses the values found in the decision factor cells to calculate advertising pages. Note that the equation is written in symbolic form as:

$$\text{AD PAGES} = f(\text{AdvCPM} * \text{Circ}) * f(\text{Prom})$$

Here the expression "f()" means, "is a function of what is included between the parentheses." The advertising page estimate is dependent on the average page rate as represented by the product of advertising CPM and circulation. The ad page estimate is also influenced by the promotion level, so the second term on the right side of the equation adds this impact.

To find the exact form of the equation to be entered into the spreadsheet you will need a curve fitting program of the kind listed in

```
        No. Subs (000)       100.00 Decision Variable
              Adv CPM         25.00 Decision Variable
       Adv Prom ($000)       100.00 Decision Variable

         No. Adv Pages       866.61 f(AdvCPM * Circ) * f(Prom)

     Adv Revenue ($000)      2166.53 Adv Pages * Adv CPM * Circ

      Edit & Prod ($000)     1104.93 Edit + Prod/Page * No. Pages
      Circulation ($000)      304.00 Prom + Fulfill * Postage
      Advertising ($000)      424.98 Fixed + 15% Commission
         Gen &Adm ($000)      300.00 Fixed
                            ──────────
         Tot Cost ($000)     2133.91 Sum of Costs
                            ══════════
          Profits ($000)       32.61 Revenues - Costs
```

Table 11.1 . *A simple strategy model of a controlled circulation magazine written on a spreadsheet program. It has only one critical* cell—the *one calculating the number of advertising pages as a function of the advertising CPM, the circulation (ratebase) and the advertising promotion budget.*

```
          Sub Price        17.00 Decision Variable
    Sub Prom ($000)        500.00 Decision Variable
          Adv CPM          30.00 Decision Variable
          Adv Prom        100.00 Decision Variable

      No. Paid Subs        146.05 f(Price) * f(Sub Prom)
      No. Adv Pages        107.75 f(AdvCPM * No. Subs) * F(Adv Promo)

      Sub Rev ($000)      2482.85 Sub Price * No. Subs
      Adv Rev ($000)       472.11 Adv Pages * Adv CPM * No. Subs
                         ─────────
      Tot Rev ($000)      2954.96 Sum of Revenues

         Edit ($000)       300.00 Edit Fixed + Edit/Page * No. Pages
         Prod ($000)      1137.04 Prod/Page * No. Pages
         Circ ($000)       920.62 Prom + Fulfill * Postage
         Advt ($000)       270.82 Fixed + 15% Commission
          G&A ($000)       300.00 Fixed
                         ─────────
    Tot Cost ($000)       2928.48 Sum of Costs
                         ═════════
      Profits ($000)        26.48 Revenues - Costs
```

Table 11.2. *A paid circulation magazine has an additional calculation cell to predict the number of paid subscriptions based on the subscription price and the subscription promotion budget.*

Spreadsheet and Model Design

Appendix A.

The price impact part of the equation is of the form:

$$\text{AD PAGES} = a/\exp((\text{PAGERATE}^2)/b)$$

And specifically for this magazine:

$$\text{AD PAGES} = 2.17/\exp((\text{PAGERATE}^2)/15)$$

Since the page rate is found by multiplying the advertising CPM by the rate base or circulation, the spreadsheet entry would actually be written:

$$2.17 * @\exp((\text{A2} * \text{A1}/1000)^2/15)$$

The "@exp" is the Lotus symbol for the raising 2.71828 to the power of the parenthetical function that follows. A2 and A1 are the advertising CPM and circulation rate base which are multiplied and divided by one thousand (for cost per *thousand* readers).

The second half of the equation to include the promotion impact is of the diminishing returns form:

$$\text{PROMOTION IMPACT} = a + b * (1 - 1/\exp(\text{PROM} - \text{C}))^d$$

and specifically

$$\text{PROMOTION IMPACT} = 100+900*(1-1/@\exp(\text{A2}/150))^{0.8}$$

so the full entry in the cell for advertising pages is

$$2.17*@\exp((\text{A2}*\text{A1}/1{,}000)^2/15)*(100+900*(1-1/@\exp(\text{A2}/150))^{0.8})$$

It looks forbidding when written out this way with all the actual constants, but the form of these equations soon becomes familiar. The rest of the spreadsheet is straightforward accounting: Editorial costs were assumed to be constant over the range of values to be tested in the model. Production costs are calculated from the total number of advertising pages per year, plus editorial pages multiplied by the circulation, to give a total for the number of pages printed. Circulation costs are a constant for salaries and overhead, plus fulfillment and postage costs per copy. Advertising costs are the fixed salaries, plus a percentage of total advertising revenues. General and administrative costs were assumed to be fixed.

The last two lines indicate total expenses and net profits, so we can now use this spreadsheet to explore variations in the decision factors. All you have to do is move the cursor to the decision cell and type in a new number.

Table 11.2 shows a somewhat more elaborate spreadsheet model. This is a paid circulation magazine, and so the number of subscribers must first be calculated as a function of the subscription price and promotion level. Then the number of advertising pages sold can be calculated as a function of the rate base, the CPM, and the advertising promotion budget. Expenses can then be calculated, and total expenses subtracted from total revenues to give profits.

Table 11.3 is a summary of how the number of advertising pages changes with changes in the subscription price and the number of subscriptions for the model in Table 11.2. Then, for each entry in Table 11.3, you can calculate profits. This is shown in Table 11.4.

Spreadsheets make good first drafts of a magazine strategy model because they are simple to create and easy to understand. They are also somewhat oversimplified and slow, because each change in the decision factors must be entered manually and the results recorded somewhere (as in Tables 11.3 and 11.4 above) to get a real sense of how profits respond to a range of values of one or more of the decision factors.

Overall Structure of the Model

A more sophisticated model would require a very elaborate spreadsheet or custom programming. You may write one yourself, or use a magazine strategy model that is available to run on IBM compatible micro-computers—see Appendix C for information on how to get more information. We will spend a few pages here to rough out how one might be constructed.

Program flow diagrams are usually drawn from top to bottom the way the program runs, but it has been my experience that programs are written from inside out and it will be easier to understand the magazine model if it is introduced in that way.

The program starts with a set of data about the magazine and its market (Table 11.5). This includes values for all the control factors for all five years, and with the fitted equations for how circulation and advertising

Sub Price	No. Subs	Advertising Cost per Thousand				
		$30.00	$32.50	$35.00	$37.50	$40.00
$17.00	146050	108	68	42	24	14
$19.00	121991	239	174	123	85	57
$21.00	99878	438	353	281	219	168
$23.00	80154	679	591	510	434	366
$25.00	63051	918	843	769	697	627
$27.00	48616	1120	1065	1008	951	893

Table 11.3 Assuming a fixed subscription promotion budget, the number of subscriptions varies strictly as a function of price (left two columns). Each combination of rate base and advertising CPM results in a different number of advertising pages sold.

Sub Price	No. Subs	Advertising Cost per Thousand				
		$30.00	$32.50	$35.00	$37.50	$40.00
$17.00	146050	$26	($36)	($88)	($127)	($155)
$19.00	121991	$284	$214	$143	$78	$22
$21.00	99878	$485	$438	$376	$307	$236
$23.00	80154	$572	$572	$550	$510	$459
$25.00	63051	$518	$562	$588	$596	$588
$27.00	48616	$342	$413	$471	$517	$550

Table 11.4. Each cell in Table 10.3, which listed the number of advertising pages sold, has associated with it a profit level—losses at the very high rate bases; increasing profits up to a subscription price of around $25.

Factor	Year 1	Year 2	Year 3	Year 4	Year 5
Sub price	14.00	15.00	16.00	17.00	18.00
Dir mail Prom	750000	800000	800000	850000	850000
Adv prom	60000	72000	72000	84000	84000
Ad pagerate	5148	7531	7753	8236	8477

Table 11.5. The first step in creating a full-scale strategy model is to list the factors to be considered (left column) and then the values planned for each factor for the years of the projection.

pages change with changes in cover price, draw, subscription price, subscription promotion, etc.

In the central section of the program the computer will run a five-year projection based on the given set of values for the control factors. This part of the program calculates the number of single-copies sold, the number of new subscriptions (by source and price), the number of renewals (by source and price), and the number of advertising pages sold for each year. Note that the calculation for a given year will depend on the previous year's new and renewed subscriptions, so the computation is a progressive one.

When circulation and advertising are known the program can determine the total revenues and, in a parallel calculation, find the costs. It is then a simple matter to find the profits for each of the five years.

Then one of the factors is set to a new value. For example, if the original data had the first year subscription price at $14, the next run might put the price at $15 in the first year, and set all the subscription prices for the remaining years proportionately higher. Thus, we have a new set of factor values and the program runs the central section to recalculate the five-year profits. For the third run the cover price might be set at $16, all other cover prices raised proportionately from their initial values, and again profits are calculated for the five years.

In this way, the program steps through a range of values for a single factor in the first year, automatically resetting the values for the factor in the later years. Each five-year projection should be displayed as a line on the screen so that a table is built up that represents a full range of values for the control factor and the resulting profits (Table 11.6).

Having completed the calculations for the desired range and displaying the profits, the user is then asked to decide on what values to choose for the factor. In this case, the user would probably set the subscription price in Year 1 at $18 or $19 because this maximizes the profit for all five years (the Pres Value in the last column). Later year prices would be raised proportionately to the new first year price (Table 11.7).

The program then asks if another factor is to be tested. If so, a set of runs is made for the range and step size of the second factor with the new subscription prices. Again, a new choice for the second factor may be selected and then a third factor may be tested. In this way, every control factor is individually checked through a settable range, and with settable steps within the range. After all the factors have been tested once, it is advisable to go back and recheck the first tested factor to see if optimum

144   **Spreadsheet and Model Design**

Sub Price	Paid Subs 000	Ctld Subs 000	Tot Circ 000	Adv Pgs	Yr 1 Prof $000	Yr 2 Prof $000	Yr 3 Prof $000	Yr 4 Prof $000	Yr 5 Prof $000	Pres Value $000
14.00	82	0	82	660	900	2194	2544	2870	3258	7375
15.00	79	0	79	681	948	2413	2787	3149	3549	8047
16.00	76	0	76	701	986	2580	2951	3328	3724	8503
17.00	73	0	73	722	1017	2697	3043	3418	3801	8768
18.00	70	0	70	742	1040	2769	3073	3432	3794	8867
19.00	68	0	68	762	1055	2800	3050	3383	3719	8823
20.00	65	0	65	782	1064	2796	2981	3281	3590	8660

Table 11.6. *The main section of the strategy model shows how five-year profits change as a result of the change in one factor, in this case the subscription price.*

Factor	Year 1	Year 2	Year 3	Year 4	Year 5
Sub price	18.00	19.25	20.50	21.95	23.00
Dir mail Prom	750000	800000	800000	850000	850000
Adv prom	60000	72000	72000	84000	84000
Ad pagerate	5148	7531	7753	8236	8477

Table 11.7. *As a result of the runs shown in table 11.6, the decision is made to increase the subscription price in Year 1 to $18, and later year prices are increased proportionately. This represents a new strategy and a much more profitable one.*

Spreadsheet and Model Design

profits are still achieved at the set value, now that the other factors have been tuned to different values.

Now we will see how each revenue stream, and then each cost, is calculated in turn and incorporated into the model.

Single-copy Sale

The model must first calculate single-copy sale because this will affect the number of subscriptions sold by bind-in cards. The three most frequently chosen factors for single-copy sale will be cover price, draw, and newsstand promotion. The equation for sale as a function of cover price was:

$$SALE1 = a/exp((PRICE - c)^2/b)$$

Your data might look something like this:

PRICE	SALE
2.00	50,000
2.50	40,000
3.00	30,000

The equation that fits these points is:

$$SALE1 = 66/exp((PRICE - .521)^2/7.75)$$

Note that since we have to include the impact of other factors as well on the newsstand sale, specifically draw and promotion level, we are calling this first factor "SALE1."

The impact of newsstand draw would be in the form:

$$SALE2 = a + b * (1 - 1/exp(DRAW/c))^d$$

This equation form needs three points plus the value when the draw is zero—obviously zero. Let's suppose your data looks as follows:

DRAW	SALE	PERCENT
100,000	50,000	100
150,000	70,000	140
200,000	80,000	160
0	0	0

Note that now I have added a third column to the table, representing the percentage change in the SALE value as a result of changes in the DRAW. Since the three factor equations have to be multiplied to give the final value of SALE, we use a percentage for SALE2 and SALE3. The equation of this curve is:

$$SALE2 = 0 + 176 * (1 - 1/exp(DRAW/60))\char`\^2.75$$

Finally, the impact of promotion is:

$$SALE3 = a + b * (1 - 1/exp(PROM/c))\char`\^d$$

PROM	SALE	PERCENT
0	45,000	90
100,000	50,000	100
150,000	52,500	105
200,000	54,000	108

Here it is assumed that even if the promotion were reduced to zero, there would still be a sale of 45,000, or 90 percent of the original value, and additional dollars spent would produce a small increase in sale.

Now we can combine the impact of the three factors:

$$SALE = SALE1 * SALE2 * SALE3$$

Subscriptions

Subscriptions are by far the most complicated part of the program. You start by producing a price impact factor for each major source. This uses an equation of the same form as was used above for cover price:

$$PRICE\ IMPACT = a/exp((PRICE - c)\char`\^2/b)$$

New subscription sales from cards, direct mail, television commercials, etc., can be calculated following the promotion equations given in Chapter 6, and similar to that used for single-copy sales above. For each source, the gross new subscriptions will be comprised of several categories—bad debt (the percentage that won't pay), one-year subscriptions, two-year subscriptions, and three-year subscriptions, or whatever terms are appropriate from that source.

Spreadsheet and Model Design   147

Next, the renewals are calculated for each source year by year through the projection, with bad debt and different terms. Note that renewal rates are affected by the renewal prices using the price impact factor equation.

When all sources and renewals have been calculated, the total circulation can be accumulated for each year and the rate base established. You can use the *integer* function to set the rate base at the nearest even number under the circulation. In the following equation, the rate base will be set to the nearest even 10,000 under the circulation.

$$\text{RATE BASE} = 10{,}000 * \text{int(CIRCULATION/10,000)}$$

For example, if the circulation were 173,000, the division reduces this to 17.3. The *integer* function takes everything to the left of the decimal point, so we have 17. Then the multiplication returns the total to 170,000—the nearest 10,000 under the achieved circulation.

Advertising

The factors influencing the sales of advertising are usually CPM, advertising promotion (or total marketing expenditure), and rate base. The first two are control factors, and the third has just been calculated so the number of advertising pages can be calculated using the equations and methods described above and in Chapter 5.

Revenues

Single-copy sales income is the single-copy price, times the number of copies sold, times a discount factor that provides net income to the publisher per copy paid by the distributor. This, then, must be multiplied by the number of issues per year to get a total revenue from single-copy sales per year. If there is a retail display allowance, it can be deducted from revenues or added as a cost at a later date.

Subscription income is best handled on a cashflow basis; that is, whatever new or renewed subscriptions are sold in the year are "booked" in that year—including the full two- and three-year subscription prices.

Gross advertising revenue is the total advertising pages multiplied by the average CPM and by the rate base in thousands. Since CPM is probably a rate card average, you will have to deduct a percentage that goes to the advertising agency plus a percentage for multiple insertion or other discounts. Make this deduction at this stage, rather than as a cost factor, since it is money that is never received at the magazine and would artificially inflate the sales figures.

Costs

One by one the appropriate costs can now be determined. It will be necessary to calculate the number of editorial pages based on the number of advertising pages sold. Editorial cost may be a fixed sum, plus a variable cost based on the number of editorial pages. Don't forget to include inflation as a factor in this equation.

Production costs include some factors dependent on the number of editorial pages, and some that are based on the total MCP (thousands of copy pages).

Single-copy sales costs are staff plus promotion. Subscription costs are staff plus the accumulated promotion for all the various sources, plus postage and fulfillment. Advertising costs are staff plus commissions, plus promotional expenses.

Administrative costs may be fixed or variable. If variable, they are probably a percentage of total revenues. Don't forget the escalation caused by inflation.

And finally, we get back to the original equation:

$$\text{Profits} = \text{Revenues} - \text{Costs}$$

and can calculate profits for the year, given the values for the factors in this run. As each year's results are found, they are printed as a line in a results table that might look something like Table 11.6.

After each decision, the user must be given the option to rerun with the same or a different control factor, or to record that the factors have been set to their optimum values.

Optimizing Routines

Experienced programmers may observe that the search procedure outlined here could be programmed to run automatically, and search for the optimum set of values.

This would hide a critically important kind of information from the publisher that is revealed as the factor steps through its range of values. Many of the factors thought to be important to the business plan may turn out to have no real impact on profits through a wide range of values. For example, as draw steps from 50,000 copies to 250,000 copies in the sample above, the profits may actually ride a flat plateau with no important improvement or loss. In that case, the publisher can make the decision on draw based on criteria other than profits, such as maintaining a slow but steady circulation growth over the years.

The second virtue from seeing the profits step by step is that when a factor has an important effect on profits, like the cover price in the example above, the publisher will want to make certain that the curve used in the model to calculate the impact on profits is as accurate as possible. You might test subscription prices over a much wider range than thought necessary before running the model.

Each set of runs that leads to a recommended five-year plan can be displayed on the monitor and only the final table printed out. However, a record of how profits change with changes in each of the factors will make interesting and useful reading. It is easy to get lost in the multiplicity of options, therefore. a printed copy of each run should be made for later review.

Program Modification

Once through the experience of creating the model, revisions and rewrites are usually easy. The structure of the program is clear:

1. Calculate single-copy sale as a function of the control factors.

2. Calculate subscriptions from each source by term as a function of the control factors.

3. Calculate rate base as an even number under the sum of paid circulation.

4. Calculate advertising pages as a function of control factors and rate base.

5. Calculate editorial pages and total pages as a function of advertising pages.

6. Calculate revenues from all sources (include those other than direct magazine revenues here).

Spreadsheet and Model Design

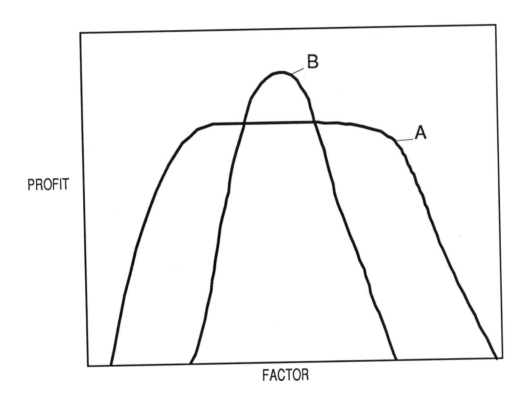

Figure 11.1. Profit sensitivity to changes in a factor tell you how much effort or research to invest in discovering as much as possible about the factor. A flat plateau (line A) indicates that over a wide range of values for the factor the profits are relatively unchanged. On the other hand a sharp peak (line B) indicates that profits are highly dependent on choosing exactly the right value for the factor and it is advisable to do as much testing and research as possible to convince yourself that the impact of that factor is understand and measured accurately.

Spreadsheet and Model Design   151

7. Calculate all costs.

8. Print a line of important data and five-year profits.

9. Step the control factor to its next value within the desired range.

10. Repeat steps 1 through 9 until all factors have been optimized

The program is dependent on the accuracy of the functional relationships between newsstand sale and its control factors, subscription sales and their control functions, and advertising sale and its control functions. So, when a factor is found to provide a steep climb to the optimum profit, and then a steep decline, it is a signal for the user to be as sure as possible about the particular functional relationship (Figure 11.1).

When in doubt, or when the functional relationship cannot be made any more reliable with additional research, it is wise to make runs with "best case," "worst case," and "most likely" values. For example, you might consider a 10 percent increase in advertising rates to produce, at worst, a 30 percent loss in pages; at best, a 10 percent loss in pages; but most likely, a 20 percent loss in pages. Each set of assumptions is used to generate an equation and each assumption then is the basis of a different strategic model. Now observe the sensitivity of profits to each model. The new curve will change the calculated profits almost certainly, but it may not change the tactics that produce maximum profits.

And having satisfied yourself that you have found the range of profits available from the model at this strategy, you can now move on to an alternate strategy, with a fairly major modification in the model, and see if the resulting profits differ importantly from those found with the first. In either case you can now be sure you have discovered the best you can do with the strategy.

Chapter 12

A CITY MAGAZINE

When running a magazine, what may seem like a simple decision—how much to budget for subscription promotion next year, for example—can have a domino effect of far-reaching consequences. If you put a few more pieces in the mail, you'll sell more subscriptions. But some of those new subscriptions may be people who normally bought the magazine at the supermarket checkout counter. If so, the percentage of single-copy sales will drop. But, overall, one would expect that circulation will increase, so you'll want to raise the rate base and the page rate. As a result, you may lose a few pages of advertising.

When you try to assess how profits are affected by a few more direct-mail pieces, it turns out to be such a tangle that you quit and make it easy on yourself. If you can afford it, more has to be better. Right?

Well, more doesn't necessarily mean better, as we have said often enough. In fact, more may even be substantially worse if it is not justified and balanced by a "more" or a "less" at some other control point of the magazine.

The Problems of Success

Let's examine one of the more successful magazines on the market, a city magazine that fought and won a tough head-to-head battle with two competitors. As a result, this magazine managed to entrench itself so firmly that it is currently selling over 1,800 pages a year at a black-and-white cost per thousand (CPM) of $15 a page. The monthly issues are so fat they are beginning to have binding problems, and the postage bill is incredible. In short, they are having all the happy problems of success.

It wasn't always thus. Here are the past three years in the magazine's history (year 0 is the current year), indicating that the breakthrough came last year (year -1) when the advertising increased by more than 30 percent. But it is also evident that the readers are somewhat less enthusiastic than the advertisers. The question facing the publisher is how to get some growth with this magazine while maintaining the current level of profitability.

Year	Sub prom	Sub price	1-yr subs	2-yr subs	3-yr subs	Tot subs	Adv prom	Page rate	CPM	Adv pages	Prof
-2	$500	$9.00	106	21	37	165	$12	$1819	$15.00	1259	$122
-1	500	9.00	102	21	50	172	12	1902	15.00	1656	423
0	500	10.50	95	23	53	171	12	1889	15.00	1831	944

We will ignore the small numbers of single copies sold for this analysis and concentrate on direct-mail subscription promotion. The subscription response to direct-mail efforts was a comfortable five percent at a price of $10.50 for 12 issues. However, bad debt is 20 percent and growing, and the conversion rate (first renewal) is only 40 percent.

(In fact, the publisher switched his offers to eight-issue terms in order to cut the apparent price and raise the response. Although the response to such an offer is often higher than it would be for longer terms, the necessity to renew more frequently and the relatively low renewal rate put the rate base on a much less secure footing. It's interesting to speculate on whether the strategy will work, but for this example we will assume we are only dealing with standard one-, two-, and three-year subscriptions.)

Increasing the current circulation any further will be exceedingly expensive. The publisher has already bumped up against the ceiling of the universe of names available to him. While the city is large, mailing more than one and a half million pieces a year for three or more years means he has already reached the prime prospects again and again. Still larger mailings must substantially reduce the average return. In fact, we estimate that the current response to mailings will drop to 2.5 percent if the mailings are doubled. There just aren't any more people out there who are worth mailing to.

The other subscription control variable, the price, could be used to bring in more dollars. However, if the response were to drop drastically, it could be an expensive mistake. Experience with previous price increases indicates that a price rise to $12 a year would probably cut the gross response to 4.7 percent, and an increase to $15 would cut it to 3.9 percent, both before bad debt.

The publisher also has questions about the advertising CPM and the money spent to promote the sale of pages. While he doesn't think he has approached saturation yet (there are thousands of restaurants and retail stores in the city and its suburbs), getting the additional sales will take personal sales calls because these potential advertisers don't normally think of advertising in a slick magazine.

He says the present advertising promotion budget of $12,000 a year brings in about 200 pages of advertising they would not get otherwise. It is estimated that an additional 100 pages would be sold if the budget were raised to $20,000, which makes it clear they should be spending more on this sort of promotion than is presently being spent. The profit per page of advertising is a lot more than the $80 a page it costs to promote the sale.

Finally, the CPM is not excessively high for a magazine that offers the only reasonable alternative to local newspapers. The concern is that with the rate base now approaching 200,000, the page rate is getting to the point where the magazine may start losing the smaller advertisers. The advertising director guesses that if the present CPM were raised from $15 to $20, they would lose a full third—600 pages a year—from the mom and pop stores and restaurants. Since these advertisers are already complaining about poor visibility in the magazine (the wages of success), a substantial price increase might be all the excuse they'd need to drop out.

The Strategic Plan

The publisher built a model such as we have been describing here. After several bugs were ironed out, it was able to reproduce the history of circulation, advertising, and the year-by-year bottom-line profit with satisfactory accuracy. With some confidence, then, the publisher felt ready to explore the future.

The first question he asked was, "How much do we lose in profits if we make no changes in what we're doing or charging, but include an increase of 6 percent in the costs of doing it (paper, printing, fulfillment, postage, salaries, overhead—everything)?" The model projections were about as discouraging as they could be.

Year	Sub prom	Sub price	1-yr subs	2-yr subs	3-yr subs	Tot subs	Adv prom	Page rate	CPM	Adv pages	Prof
+1	$500	$10.50	93	22	60	175	$12	$1926	$15.00	1858	$565
+2	500	10.50	91	23	67	181	12	1999	15.00	1814	244
+3	500	10.50	91	22	68	182	12	2002	15.00	1820	211

Just as he felt he had climbed out of trouble (the Year 0 pretax profit was a very satisfactory 17.5 percent of sales), later years promise a complete reversal—a slide back into tiny profits. Inflation will eat him up if he doesn't use one revenue source or another to keep pace.

Being so close to saturation in circulation and advertising, however, means that price increases will cut down on both subscriptions and advertising pages. He could try to make up the losses by promoting more heavily—but wouldn't that be expensive?

So the second what-if question: "What if we increase subscription prices?" Let's try a series of prices starting with $10 for the one-year subscriptions (with proportionate increases in two- and three-year subscriptions). What happens to the three-year profits? (Note that the accumulated profits for the three years are examined. Two- and three-year subscriptions have a time-lag effect that may bring unpleasant surprises.)

Year 1 Sub Price	Three-year Profits
$10.00	$ 890,269
11.00	1,123,964
12.00	1,247,164
13.00	1,239,943
14.00	1,081,871
15.00	752,670
16.00	232,989

Subscription Promotion = $500,000
Advertising CPM   = $15
Advertising Promotion = $12,000

The accumulated three-year profits are shown here at each subscription price of $10 to $16, indicating that the $12 price yields the maximum profits of just under $1.25 million—certainly an improvement over the less than $1 million predicted originally for the $10.50 price.

Now that we have what seems to be the best subscription price, let's see the year-by-year details.

Year	Sub prom	Sub price	1-yr subs	2-yr subs	3-yr subs	Tot subs	Adv prom	Page rate	CPM	Adv pages	Prof
+1	$500	$12.00	87	21	59	167	$12	$1846	$15.00	1930	$678
+2	500	12.00	84	22	64	170	12	1876	15.00	1926	308
+3	500	12.00	83	20	64	167	12	1841	15.00	1965	261

The number of subscriptions is lower than before, but not substantially. The small changes in subscriptions from year to year come about because of the number of two- and three-year subscriptions that are carried forward.

Perhaps, given the higher subscription price, it would be wise to increase the promotion effort? An optimization run now is made with the subscription price fixed at $12 and advertising CPM and promotion unchanged, but with subscription promotion efforts allowed to step from $300,000 to $700,000.

Subscription Promotion	Three-year Profits
$300,000	$ 679,236
400,000	1,069,099
500,000	1,247,164
600,000	1,239,116
700,000	1,062,080

The results may be surprising. The publisher has evidently already found the best level of subscription promotion effort—$500,000. Any higher or lower effort reduces the three-year accumulated profit.

So far, so good. Now let's turn to the advertising side. Each year the rate base is adjusted automatically by the model to be just under the actual circulation for the year. That is why the page rates change slightly from year to year in the above tables. Now let's see what a substantial change will do. We keep the subscription price at $12, the subscription promotion at $500,000, the advertising promotion at $12,000, but step the advertising CPM up from $15.

Advertising CPM	1980-1982 Profits
$15	$1,247,164
16	1,693,017
17	2,074,584
18	2,391,866
19	2,644,863
20	2,833,575
21	2,958,001
22	3,018,143
23	3,013,999
24	1,945,569

Subscription Price = $12
Subscription Promotion = $500,000
Advertising Promotion = $12,000

The results indicate that quite remarkable gains in profits are possible here. They suggest that the CPM can be taken all the way up to $22 before the profits start to decline. A higher CPM has to mean a substantial loss in advertising pages, but obviously the loss is more than made up by the higher page rates.

Again, having discovered the optimum value, let's see how we actually get there year by year.

Year	Sub prom	Sub price	1-yr subs	2-yr subs	3-yr subs	Tot subs	Adv prom	Page rate	CPM	Adv pages	Prof
+1	$500	$12.00	87	21	59	167	$12	$2708	$22.00	1158	$1211
+2	500	12.00	84	22	64	170	12	2751	22.00	1132	879
+3	500	12.00	83	20	64	167	12	2701	22.00	1183	928

It's just what we expected—a substantial drop in advertising pages at the higher page rate—but note how the profits have improved.

Since the higher CPM means a tougher selling environment, let's test an increase in advertising promotion to see if the profits can be bettered. We'll hold the subscription price at $12 for a one-year subscription, the subscription promotion effort at $500,000, and the CPM at $22.

Advertising Promotion	1980-1982 Profits
$10,000	$2,975,053
20,000	3,147,377
30,000	3,238,619
40,000	3,280,682
50,000	3,292,916
60,000	3,287,058
70,000	3,270,228

Subscription Price = $12
Subscription Promotion = $500,000
Advertising CPM = $22

It is apparent that profits don't respond very rapidly to an increase in promotion effort from $10,000 a year to $50,000 a year, but they do go up about 10 percent. It is worth spending the additional promotion money and the result is a small increase in pages, as shown here.

Year	Sub Prom	Sub Price	1-Yr Subs	2-Yr Subs	3-Yr Subs	Tot Subs	Adv Prom	Page Rate	CPM	Adv Pages	Prof
+1	$500	$12.00	87	21	59	167	$50	$2708	$22.00	1306	$1319
+2	500	12.00	84	22	64	170	50	2751	22.00	1277	971
+3	500	12.00	83	20	64	167	50	2701	22.00	1334	1003

By successively testing and adjusting each of four factors, we were able to increase this magazine's profits from $1 million to over $3.25 million. We could even fine-tune the strategy by going back over the same four factors, one at a time, and looking for the best settings for each of the three years. And then it would be wise to check the other factors such as newsstand draw, kinds of promotion effort, and so on.

Do You Trust the Model?

Is all this theory reliable? Would you bet your magazine on the advice of a dumb machine? If you are skeptical you can slide up to the new price levels a bit more carefully than indicated here. In effect, you sacrifice potential profit for security—not a new idea.

If it were my decision, I'd go for the subscription price increase at once. The $12 one-year price doesn't seem to be so far from the present $10.50 that the increase would have a terrible effect on return. I'd watch the response closely, of course, but I'd be comfortable with the risk and also expect the reduced response, if any, to be short lived. Further increases should continue to be tested at each subsequent mailing, because price increases are absorbed as people forget.

On the advertising side, I'd raise the advertising promotion budget to $25,000 the first year and make sure it was well spent. I'd tell the advertising director there is more where that came from if he can handle a CPM increase, and I'd take the rate card CPM up to $18 or $19 and see what happens.

Year	Sub prom	Sub price	1-yr subs	2-yr subs	3-yr subs	Tot subs	Adv prom	Page rate	CPM	Adv pages	Prof
+1	$500	$12.00	87	21	59	167	$25	$2339	$19.00	1596	$1173
+2	500	12.00	84	22	64	170	50	2751	22.00	1277	971
+3	500	12.00	83	20	64	167	50	2701	22.00	1334	1003

At these values the model predicts 167,000 subscriptions and 1596 advertising pages. If the actual results were no worse, the next step to $50,000 in advertising promotion and $22 in CPM could be taken with much more confidence in 1981.

Again, I'd watch the loss in advertising pages carefully. But if they came out close to the predictions, we'd be well on the way to the $3 million in profits for the three years!

Chapter 13

STAYING ON TOP

I've worked on successful magazines and I've worked on struggling ones—and believe me, successful is better. Yes, there are politics, cutthroat competition from inside as well as out, stress, and the fact that you live in a goldfish bowl. There are also compensations in that you can afford to experiment and test. There is also compensation in the compensation.

Successful magazines have many of the same goals as struggling ones, including the efficient conservation and use of revenues. So in addition to analyzing troubled magazines, we'll pattern this chapter's model after one of the bigger and better known books, one of the dramatic success stories of the sixties. This magazine easily fought off several tough new competitors in the seventies, and the future continues to look promising.

Since it is a privately held company we have no legitimate access to their data, but there is much we can infer from what is public and what we see when we buy a copy. For the rest, I'll build some assumptions into the model. Only the publisher will know if I'm off base and he won't tell.

This magazine is unique in that the publisher makes no effort to sell subscriptions. Indeed, it is not easy to subscribe, even though you want to. But the newsstand sales are remarkable. For the ten years of the seventies the sale never fell below 90 percent of the draw, and even today, with a much tougher environment, the sales are often comfortably in the 80 percent range. It is obvious that they could sell many more copies if they distributed more, but, for reasons not entirely clear to outsiders, the publisher holds tight reins on the print order.

Here is a recap of the period when the magazine was just beginning to feel some softness in newsstand sales. It will be useful for us to spend some time on these figures we can to identify the strategic questions that face the publisher.

Year	Cover price	Draw 000	Sale 000	Rate base 000	Adv prom $000	CPM	Adv Pages	Prof $000
-2	$1.25	2750	2483	2350	400	$6.85	1900	8,032
-1	1.50	3100	2706	2550	500	7.00	2142	11,188
0	1.50	3300	2847	2750	600	7.10	2246	10,855

The first thing you see is that this is one of the big and profitable magazines. The profits of almost $11 million represent over 18 percent of sales, which is well above average. The experience of this magazine confirms what most of us know: Once you get past breakeven the potential profits in magazine publishing are very large. It also has a large circulation (approaching three million), and, advertising (2,246 pages in the current year).

Don't let the big numbers faze you. Just think some zeroes off the right end and you'll find that the ratios and percentages stay fairly much the same. There are efficiencies in size, but there are inefficiencies, as well, and they tend to balance.

The cover price is a little below average for a monthly magazine and the publisher seems to be pushing the draw each year, which accounts for the fact that newsstand sales have fallen to 87 percent of the draw this year (year 0)—down from over 90 percent two years ago. One obvious concern is the way the rate base lags behind actual circulation by a year. This is always a problem in a growth situation, but it is an even bigger one for a magazine that depends on the vagaries of customer impulse at the newsstand.

As always, we look first for the factors that influence revenue streams. What influences the number of advertising pages being sold here? At first glance, the growth seems to be caused by an increase in advertising promotion but, as we saw in Chapter 3, the advertising pages in major consumer magazines (a category to which this one obviously belongs) is largely dependent on the profits of corporations who advertise. The years we are examining followed a recovery from a recession when corporate profits rose dramatically. This probably has more to do with the increase than the promotion.

(The statements in this example assign all the optional promotional expenditures—advertising in *The New York Times* and *Advertising Age*, displays at major airports, etc.—to advertising promotion. A fixed 20 percent of net advertising sales revenues each year is also deducted to cover sales staff salaries, commissions, overhead and other selling expenses.)

Staying On Top

Other factors that affect advertising page sales include the cost-per-thousand price (CPM)—especially if it is significantly different from that of the competitive media reaching the same market—and the small increases in CPM over the last three years of these statements which indicate that the publisher is concerned about competition. This restraint undoubtedly helped push up advertising sales.

Qualitative factors, such as the direction and creativity of the sales effort, the credibility of the readership research, the ambiance the magazine provides, and the ebb and flow of agency preferences, are all important, but we will not concern ourselves with these or other such factors at this time.

Keeping Up with Inflation

The one glaring problem the publisher faces is the flattening in the profitability for the current year despite increases in advertising pages, circulation, rate base and CPM. Salaries, overhead, paper and printing are the culprits. The inflationary spiral has caught this publisher in its whirl and he has to think about raising prices more quickly in order to keep up.

If you project profits over the next three years, assuming no change in any of the control factors, the dangers become very apparent.

Year	Cover price	Draw 000	Sale 000	Rate base 000	Adv prom $000	CPM	Adv Pages	Prof $000
+1	$1.50	3300	2847	2800	600	$7.10	2386	9487
+2	1.50	3300	2847	2800	600	7.10	2485	7459
+3	1.50	3300	2847	2800	600	7.10	2684	5168

Here, cover price, draw, CPM and advertising promotion are held at current levels. Advertising pages continue to increase because the continued promotion effort and an unchanged CPM, when the competitors are probably raising theirs, will be a powerful attraction to advertisers. However, cost increases will eat up more than half the profits by the third year!

The publisher will not sit still for this, but what should he do? Obviously, price increases are in order, but how much? And what about investing in a larger draw or more advertising promotion? Let's make our decisions in sequence. Using a model of the magazine that produced the above two tables, we will move our control factors through a range of values and calculate profits at each level, thereby discovering the optimum.

We start with cover price. We know the audience will not be overjoyed about another increase in cover price—but we also know that in an inflationary world they won't be surprised or shocked. In other words, we can expect to lose some sales with higher prices, but it won't be disastrous unless we are very extreme.

A price elasticity curve has been built into the model, reducing the sales as cover price increases. This seems to be a reasonably conservative assumption.

Cover Price	Sales Impact
$1.50	100%
1.75	95
2.00	87
2.50	60

Here are the results of a series of runs of three-year profitability. Each run takes a different cover price and calculates profits for three years. Draw, CPM, and advertising promotion are held at the original levels. Accumulated profits for three years rise to a peak somewhere near $1.80 and then drop off.

Cover Price	Circulation	3-yr Profits
$1.50	2,847,000	$22,113,949
1.60	2,803,969	25,543,987
1.70	2,744,715	26,241,120
1.80	2,669,429	26,433,069
1.90	2,578,111	26,043,307
2.00	2,470,762	24,995,305
2.10	2,347,381	23,212,535
2.20	2,207,969	20,618,466
2.30	2,052,524	15,972,804
2.40	1,881,048	10,790,469
2.50	1,693,541	4,994,932

If the price elasticity is incorrect the maximum profit point shifts up or down a little. For example, if the elasticity is a lot steeper than 5 percent at $1.75, then the maximum profit point shifts down to $1.60. If there is little or no loss in sales as the price is increased the maximum profit point goes to $1.95, or even higher. A careful publisher will experiment with the $1.75 price in a limited market and watch closely how sales differ from that market's previous history and the national sales elsewhere.

Let's suppose that a test confirms the given elasticity. A fixed price of $1.75 for the three years would then produce the year-by-year profits shown here.

Year	Cover price	Draw 000	Sale 000	Rate base 000	Adv prom $000	CPM	Adv Pages	Prof $000
+1	$1.75	3300	2709	2750	600	$7.10	2343	11,541
+2	1.75	3300	2709	2700	600	7.10	2397	9,099
+3	1.75	3300	2709	2700	600	7.10	2588	6,793

The publisher should test a second price increase in the next couple of years and recalculate profits, but this is more detail than would serve any purpose for this chapter. We will simply take it that the maximum profitability is at a cover price of $1.75. Note that the rate base falls to 2,700,000 in this scenario.

Now let's see whether it would be advisable to raise the draw and therefore the sale and the rate base at the higher cover price. The next series of runs is made at a cover price of $1.75, and the draw increased from a minimum of 3 million copies to a maximum of 4 million copies in steps of 100,000.

Draw	Year One Circulation	3-Yr Profits
3,000,000	2,506,331	$26,362,154
3,100,000	2,574,759	25,443,911
3,200,000	2,642,337	26,442,611
3,300,000	2,709,070	27,432,411
3,400,000	2,774,985	26,315,951
3,500,000	2,840,076	27,210,298
3,600,000	2,904,358	28,096,603
3,700,000	2,967,842	26,784,507
3,800,000	3,030,537	27,577,049
3,900,000	3,092,453	26,157,264
4,000,000	3,153,600	26,857,133

Note, first of all, that the profits remain between $26 million and $28 million through most of this range of draw. Additional copies put on the newsstands generate only enough revenues in newsstand sales and advertising to pay for the manufacture and distribution of the copies.

While we sell 2,709,076 copies, or about 82 percent, when the draw is 3,300,000 and the cover price is $1.75, we sell 2,774,985 at 3,400,000, or only 65,909 of the additional 100,000 copies. This represents a marginal sale of 66 percent of the increment in draw. The cost of manufacturing three copies in order to sell two dissipates the revenues from the newsstand buyer, as well as the advertiser who pays for the addition to the ratebase. (The profits seem to bounce up and down as the draw is increased because the rate base moves in steps rather than as a smooth curve and profitability is better when there is practically no bonus in the rate base.)

Since there was no important change in profits with the increase in draw, we will leave our draw at 3,300,000 for the three years and go on to the next important factor.

The CPM is often the most critical of the variables under the control of the publisher. The direct consequence of an increase in CPM is assumed to be a loss in advertising pages. In a highly competitive market where there are alternative ways to reach an audience, advertisers carefully examine one medium's price efficiency in comparison to another's. However, there are no truly interchangeable, hence direct, magazine competitors. Each offers both an audience and an ambiance that are unique. Higher CPMs can add to the desirability of that ambiance as easily as they can detract from it.

The consequences of a higher CPM are not necessarily bad in other respects, either. When you raise the CPM you add dollars that sink directly to the bottom line. More specifically, when the CPM was $7.10 the costs associated with advertising were:

Discounts and agency commissions	$1.78
Selling costs	1.06
Administrative costs	0.53
Manufacturing one page	2.52

Total	$5.89

This leaves a net of $1.21 toward promotion and profit. When you raise the CPM to $8.10 the costs are:

Discounts and agency commissions	$2.03
Selling costs	1.21
Administrative costs	0.61
Manufacturing one page	2.52

Total	$6.37

This leaves a net of $1.73. Therefore, an increase in CPM by 14 percent produces an increase in profits of 43 percent. You'd have to lose a lot of advertising pages before the profits are reduced as a consequence of a higher CPM.

Here is what the model predicts for profits for the three years with the CPM stepped from $7 to $12.

CPM	Ad Pages	Three-year Profits
$ 7	2516	$26,365,064
8	1290	32,397,973
9	716	33,308,377
10	423	32,795,981
11	263	31,982,344
12	170	31,204,154

According to this table, the maximum profits aren't reached until the CPM is raised to $9. Note that this is true even though the number of advertising pages has fallen to less than a third of the number at $7! Can this be true? At a guaranty of 2,700,000 and the CPM at $7, the page rate is $18,900. Raise the CPM to $9, and the page rate goes to $24,300. Revenues and costs are as follows:

CPM	$7	$9
Advertising Pages	2,516	716
Gross Revenues	$47,552,400	$17,398,800
Discounts (25%)	11,888,100	4,349,700
Selling Expense (20% of net)	7,132,860	2,609,820
Administrative (15% of net)	5,349,645	1,957,365
Manufacturing ad pp	20,972,873	5,968,433
	------------	-----------
Profit	$2,208,922	$2,513,482

Despite a loss of over 1,800 pages in advertising and a reduction of gross revenues of $30 million, there is an additional profit of more than $300,000 at the $9 CPM. The reason is not hard to find. The manufacturing cost represents 44 percent of the gross income at the $7 CPM, but only 34 percent of the income at $9.

The situation becomes even more extreme in the second year when manufacturing costs are expected to be 6 percent higher. In that year, the cost to print 2,516 advertising pages will be $22,231,245, reducing profits to only $950,550. However, if you were printing 716 advertising pages at the $9 CPM, the manufacturing cost would only be $6,326,539, leaving a profit of $2,155,425. By the third year the $7 CPM actually produces a loss.

Here are the yearly statements when the best setting for all three factors has been made. For simplicity, we are holding them at the same levels throughout this three-year period, that is, the cover price is held at $1.75, the draw at 3,300,000, and the CPM at $9.

168

Year	Cover price	Draw 000	Sale 000	Rate base 000	Adv prom $000	CPM	Adv Pages	Prof $000
+1	$1.75	3300	2709	2750	600	$9.00	716	12,345
+2	1.75	3300	2709	2700	600	9.00	732	11,054
+3	1.75	3300	2709	2700	600	9.00	791	9,909

In the real world you probably couldn't stand to see advertising pages and total revenues fall this way. It would look too much like a faltering magazine. But it would be worthwhile to try a gradual increase in the prices which might produce even higher total profits than indicated here.

The decline in profits from year to year caused by the escalation in costs, so a somewhat more gradual increase in prices would probably hold the profits in the $10 to $12 million range throughout the period.

The last factor we will consider is the advertising promotion. With the other factors held at their optimums we now step the advertising promotion from a minimum of $100,000 a year to $600,000. The results may be unexpected.

Advertising Promotion	Ad Pages	3-Yr Profits
$100,000	568	$33,668,924
200,000	632	33,857,357
300,000	670	33,853,606
400,000	693	33,733,291
500,000	707	33,543,275
600,000	716	33,308,377

Over 60 additional pages of advertising are sold because of the addition of $100,000 to the promotion budget, but the profits increase only marginally. Any further increase in promotion does not sell enough pages to pay for itself. Eventually, an additional page of advertising actually loses money for the magazine because of the escalating manufacturing costs ($2.68 per thousand pages in year 3).

In year 3 the cost per advertising page is:

Discounts and Agency Commissions	$6,075
Selling Costs	3,645
Administrative Costs	1,863
Manufacturing Costs	8,847
Total	$20,430

Income from a page at the $9 CPM and 2,700,000 rate base is $24,300. Thus, there is a profit of $3,897 on each page. If it will cost $4,000 in extra promotion to sell a page, however, it obviously doesn't pay to do so. We must sell at least 25 extra pages of advertising for our $100,000 in promotion and, according to the table above, we don't do so at levels over $300,000.

This is an estimate, of course, and would be checked against experience, and the expectations of the promotion director and the advertising director. The net of $3,897 in 1982 is real, however, and tells you where the breakeven in promotion is reached.

The unpleasant news for this magazine is that it will be difficult, if not impossible, to maintain profits at the same percentage of total sales as has been achieved up to now. If the goal were to keep profits at a constant percentage of sales, the publisher would have to increase prices even more rapidly—and only a very tolerant market of readers and advertisers would accept such increases without reducing their purchases.

However, if gross revenues are the same at higher prices—that is, if the advertiser spends the same amount of money but simply distributes it over fewer pages because of the higher CPM—then the publisher may find himself very well off. His income remains the same but his costs have been reduced because there are fewer pages to be printed.

Repeatedly, through these and other such projections, we have reached the same conclusion: Maximum profits occur at two "nodes" as prices and margins vary. There is a peak at a low-price, low-margin, high-volume place in the spectrum; there is a peak at the high-price, high-margin, low volume place in the spectrum. The low-margin strategy is extremely sensitive to small changes in the market; the high-market strategy often produces a larger overall profit and has more tolerance for error.

Chapter 14

BALANCING REVENUE STREAMS

Experience with dozens of different magazines and other products, too, indicates that a product can usually afford to lose substantial unit sales when prices are raised, and still produce more overall profit than at the lower prices. And in an inflationary economy, large percentage price increases on a relatively inexpensive item will seem small compared to the increases in more costly items in the budget like food, shelter and clothing.

That's all the hint you will get at this stage, as we look at a consumer magazine that sells single copies and subscriptions in almost equal quantities. The example has been patterned after a real magazine, and it turns out that the three revenue streams require a very delicate balancing act if optimum profits are to be achieved.

The magazine was first introduced in the early seventies, and it is a wonderfully creative departure from the norm, both in format and style. It caught on slowly, struggling for attention, distribution and display. Then, tasting success after only three or four years of publication, the publisher overextended company resources into other publishing efforts, as well as in broadening the content of the magazine, and within a year the new venture faced financial disaster. However, an infusion of new capital and a return to the original focus soon saw the magazine past its problems and today it is doing very well.

A cover and subscription price increase in the middle of first year in the table appeared to have a slight effect on newsstand sales. In anticipation of subscription sales resistance at the $18 price, the publisher increased promotion mailings in the next year. The resistance never developed, however, and the new subscriptions added handsomely to profits.

Yr	Avg N/S $	Draw 000	Sale 000	Sub Price $	Sub Prom $000	Tot Subs 000	Tot Circ 000	Rate base 000	Adv Prom $000	CPM $	Adv Adv Pages	Prof $000
-2	0.93	600	338	16.00	1000	204	542	525	100	15.00	1191	2398
-1	1.00	600	322	18.00	1500	290	612	600	100	16.00	1181	3874
0	1.00	600	322	18.00	1500	349	671	650	100	16.00	1185	4553

The cover price was increased from $.85 to $1 in July of the first year in this table, so we have an average price for that year ($.93). Similarly, the one-year subscription price at $16 is an average of $14 in the first half and $18 in the second half. Two- and three-year subscription prices were raised proportionately.

The rate base, raised every year in the magazine's history, is set to the nearest 25,000 in circulation. Advertising promotion was constant at $100,000 a year, and the increase in CPM between the first and second years apparently accounts for the small drop-off in advertising pages.

As you see from these numbers, a continuing area of concern is the static advertising page count at a time when print media all around it were enjoying very large page increases.

The computer model has several critical relationships built into it that are based on historical data. They answer the questions:

1. How does a price increase affect newsstand and subscriptions sales?

2. How does an increase in subscription promotion effort affect subscription sales?

3. How bad is the bad debt?

4. How do subscribers convert and renew?

5. How would the newsstand sales react to an increase in draw?

6. How does the advertiser respond to an increase in CPM? To changes in advertising promotion?

The point of maximum profit will depend on the nature of these assumed relationships. However, finding maximum profit points or an exact prediction of profits is not the most important thing we can do. Instead, in this analysis we are more interested in identifying those factors that have a major effect on profits, and those that have a small, or negligible effect. This information will then enable us to concentrate our attention on only the most important factors.

If the publisher makes no changes over the next three years—constant CPM, cover price, subscription and advertising budgets, and draw—he can expect to earn almost $15 million in profits despite cost increases and a static level of advertising pages. This gives us a benchmark figure to measure other changes by—just over $4 million more profits in the next three years compared to the past three years.

Yr	Avg N/S $	Draw 000	Sale 000	Sub Price $	Sub Prom $000	Tot Subs 000	Tot Circ 000	Rate base 000	Adv Prom $000	CPM $	Adv Adv Pages	Prof $000
+1	1.00	600	325	18.00	1500	398	722	700	100	16.00	1185	4746
+2	1.00	600	327	18.00	1500	441	767	750	100	16.00	1185	4921
+3	1.00	600	326	18.00	1500	475	801	800	100	16.00	1185	5256

Increasing the CPM

To explore the profit changes as a result of CPM, we hold constant all other factors—cover and subscription prices, subscription promotion, advertising promotion, and draw—and step CPM from $16 to $20. The profits shown here are accumulated three-year totals at each CPM.

Advertising CPM	Ad Pages in last year	Three-year Profits
16	1185	$14,922,952
17	1096	15,480,292
18	995	15,736,166
19	882	15,646,884
20	757	15,165,867

The effect of increasing the CPM is to reduce advertising pages— down 89 pages (7.5 percent) with a CPM increase from $16 to $17; down 101 pages (9.2 percent) with an increase from $17 to $18; and down 125 pages (14 percent) with an increase from $19 to $20.

The improvement in profits is relatively small—only 5 percent on a CPM change of 12.5 percent. It seems the magazine is close to saturation as far as advertising is concerned. The loss in advertising pages in the first two years of history, when other magazines were doing so well, was a clear signal that the magazine had exhausted its market as approached by the sales force and must look for growth among other categories, or that a change in selling technique or magazine "positioning" is in order.

At this point, quantitative methods must be put aside and creative juices made to flow. Many companies and industries reach this situation at some time during their corporate lives, though normally later than this one. (I guess the young are getting old much faster these days.)

Corporations respond in different ways. Some do nothing and experience the slow decline of old age and high, though declining, profits. Business strategies call such companies "cash cows" and often advise milking them for everything they are worth.

Other companies wriggle on the hook. They make acquisitions, involve themselves in new ventures and introduce new products. In effect, they go back to their good old entrepreneurial days in an attempt to regain their lost youth. This strategy works to the extent that the managers have the vision and luck necessary to any successful entrepreneurial enterprise.

A third option is to make little or no change in the product itself, but a major change in the way it is packaged, distributed or sold. Perrier had entered a static market of bubbly water and either stumbled, or was inspired, to position itself as a high-fashion, high-class drink, that was low in calories and non-alcoholic.

Similarly, in 1960 Hanes was a clothing manufacturer facing a bleak future of tough competition and rising costs. Its management decided to gamble by selling its goods through new outlets and by methods never before used by apparel manufactures. L'Eggs moved into supermarkets and the results were astounding.

In the magazine business, *Sports Illustrated* is probably the best example of a magazine struggling and losing buckets of money until it rebilled itself as, and convinced advertisers that it was, a third newsweekly. Today it has an unchallenged place in the market, offering readers the topicality of the news magazines and the special interest and appeal of the sports magazine.

We will not go into these qualitative matters here, so the best course would be to put through the increase in CPM. Here is the year-by-year result:

Yr	Avg N/S $	Draw 000	Sale 000	Sub Price $	Sub Prom $000	Tot Subs 000	Tot Circ 000	Rate base 000	Adv Prom $000	CPM $	Adv Adv Pages	Prof $000
+1	1.00	600	325	18.00	1500	398	722	700	100	18.00	995	4982
+2	1.00	600	327	18.00	1500	441	767	750	100	18.00	995	5192
+3	1.00	600	326	18.00	1500	475	801	800	100	18.00	995	5561

Nothing is changed except the CPM, but the net improvement in profits is about $250,000 for each of the three years, despite the loss in advertising pages.

Increasing Advertising Promotion

Now let's see if raising the advertising promotion has any important effect. Here we raise the budget in steps of $25,000:

Advertising Promotion	Ad Pages Last Year	Three-Year Profits
$100,000	995	$15,736,166
125,000	1056	16,236,411
150,000	1093	16,510,314
175,000	1116	16,646,935
200,000	1130	16,700,289
225,000	1138	16,703,140
250,000	1143	16,675,359

The advertising pages respond—over 60 additional pages for an expenditure of only $25,000, and the profits go up about half a million. Still further expenditures for promotion don't produce quite so many pages of space, however, and toward the end, when you add $25,000 to a budget of $200,000, you sell only eight additional pages. Profits increase a little, indicating that at this point advertising pages are throwing off about $3,000 in bottom-line profit per page ($25,000 divided by eight pages) at the $18 CPM.

Does this seem realistic? It's hard to be sure without being privy to a lot of what is going on between the advertising director, the sales staff, and their agency and advertising clients. The promotion expenditures in this table are raised at the same time the $18 CPM has been imposed, so it is possible that some part of the expected loss in pages can indeed be made back with increased promotion.

We would make both changes—the increase in CPM to $18 and the increase in advertising promotion to $200,000, and here is how it looks year by year.

Yr	Avg N/S $	Draw 000	Sale 000	Sub Price $	Sub Prom $000	Tot Subs 000	Tot Circ 000	Rate base 000	Adv Prom $000	CPM $	Adv Adv Pages	Prof $000
+1	1.00	600	325	18.00	1500	398	722	700	200	18.00	1130	5288
+2	1.00	600	327	18.00	1500	441	767	750	200	18.00	1130	5514
+3	1.00	600	326	18.00	1500	475	801	800	200	18.00	1130	5899

What About the Cover Price?

The next obvious place to look is the cover price, and maybe we should have started with the cover. Here is the effect of cover price increases of the newsstand copies, as well as a proportionate increase in subscription prices:

Cover Price	Subscriptions in last year	Newsstand Sales in last year	Three-year Profits
$1.00	474,802	326,134	$16,700,289
1.25	440,299	314,417	20,980,089
1.50	391,550	296,400	22,534,745
1.75	328,667	270,414	20,803,061
2.00	253,548	234,235	14,448,762

Now we're really beginning to see some changes. At $1.50 there are almost $6 million more profits over the $1 price, even though there are 20 percent fewer subscriptions on the list in the last year and 10 percent fewer newsstand purchasers. Note, too, how quickly the profits fall down the other side when the price goes on to $2.

Price is the one factor we really must watch because of the very steep and narrow peak of profits. It means careful testing of subscription prices every step of the way. It also means careful testing of newsstand prices at localized geographical areas if that is possible. There should also be some healthy skepticism about whether data gathered in today's tests under today's economic conditions will automatically apply next year under unknown new economic conditions.

Here are the specific year-by-year figures at the $1.50 cover price, $18 CPM, and $200,000 advertising promotion budget:

Yr	Avg N/S $	Draw 000	Sale 000	Sub Price $	Sub Prom $000	Tot Subs 000	Tot Circ 000	Rate base 000	Adv Prom $000	CPM $	Adv Adv Pages	Prof $000
+1	1.00	600	267	27.00	1500	347	615	625	200	18.00	1130	7176
+2	1.00	600	286	27.00	1500	367	653	625	200	18.00	1130	7233
+3	1.00	600	296	27.00	1500	392	688	675	200	18.00	1130	8125

The rate base has dropped almost 100,000 compared to our last detailed run. However, three-year profits are more than $5.8 million higher on only $4 million more in gross revenues.

Draw and Subscription Promotion

After the cover price increase, the next factor is a little anticlimactic. An increase in draw adds a few thousand dollars per year at the 750,000 level, about a 10 percent higher newsstand sale for each of the three years, and provides a few more subscriptions, but it is clear that distributing 150,000 more copies, even to sell only 33,000, is worthwhile.

Draw	Subscriptions in last year	Newsstand Sales in last year	Three-year Profits
600,000	391,550	296,440	$22,534,745
650,000	392,904	308,915	22,697,498
700,000	394,108	320,005	23,037,622
750,000	395,178	329,865	23,067,362
800,000	396,130	338,630	23,041,451

Remember our previous discussion on sales of marginal copies? A magazine selling about 50 percent of its total draw can't possibly hope to sell 50 percent of an increase in draw. The tables in Chapter 5 say that the marginal percent of sale is only 20 percent of the increment. At that sale, and even including additional revenues from a higher rate base, we can scarcely pay for the paper and printing.

Yr	Avg N/S $	Draw 000	Sale 000	Sub Price $	Sub Prom $000	Tot Subs 000	Tot Circ 000	Rate base 000	Adv Prom $000	CPM $	Adv Adv Pages	Prof $000
+1	1.50	750	298	27.00	1500	347	646	650	200	18.00	1130	7255
+2	1.50	750	318	27.00	1500	370	687	675	200	18.00	1130	7588
+3	1.50	750	330	27.00	1500	395	725	700	200	18.00	1130	8225

But we accept the new draw of 750,000 copies and go to the last factor, the subscription promotion budget. Here, we step subscription effort up in $100,000 increments from the current $1,500,000.

Subscription Promotion	Subscriptions in last year	Newsstand Sales in last year	Three-year Profits
$1,500,000	395,178	329,865	$23,067,362
1,600,000	408,678	327,598	23,441,797
1,700,000	421,306	325,477	23,540,371
1,800,000	432,953	321,750	24,385,635
2,000,000	452,814	320,185	24,380,109

We can sell over 57,000 subscriptions by increasing subscription promotion by $500,000, at a net cost of less than $9 per subscription. With the subscriber contributing $27 to the production cost of the year's issues, and advertisers paying for a higher rate base, profits are improved by more than $1.3 million.

Yr	Avg N/S $	Draw 000	Sale 000	Sub Price $	Sub Prom $000	Tot Subs 000	Tot Circ 000	Rate base 000	Adv Prom $000	CPM $	Adv Adv Pages	Prof $000
+1	1.50	750	292	27.00	2000	378	670	675	200	18.00	1130	7493
+2	1.50	750	309	27.00	2000	415	725	700	200	18.00	1130	7962
+3	1.50	750	320	27.00	2000	453	773	750	200	18.00	1130	8925

Summing it Up

In order of impact, then, the improvement in profits comes from increases in:

Cover price to $1.50	$5.8 million
Sub Promotion to $2 million	1.3 million
Ad Promotion to $200,000	1.0 million
CPM to $18	0.8 million
Draw to 750,000	5 million
Total change	$9.4 million

As a real course of action you would certainly test price increases at the newsstand, as well as in subscription mailings. You would also test new lists and new techniques of reaching subscribers in anticipation of a substantial increase in subscription promotion effort over the next three years. You might loosen the purse strings on the advertising promotion budget a little, and press the advertising director for an increase in rate card CPM of 10 to 15 percent. You would allow the draw to drift up, watching closely to be sure that the sales percentage on the increase is not less than 20 percent.

Note that we have forecast $9.4 million more in profits, whereas a no-change strategy would have produced $5.2 million. The improvement of $4.2 million comes out of $14.7 million more in sales. Or put another way: The no-change strategy produces 22.4 percent profits on sales and the optimum takes profits to over 30 percent of sales.

Chapter 15

THE FACE OF FAILURE

One would think we could certainly recognize the inevitability of failure, yet it is amazing how far past reason many publishers take their mistakes. Of course no one wants to give up on a loved one, and it always seems as if the turn-around is about to arrive. Why, then, does it stay just out of reach and for so long?

An article in *The Harvard Business Review* offers some interesting statistics. The authors polled 200 of the Fortune 500 companies for their experiences with new products—not merely extensions of their current lines of business but new ventures to which they applied all of their considerable marketing skills. It turns out that only four out of ten new ventures reached profitability in the first four years. The average time to pay off the initial investment was eight years for these companies, which certainly cannot be accused of undercapitalization or lack of managerial skill. This means that half of all new ventures started by major corporations take more than eight years to pay off their initial investments!

Magazines have a better track record for new ventures, but there comes a time for us to face the fact that our new magazine isn't going to make it, that still one more financial transfusion is another wasted year, and any more lies to our backers will only make our nose grow longer and longer, like Pinoccio's.

It may be the toughest decision you'll ever make and no one will love you for it. This is an area so charged with emotional energy that it is probable this chapter will only help you after the fact—post mortem, literally. But look at it this way: The experience of failure, like the experience of getting fired, is an important addition to your fund of knowledge. You'll be a better publisher for it next time.

In any case, the challenge to the publishing strategist is to recognize an impossible situation early enough to keep the losses to a minimum. The technique isn't any different from what we have being doing up to now. You still look for a point of maximum profitability, but if the point of maximum profitability is a negative number, it is nature's way of telling you to get out.

Let's take a typical situation—for instance, a subscription magazine with 90,000 one-year, $12 subscriptions. Renewal rate is 60 percent and it can be assumed the rate will fall if subscription price is raised. To replace the 36,000 nonrenewers last year, the publisher dropped 1,600,000 direct-mail pieces and the gross response was a tolerable 3 percent before 25 percent bad debt. The net paid subscriptions acquired from the mailing was 36,000, just enough to maintain the 90,000 circulation.

Here is last year's performance in the critical areas we will be discussing:

Sub Price	Number of Pcs Mld	Number of Subs	CPM	Sales Expense	Ad Pages	Profit
$12	1,600,000	90,000	$20	$300,000	600	$-78,000

You have been hired to advise the publisher about his prospects. To start, you have meetings with the staff and you find the typical and familiar relationships. We'll sketch the curves and then read off the values for computational convenience.

We know that if we raise the subscription price the percent return will lower. Figure 15.1 shows what happens to circulation over a range of subscription prices.

Note that the number of subscriptions will rise if you keep the price at $12, because inflation will have driven the prices of other magazines and books up so that this one looks more attractive by comparison. If you left the subscription price at $12 and checked with your subscription manager about a range of promotion levels the estimates look like Figure 15.2.

On the advertising side, last year you sold 600 pages at an average CPM of $20, or $1,800 per page on the 90,000 rate base. If you were to raise your CPM you'll lose pages. The advertising director estimates as shown in Figure 15.3.

The advertising director tells you he could sell more pages if you allowed him to hire another salesperson and maybe spend some money on promotion. His estimates are given in Figure 15.4.

It is not a hopeful situation. Increasing prices will reduce

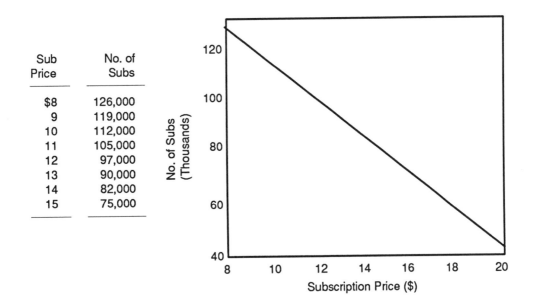

Sub Price	No. of Subs
$8	126,000
9	119,000
10	112,000
11	105,000
12	97,000
13	90,000
14	82,000
15	75,000

Figure 15.1. Subscription price elasticity.

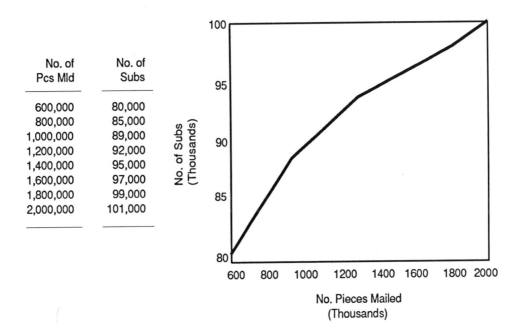

No. of Pcs Mld	No. of Subs
600,000	80,000
800,000	85,000
1,000,000	89,000
1,200,000	92,000
1,400,000	95,000
1,600,000	97,000
1,800,000	99,000
2,000,000	101,000

Figure 15.2. Subscriptions at different levels of promotion

The Face of Failure

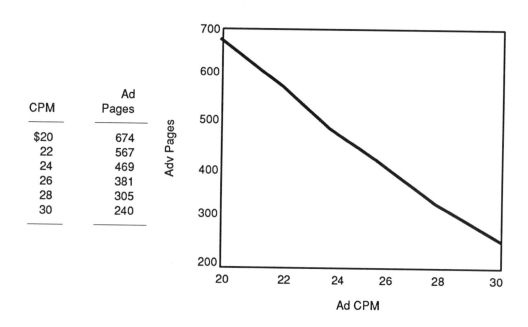

CPM	Ad Pages
$20	674
22	567
24	469
26	381
28	305
30	240

Figure 15.3. Advertising price elasticity.

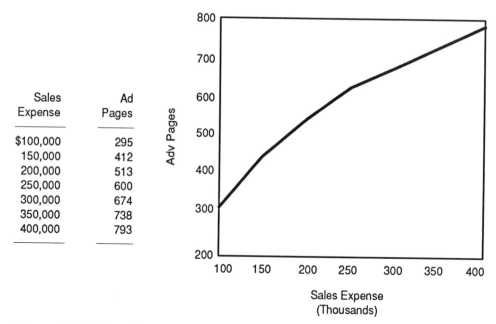

Sales Expense	Ad Pages
$100,000	295
150,000	412
200,000	513
250,000	600
300,000	674
350,000	738
400,000	793

Figure 15.4 Advertising at different levels of sales effort.

184

The Face of Failure

circulation or advertising pages fairly steeply; increasing mailing efforts or advertising sales expenses don't seem to produce important changes in sales. What should you do—particularly looking into a recession which may hurt advertising and circulation sales, without any let up in inflation?

The title of this chapter gave you a hint but let's try to imagine ourselves in this fix. A stubborn publisher would trim costs— probably for the third or fourth time—and hold the line on prices. But by this time, cost cutting is likely to hurt sales. A cautious one would do the same and get the word around town that he's ready for another job. A curious publisher would call the local university that has a management school and get a couple of young graduate degree candidates to convert these figures into equations which they can then program on a small computer.

There are only a few additional pieces of data they would need.

Ratio of net advertising income to rate card gross:	75%
Mailing cost per subscription package:	$.30
Editorial and administrative costs:	$825,000
Manufacturing cost per thousand pages:	$3
Inflation in all costs :	10%

You then run the programs and explore each of the strategic decisions in turn. For example, suppose you tested a range of subscription prices to see how they affect profits:

Sub Price	Number of Pcs Mld	Number of Subs	CPM	Sales Expense	Ad Pages	Profit
$8	1,600,000	126,000	$20	$300,000	674	$-149,000
9	1,600,000	119,000	20	300,000	674	-114,000
10	1,600,000	112,000	20	300,000	674	-98,000
11	1,600,000	105,000	20	300,000	674	-100,000
12	1,600,000	97,000	20	300,000	674	-119,000
13	1,600,000	90,000	20	300,000	674	-154,000
14	1,600,000	82,000	20	300,000	674	-204,000
15	1,600,000	75,000	20	300,000	674	-265,000

Not wonderful, even though advertising pages increased to 674 because you held the line on CPM. You'd probably be tempted to drop the price to $10 and see what happens at different levels of direct-mail effort:

Sub Price	Number of Pcs Mld	Number of Subs	CPM	Sales Expense	Ad Pages	Profit
$10	600,000	93,000	$20	$300,000	674	$-56,000
10	800,000	98,000	20	300,000	674	-42,000
10	1,000,000	103,000	20	300,000	674	-41,000
10	1,200,000	106,000	20	300,000	674	-51,000
10	1,400,000	110,000	20	300,000	674	-71,000
10	1,600,000	112,000	20	300,000	674	-98,000
10	1,800,000	115,000	20	300,000	674	-131,000
10	2,000,000	116,000	20	300,000	674	-170,000

A little better, but still not profitable. Maybe the CPM is pegged too low. You try a range of CPMs.

Sub Price	Number of Pcs Mld	Number of Subs	CPM	Sales Expense	Ad Pages	Profit
$10	900,000	100,000	$20	$300,000	674	$-40,000
10	900,000	100,000	22	300,000	567	-27,000
10	900,000	100,000	24	300,000	469	-38,000
10	900,000	100,000	26	300,000	381	-66,000
10	900,000	100,000	28	300,000	305	-106,000
10	900,000	100,000	30	300,000	240	-154,000

Ugh. Okay, kick the CPM up to $22 and give the advertising director a range of sales expense:

Sub Price	Number of Pcs Mld	Number of Subs	CPM	Sales Expense	Ad Pages	Profit
$10	900,000	100,000	$22	$100,000	248	$-91,000
10	900,000	100,000	22	150,000	347	-60,000
10	900,000	100,000	22	200,000	431	-39,000
10	900,000	100,000	22	250,000	504	-29,000
10	900,000	100,000	22	300,000	567	-27,000
10	900,000	100,000	32	350,000	620	-38,000
10	900,000	100,000	32	400,000	667	-45,000

The Face of Failure

Nothing seems to help. Even at best, we wind up losing another $27,000 this year—and it can only get worse.

There's no doubt about it, is there? FOLD!

Total cost to fold—maybe $5,000 for the computer and programming, plus separation allowances for the staff, legal fees in bankruptcy—if that's necessary—and pride. On the plus side, you take the computer home for your kids to play with and you sell the 90,000 subscriber names, plus expires, to your competitor for enough to pay off your creditors, the IRS, and give you a luxurious summer in Florida.

Chapter 16

CHALLENGE I: A SUBSCRIPTION MAGAZINE

We have had a detailed look at the philosophy and the methodology of strategic analysis of magazines. Now we will try some exercises. You can solve the problems by brute force with reams of paper and a hard-driven calculator, or you can rely on guesswork and instincts, whichever you prefer.

Each of the next three chapters presents a magazine at a critical point in its lifetime. In each, you will be given everything you need to know about the problem faced and then have the responsibility to make the decisions that will make or break the magazine. At the end we provide tables that list the outcome for every possible combination of decisions so that you can see where in the profit ballpark you put the company, and where you might have put it. And we will indicate a line of reasoning that, with only a small amount of calculation, would have led you to the optimum set of decisions.

The first is a small paid-subscription magazine going to a devoted audience of hobbyists. There are no single-copy sales.

Frequency	Monthly
Subscriptions	$6 per year, all one-year
Renewal Rate	60 percent at $6 rate
No. of Subs	100,000
CPM	$12, which nets to $9 after agency fees and other discounts
No. of Ads	86 per issue average, or 1032 this year
Edit. Pages	53 per issue (policy is 40 edit pages plus 1 for every 2 ad pages over 60)
Edit. Cost	$1000 per page total (staff plus purchases)
Mfg. Cost	$2.50 per thousand pages

You must make three decisions: What should the subscription price be next year? How many subscriptions should you acquire through direct-mail promotion? What should the advertising CPM be next year?

Here is the report for last year:

Subscription Promotion	Circulation Ratebase	CPM	Ad Pages	Revenues	Profit
$238,610	100,000	$12	86	$1,524,014	$-165,431

The costs include postage and fulfillment on the subscriptions of $1.70 per subscription per year; advertising sales expenses of 18 percent of the net advertising revenue, and general and administrative overhead of 10 percent of net revenues. It is assumed that these percentages will stay the same at all sales levels.

You call a meeting with the subscription manager who gives you a fairly straightforward estimate of price impact on renewals. It is a classic straight-line elasticity (Figure 16.1).

The subscription manager says he will have to spend $120,000 on the renewal series no matter what price you set next year. Since these are the least costly subscriptions you can buy, you agree that the renewal series should take the first $120,000 of any subscription promotion budget you set.

For new subscriptions, the manager provides 250 feet of computer printouts showing the results in percent return for every test mailing over every list and at every price made in the last ten years. You give the stack to your administrative assistant who comes back with the following table and Figure 16.2.

Subscription Promotion	Subscription Price			
	$6	$8	$10	$12
$200,000	62,000	56,000	48,000	39,000
400,000	109,000	98,000	85,000	70,000
600,000	140,000	127,000	110,000	89,000
800,000	164,000	148,000	129,000	104,000

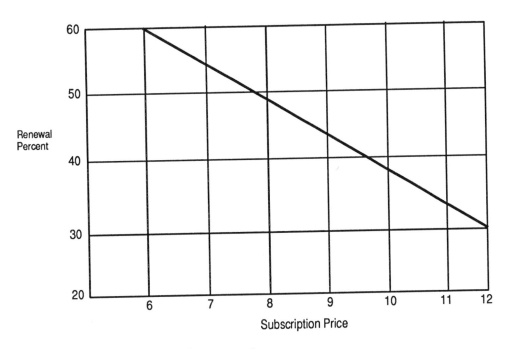

Figure 16.1. Elasticity of the renewal rate

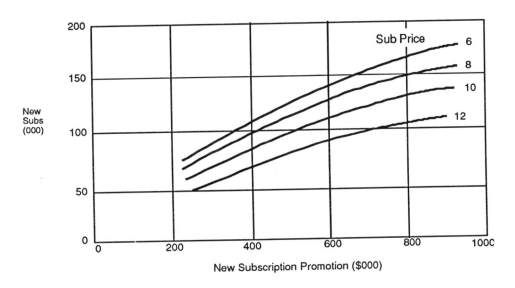

Figure 16.2. New subscriptions as a function of price and promotion.

Challenge I: A Subscription Magazine   191

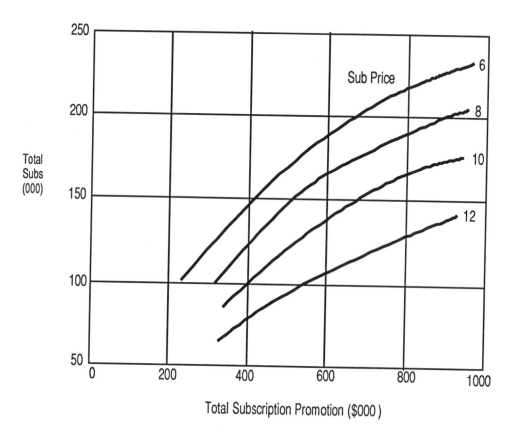

Figure 16.3. Total subscription promotion and total subscriptions.

Challenge I: A Subscription Magazine

Last year they spent $120,000 on renewals and an additional $118,610 to get 40,000 new subscriptions. This calculates out to $2.97 per new subscription. At the $800,000 budget the cost per new subscription will be $4.88 at the $6 price, and $7.69 at the $12 price.

Data for renewals and new subscriptions can be added—$120,000 for the notices which produce the renewals, plus the new subscription promotion budget and what it produces—to give us the following table and Figure 16.3.

Subscription Promotion	Subscription Price			
	$6	$8	$10	$12
$400,000	143,000	125,000	105,000	83,000
600,000	183,000	161,000	136,000	108,000
800,000	211,000	187,000	159,000	126,000
1,000,000	232,000	205,000	175,000	139,000

The next meeting you call is with the advertising director. Advertising provides a substantial part of the total revenue and, if you want to think about it that way, all the profits of the magazine (not any this year). The advertising director begins by starting a discussion of how to allocate costs between subscriptions and advertising, but you stop it at once.

The advertising director sings the expected refrain. He is afraid of raising the cost per thousand (CPM) because the competition is keen for advertising pages. But he would like you to give him a higher rate base because it would undoubtedly attract advertisers who now regard his book as too little to bother about.

When pressed for an estimate, he guesses that at a $20 CPM advertising would drop to an average of 40 pages per issue at 100,000 rate base but 50 pages at 250,000 rate base. In this magazine, advertising is billed on actual circulation rather than a guaranteed rate base. This slows receivables, but eliminates all the worries about setting the rate base too high or too low. The advertising director estimates he could sell another 3 pages per month for a total of 116 per month, if he could hold the CPM at $12 and the rate base at 250,000.

Again you toss the notes of the meeting to your administrative assistant who produces the following table and Figure 16.4.

	Ratebase			
CPM	100,000	150,000	200,000	250,000
$12	86	95	101	108
14	68	75	80	86
16	55	61	66	71
18	46	51	55	58
20	39	44	47	50

Now comes the crunch: You must choose one value from column A, one from column B, one from column C.

Column A	Column B	Column C
============	============	============
Subscription Price	Subscription Promotion	CPM
$6	$400,000	$12
8	600,000	14
10	800,000	16
12	1,000,000	18
		20
============	============	============

Make your choices and then look up your decisions in table 16.1 through 16.4 to see what your profits will be next year.

How Did You Do?

It is obvious that this magazine has been operating at the horrible end of the equation. The low circulation and rate base, combined with a low CPM, limited the advertising revenues drastically, yet they were printing a lot of advertising pages plus editorial pages to maintain the editorial/advertising

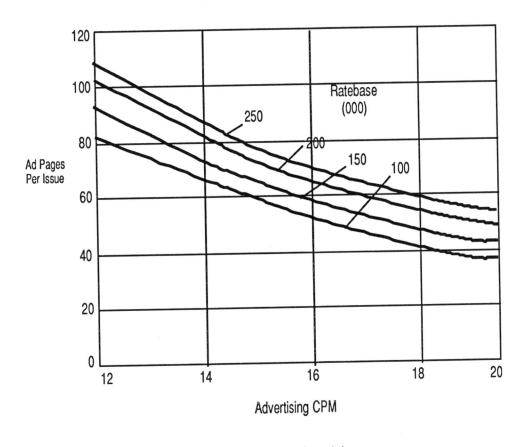

Figure 16.4. Advertising CPM impact on advertising pages.

Challenge I: A Subscription Magazine

Sub Prom	Ratebase	CPM	Revenues	Ad Pages	Profits
$400,000	143,159	$12	$2,305,912	94	$-19,043
400,000	143,159	14	2,198,577	74	-6,909
400,000	143,159	16	2,112,057	61	-6,118
400,000	143,159	18	2,040,390	51	-11,139
400,000	143,159	20	1,979,763	43	-19,170
600,000	182,800	12	3,060,841	99	77,700
600,000	182,800	14	2,915,149	79	94,170
600,000	182,800	16	2,797,149	65	95,244
600,000	182,800	18	2,700,432	54	88,429
600,000	182,800	20	2,618,139	46	77,528
800,000	211,203	12	3,619,872	103	97,244
800,000	211,203	14	3,445,353	82	116,973
800,000	211,203	16	3,304,677	67	118,260
800,000	211,203	18	3,188,152	56	110,096
800,000	211,203	20	3,089,577	48	97,038
1,000,000	231,555	12	4,028,704	106	57,715
1,000,000	231,555	14	3,832,916	84	79,848
1,000,000	231,555	16	3,675,096	69	81,292
1,000,000	231,555	18	3,544,371	57	72,133
1,000,000	231,555	20	3,433,781	49	57,483

Table 16.1. Subscription Price: $6

Challenge I: A Subscription Magazine

Sub Prom	Ratebase	CPM	Revenues	Ad Pages	Profits
400,000	125,328	12	2,227,923	91	77,247
400,000	125,328	14	2,137,030	72	87,522
400,000	125,328	16	2,063,764	59	88,192
400,000	125,328	18	2,003,076	49	83,940
400,000	125,328	20	1,951,736	42	77,139
600,000	161,236	12	2,968,719	96	205,001
600,000	161,236	14	2,844,183	77	219,079
600,000	161,236	16	2,743,798	63	219,079
600,000	161,236	18	2,660,647	52	214,171
600,000	161,236	20	2,590,304	45	204,853
800,000	186,964	12	3,515,851	100	246,088
800,000	186,964	14	3,365,998	79	263,028
800,000	186,964	16	3,245,205	65	264,133
800,000	186,964	18	3,145,150	54	257,123
800,000	186,964	20	3,060,506	46	245,910
1,000,000	205,400	12	3,195,326	102	221,677
1,000,000	205,400	14	3,746,780	81	240,730
1,000,000	205,400	16	3,610,918	67	241,973
1,000,000	205,400	18	3,498,383	56	234,088
1,000,000	205,400	20	3,403,181	48	221,477

Table 16.2. Subscription Price $8

Challenge I: A Subscription Magazine

Sub Prom	Ratebase	CPM	Revenues	Ad Pages	Profits
$400,000	105,259	$12	$2,037,757	87	$88,634
400,000	105,259	14	1,964,678	69	96,895
400,000	105,259	16	1,905,770	56	97,434
400,000	105,250	18	1,856,976	47	94,015
400,000	105,259	20	1,815,698	40	88,547
600,000	136,367	12	2,725,339	92	222,300
600,000	136,367	14	2,624,331	73	233,718
600,000	136,367	16	2,542,911	60	234,463
600,000	136,367	18	2,475,469	50	229,738
600,000	136,367	20	2,418,415	43	222,180
800,000	158,657	12	3,231,918	96	266,697
800,000	158,657	14	3,109,866	76	280,494
800,000	158,657	16	3,011,484	62	281,394
800,000	158,657	18	2,929,992	52	275,685
800,000	158,657	20	2,861,052	45	266,552
1,000,000	174,629	12	3,601.212	98	244,229
1,000,000	174,629	14	3,463,614	78	259,783
1,000,000	174,629	16	3,352,699	64	260,798
1,000,000	174,629	18	3,260,827	54	254,361
1,000,000	174,629	20	3,183,106	46	244,066

Table 16.3 Subscription Price: $10

Challenge I: A Subscription Magazine

Sub Prom	Ratebase	CPM	Revenues	Ad Pages	Profits
400,000	82,953	12	1,726,957	82	4,933
400,000	82,953	14	1,672,693	65	11,068
400,000	82,953	16	1,628,952	53	11,468
400,000	82,953	18	1,592,721	44	8,929
400,000	82,953	20	1,562,071	38	4,869
600,000	108,195	12	2,317,973	87	114,468
600,000	108,195	14	2,242,337	69	123,018
600,000	108,195	16	2,181,368	57	123,576
600,000	108,195	18	2,130,867	47	120,037
600,000	108,195	20	2,088,145	41	114,378
800,000	126,282	12	2,752,351	91	140,424
800,000	126,282	14	2,660,593	72	150,797
800,000	126,282	16	2,586,629	59	151,473
800,000	126,282	18	2,525,363	49	147,181
800,000	126,282	20	2,473,534	42	140,315
1,000,000	139,242	12	3,068,531	93	104,215
1,000,000	139,242	14	2,964,855	74	115,935
1,000,000	139,242	16	2,881,284	60	116,699
1,000,000	139,242	18	2,812,061	51	111,849
1,000,000	139,242	20	2,753,500	43	104,092

Table 16.4. Subscription Price: $12

Challenge I: A Subscription Magazine

ratio. Using marginal analysis, that last advertising page, with a page rate of $1,200 and a net of $900 a page, required a total expenditure as follows:

Manufacturing	1.5 x 100,000/1,000	=	$250
Editorial Page Mfg	2.5 x 100,000/1,000x .5	=	125
Editorial Purchase	10 x .5	=	500
Ad Department	.18 x 900	=	162
C&A Overhead	.1 x 900	=	900

Total $1127

But the net income from the page is only $900! The first 60 pages of advertising don't have to pay for any additional editorial and so they do a lot better—netting about $400 per page. It is clear the CPM and rate base should be adjusted to keep the total advertising at close to 60 pages per issue.

On the circulation side, the 100,000 subscriptions bring in $600,000 and they cost:

Acquisition cost		=	$238,610
Fulfill and Post	1.70 x 100,000	=	170,000
Manufacturing	2.5 x x 100,000/1,000 x 12	=	120,000
Editorial	40 x 12 x 1,000	=	480,000
G&A Overhead	.1 x 6 x 100,000	=	60,000

Total $1,086,610

Note we are charging the subscriptions for producing and manufacturing only the first 40 editorial pages, not the additional pages called for by the advertising pages. But with total income from subscriptions at $600,000, we have real trouble.

Now let's do the same accounting at what we have discovered is the optimum profit point. This is at $10 subscription price and $800,000 subscription promotion, which acquires 159,000, subscriptions. The advertising is 62 pages per issue at $16 CPM and a ratebase of 159,000 so the page rate is a net of $1,903.88. Here is how the last advertising page adds up:

Manufacturing	2.5 x 158,657/1000	=	$409.34
Editorial Page Mfg	2.5 x 158,657/1000 x .5	=	204.67
Editorial Purchase	1000 x .5	=	500.00
Ad Department	.18 x 1903.88	=	342.70
C&A Overhead	.1 x 1903.88	=	190.39
		Total	$1647.10

Total income from the page is $1,903.88. So we are still making a profit on these pages.

On the circulation side we run at a loss, though not nearly as large as before:

Acquisition cost		=	$800,00
Fulfil and Post	1.70 x 158,657	=	269,717
Manufacturing	2.5 x 40 x 158,657/1000	=	190,388
Editorial	40 x 12 x 1,000	=	480,000
G&A Overhead	.1 x 10 x 158,657	=	158,657
		Total	$1,898,762

But the gross income from subscription sales would be $1,586,570 for a loss of $312,192, which is made up by the advertising profits.

In the tables it is evident that profits are relatively insensitive to CPM. The reason for this is that, although raising the CPM reduces the number of ad pages fairly quickly, the gross income goes down much less quickly, if at all, because of the higher page rate. When you factor in the cost of paper and printing, plus the burden on advertising of editorial pages—which must be added—then profits don't change all that rapidly.

That "corner" in the advertising cost per page created by the need to add editorial pages when advertising goes above 60, changes the profit picture dramatically. This policy should be examined very closely, because it creates a hidden expense that will otherwise be charged to editorial or circulation but is rightfully the responsibility of advertising.

Since the profits are insensitive to CPM we can arbitrarily set the CPM at a $16 midpoint, and graph the other two variables against profits (Figure 16.5 and Figure 16.6).

Here you see that the profits rise quickly with subscription promotion

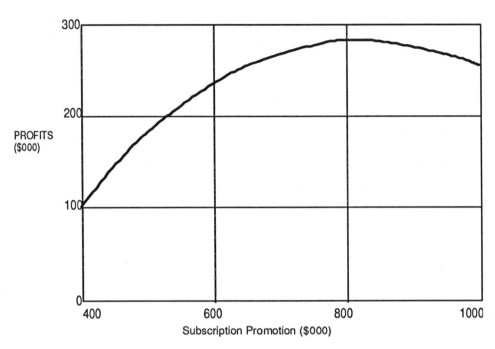

Figure 16.5. Profit sensitivity to subscription promotion peaks at $800,000.

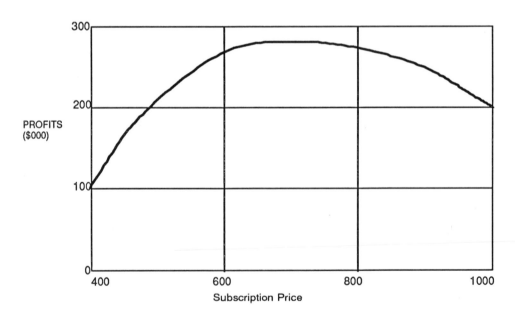

Figure 16.6. Profit sensitivity to subscription price peaks at $9.

because of the advertising value per subscriber. New subscribers bring in $16 per thousand times the total number of advertising pages, or 16 x .75 x 62/1,000 x 12, or $8.93 in addition to the subscription price. The peak is reached when the cost of acquiring the new subscriber becomes prohibitive.

The profits are also fairly sensitive to subscription price, as you see in Figure 16.6. There may be little to choose between $8 and $10. In fact, the $9 price is probably best, not least, because of the appeal of a price that doesn't cross the $10 barrier.

It is always necessary to check out the results of an analysis of this kind. The next realistic step would be a meeting with the subscription manager when you say something like, "Okay, subscription price will be $8.95. Your total acquisition budget will be $800,000. Give me a detailed breakdown of exactly how many subscriptions you can expect to sell."

And then to the advertising director, "If we boost the CPM to $16 and the subscription department tells me they can guarantee better than 160,000 subscriptions. Let's see how many pages you can sell."

Their answers should confirm their predictions and give you a budget you can hold them to.

Chapter 17

CHALLENGE II: A NEWSSTAND MAGAZINE

Your second challenge is a little more subtle. It is a tabloid newsstand magazine that your company would like to acquire. Here are the vital statistics:

Frequency	Monthly
Newsstand Draw	1,500,000
Newsstand Sale	1,230,000
Cover Price	$.45 (50 percent net to publisher)
CPM	$9 ($6.75 after commissions and discounts)
Rate base	1,200,000
Number of ads	1,036 last year
Editorial Pages	900 (75/issue)—no change for ad count
Editorial Cost	$1,000,000/year for staff and purchases
Production	$2.50/thousand pages for paper and printing
Ad Department	16 percent of net ad sales
Circ. Prom.	5 percent of net newsstand revenue
G&A	10 percent of all revenue

Last year the magazine made just under $775,000 in profits on almost $12 million in sales. Your company—a large publisher—wants to acquire this magazine since it would round out the stable perfectly, but when you the current owner laughs when you offer $4 million. Your board of directors says you may offer no more than six times earnings, and that if you value your job you'll find some way to buy the magazine because they really want it.

Being reasonably bright, you quickly explore alternative ways to structure the deal for the current owner, so that while it costs your company only $4.6 million, it represents a lot more to him. Nothing works. He wants the purchase price in cash.

Your only remaining alternative is to show the board that you can make a lot more out of this magazine than the current publisher is making, and therefore quickly get back a higher purchase price.

Your first meeting is with the newsstand circulation manager. He tells you that the 82 percent sale they have at the $.45 cover price is ideal. A higher percentage of sale would mean selling out in a number of outlets. A lower percentage means throwing away expensive magazines every month. He also emphasizes that he could not maintain the 82 percent sale if you raise the cover price.

We have seen in Chapter 7 how the sale is affected by draw. At very low levels of draw the sale will be equal to the draw as the magazine sells out everywhere. At very high levels of draw any additional copies distributed contribute nothing—the magazine has reached saturation. The effect of changing cover price is to raise or lower the saturation line, since a higher price will simply eliminate some potential buyers and a lower price will add some. So we can draw our graph of the magazine sales, draw, and cover price, as shown in Table 17.1 and Figure 17.1.

Your next meeting is with the advertising director. He tells you that selling over 1,000 pages a year in this business is tough. He runs a tight ship, he says, and 16 percent of the net sales dollars for staff and advertising promotion is better than what an advertising representative would charge. He is afraid to raise the CPM because the competition could take pages away from the magazine very quickly. He estimates that he would lose 300 pages of advertising if he were to raise the CPM to $10, and 600 if he took the CPM to $12.

He also is not enthusiastic about raising the rate base, because the page costs are already limiting the number of advertisers who can afford national schedules. He says he would lose 125 pages of advertising if the rate base were raised to 2 million, because the page cost would go from $10,000 to $18,000 at the same $9 CPM. He thinks he could sell another 100 pages if the page rate were cut to $7,200 at the same CPM, but that would mean reducing the rate base to 800,000, and he surely wouldn't want to do that. This is all very confusing until you pull out your trusty graph paper, plot his points, and then rough in the curves that seem to fit. Now it all begins to show a pattern. Rate base increases will move you down from curve to curve. The curves, themselves, are obviously quite sensitive to changes in CPM (Figure 17.2).

So again we come to the tough questions: Is the current publisher making as much as he can out of the magazine's sales? Could you do better? If so, how much better, and then what could you offer that would nail the purchase and at the same time get board approval?

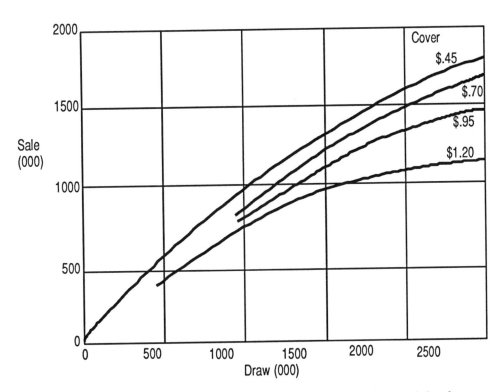

Figure 17.1 Newsstand sale as influenced by the cover price and the draw.

| Draw | Cover Price | | | |
	$.45	$.70	$.90	$1.20
500,000	467,000	459,000	446,000	420,000
1,000,000	874,000	846,000	800,000	715,000
1,500,000	1,230,000	1,171,000	1,080,000	920,000
2,000,000	1,540,000	1,445,000	1,302,000	1,064,000
2,500,000	1,810,000	1,675,000	1,478,000	1,165,000

Table 17.1. Single-copy sale versus draw and price.

Challenge II: A Newsstand Magazine

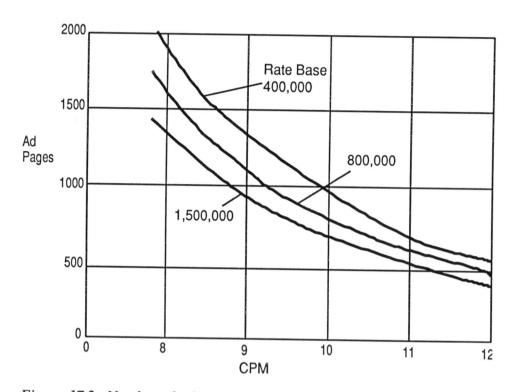

Figure 17.2 Number of ad pages sold as influenced by advertising CPM and rate base.

	CPM				
Ratebase	$8	$9	$10	$11	$12
400,000	1942	1364	994	747	575
800,000	1633	1147	836	628	484
1,500,000	1395	980	714	537	413

Table 17.2. Ad Pages vs CPM and Rate base

Challenge II: A Newsstand Magazine

Choose one from Column A, one from Column B, one from Column C, and check out the tables on the following pages to see the results of your decisions.

Column A	Column B	Column C
Cover Price	Draw	CPM
$.45	500,000	$8
.70	1,000,000	9
.95	1,500,000	10
1.20	2,000,000	11
	2,500,000	12

How Did You Do?

Amazing, isn't it? The best strategy is not very different from what has been done so far, except for one critical point—the cover price increase to $.95. Even $.70 improves profits dramatically over what was being generated at $.45. Let's make a comparison table of revenues and costs at the two prices, but with the same $9 CPM and the same $1.5 million draw.

	$.45	$.95
Cover Price		
Newsstand Revenues	3,320,995	6,155,179
Newsstand Expenses		
Editorial	1,000,000	1,000,000
Editorial Manufacturing	3,375,000	3,375,000
Circulation Promotion	166,050	307,759
G&A	332,100	615,518
Newsstand Net	-1,552,155	856,902
Advertising Revenues	8,391,600	7,590,713
Advertising Expenses		
Advertising Manufacturing	3,885,000	4,016,250
Advertising Department	1,342,565	1,214,514
G&A	839,160	759,071
Advertising Net	2,324,784	1,600,878
Total Net Profit	772,629	2,457,780

Challenge II: A Newsstand Magazine

Draw	Sale	Ratebase	CPM	Ad Pages	Revenues	Profits
500,000	467,265	450,000	8	1,885	6,351,767	357,534
1,000,000	874,712	850,000	8	1,608	10,563,075	806,194
1,500,000	1,229,998	1,200,000	8	1,475	13,943,018	775,839
2,000,000	1,539,802	1,500,000	8	1,395	16,714,576	349,934
2,500,000	1,809,945	1,800,000	8	1,333	19,283,972	148,975
500,000	467,265	450,000	9	1,324	5,283,464	268,459
1,000,000	874,712	850,000	9	1,129	8,841,803	729,159
1,500,000	1,229,998	1,200,000	9	1,036	11,713,705	772,937
2,000,000	1,539,802	1,500,000	9	980	14,079,132	476,290
2,500,000	1,809,945	1,800,000	9	936	16,262,354	95,099
500,000	467,265	450,000	10	965	4,519,312	151,515
1,000,000	874,712	850,000	10	823	7,610,588	583,246
1,500,000	1,229,998	1,200,000	10	755	10,119,090	645,897
2,000,000	1,539,802	1,500,000	10	714	12,194,016	409,092
2,500,000	1,809,945	1,°00,000	10	683	14,101,008	81,486
500,000	467,265	450,000	11	725	3,953,927	33,182
1,000,000	874,712	850,000	11	619	6,699,628	421,024
1,500,000	1,229,998	1,200,000	11	568	8,939,255	477,230
2,000,000	1,539,802	1,500,000	11	537	10,799,242	265,214
2,500,000	1,809,945	1,800,000	11	513	12,501,857	41,041
500,000	467,265	450,000	12	559	3,523,905	76,770
1,000,000	874,712	850,000	12	476	6,006,768	263,606
1,500,000	1,229,998	1,200,000	12	437	8,041,894	302,110
2,000,000	1,539,802	1,500,000	12	413	9,738,403	96,725
2,500,000	1,809,945	1,800,000	12	395	11,285,571	204,766

Table 17.3 Cover price $.45

Challenge II: A Newsstand Magazine

Draw	Sale	Ratebase	CPM	Ad Pages	Revenues	Profits
500,000	459,271	450,000	8	1,885	7,019,088	924,756
1,000,000	845,807	800,000	8	1,633	11,389,189	1,487,096
1,500,000	1,171,128	1,150,000	8	1,491	15,207,061	1,827,805
2,000,000	1,444,928	1,400,000	8	1,420	17,992,569	1,384,515
2,500,000	1,675,366	1,650,000	8	1,362	20,524,125	821,981
500,000	459,271	450,000	9	1,324	5,950,784	835,682
1,000,000	845,807	800,000	9	1,147	9,744,428	1,484,955
1,500,000	1,171,128	1,150,000	9	1,047	13,047,783	1,894,345
2,000,000	1,444,928	1,400,000	9	997	15,490,028	1,645,346
2,500,000	1,675,366	1,650,000	9	957	17,693,397	1,261,853
500,000	459,271	450,000	10	965	5,186,633	718,737
1,000,000	845,807	800,000	10	836	8,567,941	1,391,226
1,500,000	1,171,128	1,150,000	10	763	11,503,264	1,815,638
2,000,000	1,444,928	1,400,000	10	727	13,699,975	1,671,596
2,500,000	1,675,366	1,650,000	10	698	15,668,594	1,384,155
500,000	459,271	450,000	11	725	4,621,248	600,404
1,000,000	845,807	800,000	11	628	7,697,473	1,266,785
1,500,000	1,171,128	1,150,000	11	574	10,360,495	1,681,934
2,000,000	1,444,928	1,400,000	11	546	12,375,538	1,595,220
2,500,000	1,675,366	1,650,000	11	524	14,170,496	1,359,716
500,000	459,271	450,000	12	559	4,191,226	490,453
1,000,000	845,807	800,000	12	484	7,035,411	1,137,584
1,500,000	1,171,128	1,150,000	12	442	9,491,325	1,532,906
2,000,000	1,444,928	1,400,000	12	421	11,368,195	1,477,045
2,500,000	1,675,366	1,650,000	12	404	13,031,021	1,269,045

Table 17.4. Cover price. $.70

Challenge II: A Newsstand Magazine

Draw	Sale	Ratebase	CPM	Ad Pages	Revenues	Profits
500,000	446,117	400,000	8	1,942	7,202,657	1,057,708
1,000,000	799,667	750,000	8	1,659	12,024,602	2,001,539
1,500,000	1,079,856	1,050,000	8	1,525	15,764,954	2,248,031
2,000,000	1,301,907	1,300,000	8	1,446	28,700,082	1,924,091
2,500,000	1,477,883	1,450,000	8	1,407	20,665,790	799,880
500,000	446,117	400,000	9	1,364	6,224,676	1,056,435
1,000,000	799,667	750,000	9	1,165	10,457,558	2,076,671
1,500,000	1,079,856	1,050,000	9	1,071	13,748,088	2,458,242
2,000,000	1,301,907	1,300,000	9	1,016	16,332,840	2,324,551
2,500,000	1,477,883	1,450,000	9	988	18,096,511	1,516,436
500,000	446,117	400,000	10	994	5,525,133	1,000,703
1,000,000	799,667	750,000	10	850	9,336,661	2,036,715
1,500,000	1,079,856	1,050,000	10	781	12,305,435	2,479,398
2,000,000	1,301,907	1,300,000	10	740	14,639,565	2,447,678
2,500,000	1,477,883	1,450,000	10	720	16,258,721	1,830,335
500,000	446,117	400,000	11	747	5,007,549	926,710
1,000,000	799,667	750,000	11	638	8,507,324	1,951,164
1,500,000	1,079,856	1,050,000	11	587	11,238,035	2,417,844
2,000,000	1,301,907	1,300,000	11	556	13,386,733	2,441,189
2,500,000	1,477,883	1,450,000	11	541	14,898,965	1,943,382
500,000	446,117	400,000	12	575	4,613,885	849,887
1,000,000	799,667	750,000	12	492	7,876,545	1,850,980
1,500,000	1,079,856	1,050,000	12	452	10,426,190	2,322,604
2,000,000	1,301,907	1,300,000	12	428	12,433,852	2,375,045
2,500,000	1,477,883	1,450,000	12	417	13,864,758	1,955,795

Table 17.5 Cover price. $ .95

Challenge II: A Newsstand Magazine

Draw	Sale	Ratebase	CPM	Ad Pages	Revenues	Profits
500,000	420,458	400,000	8	1,942	7,687,090	1,469,476
1,000,000	714,642	700,000	8	1,688	12,235,397	2,149,966
1,500,000	920,474	900,000	8	1,585	15,187,990	1,648,280
2,000,000	1,064,489	1,050,000	8	1,525	17,274,094	499,098
2,500,000	1,165,252	1,150,000	8	1,491	18,678,138	-1,199,433
500,000	420,458	400,000	9	1,364	6,709,100	1,468,203
1,000,000	714,642	700,000	9	1,186	10,747,377	2,305,057
1,500,000	920,474	900,000	9	1,113	13,391,325	2,088,339
2,000,000	1,064,489	1,050,000	9	1,071	15,257,227	1,276,873
2,500,000	1,165,252	1,150,000	9	1,047	16,518,860	-23,290
500,000	420,458	400,000	10	994	6,009,566	1,412,471
1,000,000	714,642	700,000	10	864	9,683,005	2,320,665
1,500,000	920,474	900,000	10	812	12,106,181	2,268,827
2,000,000	1,064,489	1,050,000	10	781	13,814,574	1,660,935
2,500,000	1,165,252	1,150,000	10	763	14,974,341	607,495
500,000	420,458	400,000	11	747	5,491,983	1,338,479
1,000,000	714,642	700,000	11	649	8,895,491	2,275,252
1,500,000	920,474	900,000	11	610	11,155,320	2,322,129
2,000,000	1,064,489	1,050,000	11	587	12,747,174	1,842,156
2,500,000	1,165,252	1,150,000	11	574	13,831,572	948,421
500,000	420,458	400,000	12	575	5,098,318	1,261,655
1,000,000	714,642	700,000	12	500	8,296,521	2,204,985
1,500,000	920,474	900,000	12	470	10,432,112	2,312,342
2,000,000	1,064,489	1,050,000	12	452	11,935,329	1,915,424
2,500,000	1,165,252	1,150,000	12	442	12,962,402	1,128,832

Table 17.6 Cover price. $1.20

Challenge II: A Newsstand Magazine   213

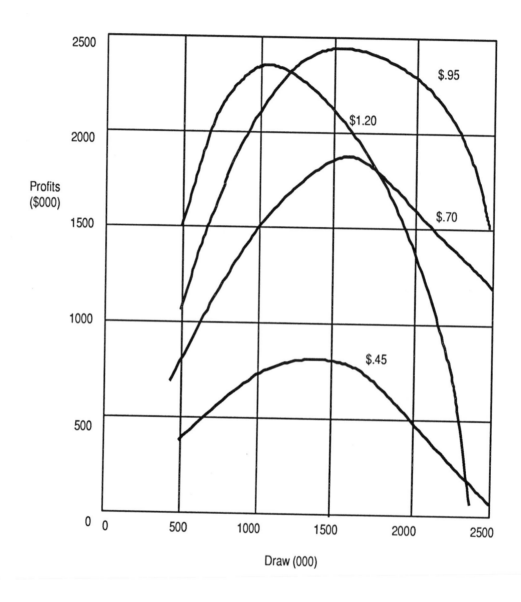

Figure 17.3. Profit elasticity for different newsstand draws and cover prices.

Challenge II: A Newsstand Magazine

While the advertising net dropped over $700,000, the newsstand net went up over $2.4 million. Although there is even more profit to be taken at a CPM of $10, ad pages drop to 781 and, from a promotional point of view, you might be wise to sacrifice a little in profits to keep the advertising page count over 1,000 per year.

With the CPM at $9, draw and cover price combine to affect profits as shown in Figure 17.3.

The curves have a curiously lumpy shape because of the way the rate base steps in 50,000 increments. This makes a magazine with a circulation at or just over, the rate base more profitable than one that is 49,000 over the rate base. As a matter of fact, if advertising were billed at actual circulation rather than a rate base guarantee, the profits would easily average $150,000 a year more than the table indicates—something to be considered when the advertising rate card is being redone. However, for a magazine this big, advertisers might be unwilling to accept a page rate based on actual circulation, since they would not be able to budget exactly.

Note that peak profits at $.95 and $1.20 are not all that different, even though the peak at $1.20 is at a much lower draw.

Okay. Let's leave the theoretical world of mathematics for a more realistic one. As acquisitions director of your company, what do you, actually do? With potential profits of almost $2.5 million projected here, you could offer $12 million to the owner and stay within the guidelines set by your board. But that would be risky. You still need to confirm that the price and draw sensitivity are as predicted.

A wiser strategy would be to spend $25,000 on an option to purchase at $7 million or $8 million. Give yourself three months in the option to test price and draw sensitivity in a small geographical area. Pick a wholesaler who will cooperate with good data, careful controls and fast reporting.

In this way you confirm the potential profits at least risk. If you are wrong you have spent $25,000 in a good cause. If you are right, or even close to right, the $8 million purchase price is made back in three years and you will be a hero to the board.

Chapter 18

CHALLENGE III: CONTROLLED CIRCULATION

"I run a tight ship," the crusty publisher growled at me. "You won't find any soft carpeting or fancy furniture around here."

He was right. It was a dusty, linoleum-floored office with an old oak desk that had been battered and gouged enough to qualify as a flea market antique. His staff worked in a bullpen just outside his glass-walled office and, as far as I could see, it consisted of about a dozen men and women who looked harried and overworked, and perhaps just a little sloppy because of being run too hard.

"As a matter of fact, I don't know why I'm talking to you at all. There's damn little chance you're going to squeeze another nickel out of this magazine, and if it weren't for that young idiot I wouldn't have to waste my time. . . and yours, of course," he added.

We all must have started in this business with someone like him as mentor, teacher, sometime taskmaster and lovable bastard. Our first job is usually on a trade magazine or newspaper—or we find "Truth" calling on the advertising managers of crummy little hole-in-the-wall machine shops, contractors, or retail store managers.

I had been foisted on him by a young whippersnapper who had inherited a business he knew nothing about. The new owner simply wanted to make sure his publisher knew what he was doing and that they were getting as much profit out of the magazine as could be expected.

It really was a good little magazine with a controlled circulation and a satisfactory advertising gross. Here are the numbers as the irascible publisher gave them to me right out of his head (they proved dead accurate when checked with the accountant).

Frequency	Monthly
Circulation (all controlled)	91,263
Acquisition Cost/sub-year	$3
Renewal Rate	60%
Cost to Renew	$.25/sub
Number of Editorial Pages	625 (40% of total)
Number of Advertising Pages	937 (60% of total)
Page Rate (average)	$2,000 ($1,500 net)
Editorial Staff Cost	$90,000/year
Editorial Purchases	$27,000/year
Advertising Staff Cost	$145,000/year
Advertising Promotion	$30,000/year
Manufacturing Cost	$2.12/1,000 pages
Fulfillment & Postage	$.15 per copy
Gen & Adm	$160,000/year

This last figure included everything—rent, heat, telephone, two-thirds of his own salary (he was one-third editor and two-thirds publisher, he said) and that of his secretary/office manager/assistant (a young typing-school graduate). Both administrative costs and advertising staff costs would go up by seven percent next year because of inflationary increases in travel and entertainment expenses, telephone and rent increases. However, the publisher was determined to hold the line on salaries. I had to feel a little sorry for those poor, overworked gnomes in the bullpen.

There didn't seem to be much I could do here. Profits were a comfortable $200,000 on $1,874,000 of gross sales. It was hard to see how to cut the costs or improve the profits in this situation. But I also knew that publishers of this kind rarely explore the range of control they have. It's dangerous to change rates in so competitive an environment, and publishers can't be blamed for being slow and careful about changing the editorial appearance of a goose that lays golden eggs every month.

So I put on my best butter-up face and lugged the heavy accounting books over to a desk in the bullpen. After some time with the books I started my usual questions to the circulation director.

She knew exactly how many subscriptions she had at any time and precisely what she would need each month to keep the circulation at the requested 90,000. She had a large universe of names to mail to, if needed. Some were expired subscribers who often resubscribed after a year or two

Challenge III: Controlled Circulation

in another location or another job. Others were people coming into the industry or people in job functions that were applicable. Renewal cost was simply a confirmation form required by the auditing bureau, and it only took one mailing to get them all.

She said she could easily increase the circulation by 50 percent or more, at a cost of $3 per subscription, just by sending a copy or two and then following up with her "Wouldn't you like to keep on getting . . ." mailing piece that had been working well for more years than she could remember. Yes, they occasionally tried other approaches, but the "Wouldn't you . . ." always outpulled the others. "We have a good editorial package," she said with some pride, "and that's all I need to bring in the subs."

By their standards it might have been, but from where I sat the magazine was a singularly unattractive mishmash of poor pictures, dull layouts and pedestrian prose. Half the book was filled with burnt-out flash pictures of plaid-jacketed men in hotel rooms looking directly at the camera while shaking hands with other plaid-jacketed men. The other half seemed to be pictures of machines, occasionally with a bikini-clad girl standing nearby and leaning forward to show her cleavage.

Did people still read magazines like this? Certainly. Those pictures and new machinery write-ups were very important to the professionals in the field. They might spend only a few minutes with the magazine, but I knew they would look at it within a few days of delivery to their in-boxes every month.

There were other magazines in the field with more or less overlapping editorial content, and although some were paid and others were controlled, the advertisers didn't seem to discriminate on that basis. Indeed, recent surveys indicate that many readers do not know whether a magazine is free or by subscription, and they pass the cost along to the company in any case.

Their own research showed no clear cut reader preference for one magazine over the other, and the advertisers seemed to buy space based on instinct and personal selling rather than on any measure of total readership, price, or cost per thousand.

There were several strategies available, but I had no confidence that any of them, alone or in combination, would produce more profit than was now being taken out of the company. And, of course, any change entailed a risk of the very satisfactory position they held. For example:

1. Change to paid circulation with a two-year period of part paid/part free. The acquisition cost would have to be much higher and the cost to renew would jump from $.25 per subscription to something like $2. Could they charge enough to make this worthwhile?

2. Make major editorial improvements so as to clearly differentiate this magazine from its competitors. They could add color, increase the number of editorial pages, make the layout more attractive, redesign the cover as well as their ancient logo—in short, do all the things which would proclaim to the advertiser and reader that this was a new, bigger, better value magazine. Would the readers be attracted or would they be furious that someone tampered with their comfortable and familiar rag?

3. Change advertising page rates. How would the advertiser react?

4. Increase the advertising sale effort by hiring another salesperson, planning a new sales promotion campaign, or simply taking a booth at another trade show.

In short, they could do all the things any publisher in these circumstances would consider and probably reject out of boredom ("We tried that back in '65 and it bombed."), or out of the sincere and possibly correct conviction that change for the sake of change is the surest way to kill a good thing.

I didn't disagree, but I needed to be convinced so I could advise the new young owner—with my professional position on the line—to keep hands off.

After a detailed examination of records and calculations, we came up with a graph that seemed to indicate what would happen if we switched from controlled to paid (Figure 18.1).

The plan included raising the circulation to 100,000 the following year. Since new subs now were costing $3 each to acquire, we had to assume a substantially larger cost of acquisition if the magazine went paid—to around $6 if the subscription price were $5, and to (a wild guess) $15 or $16 if the price were $10. That's why the curves sweep up so steeply. Any improvement in editorial product would presumably make subscription acquisition a little easier, hence the lower curve for acquisition cost at an editorial investment of $550,000 a year.

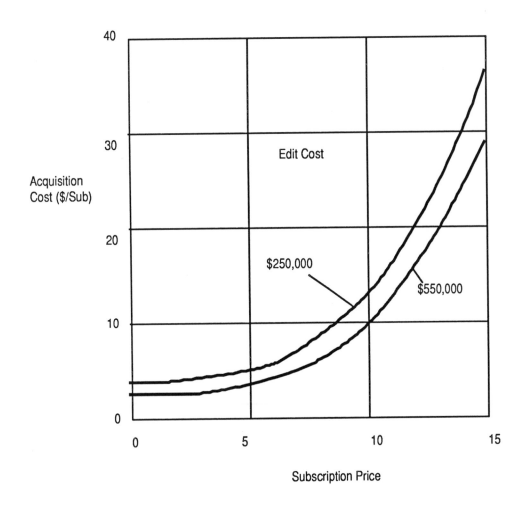

Figure 18.1 How the cost to acquire paid subscriptions would be influenced by subscription price and the quality of the editorial product.

Challenge III: Controlled Circulation 221

Last year the total cost of the editorial product was $250,000. This included the paper and printing (625 pages x 100,000 copies x $2.12/1000), plus staff ($90,000), plus purchases ($27,000). Any editor worth his saltcould spend as much as $550,000 to improve the product—by adding pages, color, more expensive purchases, additional staff—and the difference would undoubtedly be apparent to readers. Although it might not help acquisition cost much, it would do some good for the renewal percentages.

The same combined effect applies to renewals as it did in acquisitions (Figure 18.2). Raise the subscription price and there is sure to be a drop-off in renewal percentage (follow the $250,000 line down to the right). Increase the editorial investment and renewal percentage will rise (move from line to line up to the right), but less improvement as you approach the outer reaches of the editorial stratosphere.

As for advertising—a change in rates seemed very risky until they could show a substantially different or better audience than their competitors. The publisher convinced me that they already had most advertisers who might want to reach this audience and that the only way to get more pages is to have more personal contact with the advertisers. Spending $30,000 a year for promotion, he felt, was approaching the point of diminishing returns, and any important additional expenditure would produce only a negligible increase in pages (Figure 18.3).

Okay. You've got all the information. Should they go paid, and if so at what subscription price? Should they increase editorial costs or advertising promotion, and if so, by how much? Choose one value from Columns A, B, and C, and turn the page to check your results.

Column A	Column B	Column C
============	============	============
Subscription Price	Editorial Cost	Advertising Promotion
$ 0	$250,000	$20,000
5	350,000	30,000
10	450,000	40,000
15	550,000	50,000
============	============	============

Challenge III: Controlled Circulation

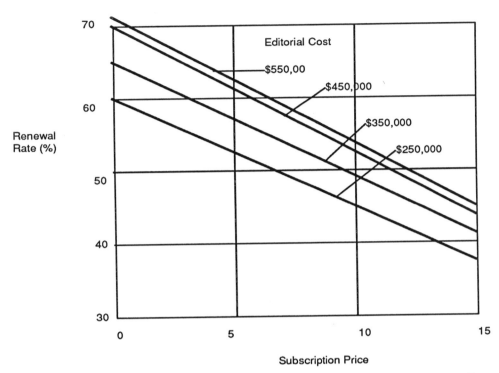

Figure 18.2 *Subscription price and editorial quality will combine to offset renewal rate.*

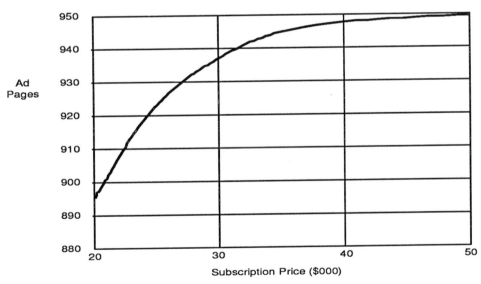

Figure 18.3 *Advertising promotion will improve the advertising page sales dramatically at the lower levels but not much after $30,000 has been spent.*

Challenge III: Controlled Circulation

Editorial Cost	New Subs Needed	Ad Promotion	Ad Pages	Ed Pages	Profits
$250,000	45,236	$20,000	895	597	$145,746
250,000	45,236	30,000	937	625	185,387
250,000	45,236	40,000	947	632	187,284
250,000	45,236	50,000	949	633	180,135
350,000	39,031	20,000	895	597	74,723
350,000	39,031	30,000	937	625	114,364
350,000	39,031	40,000	947	632	116,261
350,000	39,031	50,000	949	633	109,112
450,000	35,845	20,000	895	597	-12,694
450,000	35,845	30,000	937	625	26,947
450,000	35,845	40,000	947	632	28,844
450,000	35,845	50,000	949	633	21,695
550,000	34,209	20,000	895	597	-106,737
550,000	34,209	30,000	937	625	-67,096
550,000	34,209	40,000	947	632	-65,199
550,000	34,209	50,000	949	633	-72,348

Table 18.1 Subscription Price $0

Challenge III: Controlled Circulation

Editorial Cost	New Subs Needed	Ad Promotion	Ad Pages	Ed Pages	Profits
$250,000	52,081	$20,000	895	597	$347,783
250,000	52,081	30,000	937	625	387,424
250,000	52,081	40,000	947	632	389,321
250,000	52,081	50,000	949	597	305,613
350,000	46,652	20,000	895	597	305,613
350,000	46,652	30,000	937	625	345,254
350,000	46,652	40,000	947	632	347,151
350,000	46,652	50,000	949	633	340,002
450,000	43,864	20,000	895	597	230,142
450,000	43,864	30,000	937	625	269,783
450,000	43,864	40,000	947	632	271,680
450,000	43,864	50,000	949	633	264,531
550,000	42,433	20,000	895	597	141,603
550,000	42,433	30,000	937	625	181.244
550,000	42,433	40,000	947	632	183,140
550,000	42,433	50,000	949	633	175,992

Table 18.2 Subscription Price $5

Challenge III: Controlled Circulation

Editorial Cost	New Subs Needed	Ad Promotion	Ad Pages	Ed Pages	Profits
$250,000	58,927	$20,000	895	597	$250,622
250,000	58,927	30,000	937	625	290,264
250,000	58,927	40,000	947	632	292,160
250,000	58,927	50,000	949	633	285,011
350,000	54,273	20,000	895	597	307,524
350,000	54,273	30,000	937	625	347,165
350,000	54,273	40,000	947	632	349,062
350,000	54,273	50,000	949	633	341,913
450,000	51,884	20,000	895	597	275,589
450,000	51,884	30,000	937	625	315,231
450,000	51,884	40,000	947	632	317,127
450,000	51,844	50,000	949	633	309,978
550,000	50,657	20,000	895	597	207,794
550,000	50,657	30,000	937	625	247,436
550,000	50,657	40,000	947	632	249,332
550,000	50,657	50,000	949	633	242,183

Table 18.3 Subscription Price $10

Challenge III: Controlled Circulation

Editorial Cost	New Subs Needed	Ad Promotion	Ad Pages	Ed Pages	Profits
$250,000	65,772	$20,000	895	597	$-690,181
250,000	65,772	30,000	937	625	-650,539
250,000	65,772	40,000	947	632	-648,643
250,000	65,772	50,000	949	633	-655,792
350,000	61,894	20,000	895	597	-423,966
350,000	61,894	30,000	937	625	-384,324
350,000	61,894	40,000	947	632	-382,428
350,000	61,894	50,000	949	633	-389,577
450,000	59,903	20,000	895	597	-364,049
450,000	59,903	30,000	937	625	-324,408
450,000	59,903	40,000	947	632	-322,511
450,000	59,903	50,000	949	633	-329,660
550,000	58,881	20,000	895	597	-388,112
550,000	58,881	30,000	937	625	-348,471
550,000	58,881	40,000	947	632	-346,574
550,000	58,881	50,000	949	633	-353,723

Table 18.4 Subscription Price $15

Challenge III: Controlled Circulation

How Did You Do?

We can look at advertising promotion in a simple and straightforward way. By examining the advertising page response to promotion in Figure 18.3, we can estimate that an increase in promotion of $10,000 would bring in approximately 10 more pages of ads. The cost of this additional advertising would be paper and printing for another 6.67 pages of editorial (to maintain the 60/40 ad/edit ratio), plus the promotion itself.

It's not likely any changes in editorial staff or purchases would be necessary to fill these pages. So the figures are:

Paper and Printing (16.67 x 100,000 x 2.12/1000)	$3,534
Promotion	10,000
Total Cost	13,534
Net income (10 x $1,500)	15,000
Profits	$1,466

This differs from the table which indicates an increase in profits of $1897 because the computer is finicky about detail and it has it that $10,000 in additional promotion will bring in 10.375 pages, not 10.

In any case, the message is clear that more advertising promotion, pay. The next step of another $10,000 to raise the advertising budget to $50,000 would only bring in about 2 pages of advertising—a clear loser.

A prediction of the best subscription price is not so easily made. Going to $5 would raise the acquisition cost from $3 to $6.50. Also the renewal rate drop-off means more subs would have to be found through subscription mailings. However, the renewals would generate some revenue—$5 minus the $2 renewing cost for a net of $3—and since renewals are profitable (even with the fulfillment costs), one might be tempted to put some money in the editorial package so as to keep the renewal percentage as high as possible.

The tables show a peak profit at the $5 subscription price and $250,000 editorial cost. I have graphed the profits when the advertising promotion level is $40,000 (Figure 18.4). This shows that the peak profit actually lies between the $5 and $10 subscription prices, with both the $350,000 and $250,000 editorial investments producing a profit of over $400,000. This

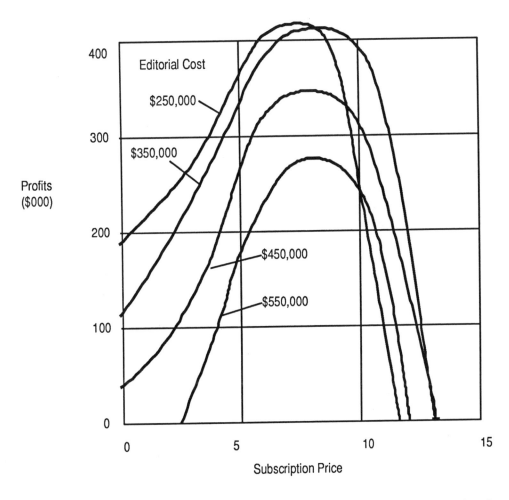

Figure 18.4. Profits as influenced by subscription price and different levels of editorial investment.

Challenge III: Controlled Circulation

is twice what can be produced at the controlled subscription rate ($0). It is surely advisable to switch to paid circulation—even at the very high cost of acquisition and renewals.

In real life you'd do a test, and that was what I recommended. A test mailing to 5,000 potential subscribers at the $5 rate and at a $7.50 rate produced a much better response than we predicted, and a further test of converting the controlled renewers to paid matched our assumptions very closely.

The accountant was turned loose on the new predictions and he budgeted the company for $500,000 in profits after two years. The publisher got a bonus and my client paid my fee with a very happy smile.

Chapter 19

TRACKING THE RESULTS

A characteristic shared by the best managers (and interestingly of the creative artist as well) is the ability to accept incomplete data, unbalanced compositions and the unknown, and function effectively. Strategic thinking depends on this talent because if all were known, if the future were a simple extrapolation of the past, the best strategies would be obvious. Let's face it, strategic decision making means choosing a course of action in an uncertain and generally hostile environment, or else who needs it?

Modelmaking is a tool of strategic thinking. It doesn't eliminate the uncertainty, it just reduces it a little—or more accurately, it defines the areas of uncertainty, makes them explicit and conscious. It marks the "Unknown Territory" clearly on your map and permits you to be logical and consistent .

But it is easy to be seduced by logic. Computer printouts are in formats similar to accountant's reports and the numbers are totaled to the nearest penny. Therefore, you may think that the printouts are as accurate and reliable as your bank statement. Be warned: They are not.

Throughout this book we have been saying "approximately," "nearly," "probably," until we long for a simple definitive statement. Alas, such is not to be. Every time a pair of factors is locked into a graph and an equation, we are making the incredible assertion that the dependent factor is directly and exactly defined by the independent factor—that newsstand sales are directly and exactly defined by draw, for example, or by draw and cover price, and nothing else. But there are other variables as well as random events that we are not aware of, or too limited in our ability to measure, that will push the sales up or down—sometimes by very large amounts. We must be prepared for these variations and learn from them.

The first test of our model is in these same graphs. Given changes in draw and price, does the single-copy sale move roughly as expected? Given price and the number of direct-mail pieces, is the subscription response on target? Does a price test at the Atlanta airport newsstand confirm your forecast?

The next test is to use the model to outline a business plan. The decision data and curves give you all the raw stuff of which budgets are made, and needs only your accounting department to explode them into month-by-month detail for as far as your courage may take you. There are several budgeting models available (see Appendix C), or you may be ambitious enough to write your own financial reporting program that will run out monthly projections of circulation, cash flow, profit and loss, etc.

And like any budget, this detailed business plan can be used as the tracking device to see how close the projection simulates the real world. It takes a little care. Variances here mean something different from normal budget variances. It isn't simply that the advertising sales staff didn't make their targets, or that the paper company slipped an unexpected price increase in on you. Those are normal budget variations that can be explained and even anticipated.

The strategic plan may have variances of a different kind. It could be an unexpectedly small reaction to a price increase given a changed economic environment, or a competitor's capable or inept response to your increased promotion budget. It is not enough to look at the immediate cause of a variance. You need to reexamine your assumptions, even your theory. And there's a good chance the variance was caused by a factor or combination of factors several layers distant from the obvious one.

That doesn't make the cause unknowable, only a little more subtle.

And you will be too.

Appendix A

CURVE FITTING PROGRAM LISTINGS

The following programs find the coefficients necessary to fit three of the most frequently used mathematical curves to given data. None of these can be easily solved explicity, therefore a trial and error routine is built into the programs so that a reasonably close fit can be made.

In each case, a crude sample graph may be viewed by the user before attempting to fit the data. It is crude because it uses the 80 column by 25 line increments for data plots. You will not need graphics capability in your computer to see the shape of the curve.

Data points are then requested and the coefficients determined, and the equation is displayed on the screen. The user may next request a table to be displayed that shows values for the dependent variable (Y) over a chosen range, and range increment of the independent variable (X). Different ranges may be requested in later runs.

Finally, a second rough graph of the data for the given range may be displayed on the screen. Negative values and values over 1 million are not plotted.

Specific notations about each program listing introduce each listing. The programs have been used extensively for simulation modeling, however, they are not crash proof. Extreme ranges of data or unlikely shapes may drive the solutions beyond the capacity of the computer arithmetic, resulting in divide by zero errors or illegal function calls.

A more complete set of curve shapes plus full graphical capabilities are available in a set of compiled programs (written in Turbo Pascal). They are available in disk form. See Appendix C for details on how these may be purchased.

Polynomial Curve

This is the most general program of the group. It uses a least-squares regression to find a polynomial of the form:

$$Y = a + b * X + c * X^2 + d * X^3 + e * X^4 + f * X^5$$

Where "Y" is the dependent variable, "X" is the independent variable, and "a," "b," "c," "d," "e," and "f" are the coefficients to be determined. The coefficients may be either positive or negative.

At the beginning of the program the user is asked to type the number of points that are available. This establishes the degree of the equation which is the maximum power of X (from 0 to 5). The higher powers provide more flexibility in the curve shape and allow for more varied data points. If the curve is a straight line, the degree is 1. If it has a single direction of curvature, the degree is 2. Each inflection point (where the curve changes from convex to concave or the reverse) adds one degree to 2. Thus, a curve with one inflection point, such as the sample shown in Figure A.1, is of degree 3.

Data points to be supplied by the user are listed in X,Y order. the number of points must be at least one more than the degree of the equation. If this number of points is supplied, the program will normally be able to find coefficients for a perfect fit. If more points than the minimum necessary are supplied, the program will fit a curve that has the least mean-square error in deviations from the supplied data.

```
100 REM Polynomial
110 CLS : FOR I=1 TO 4 : PRINT : NEXT
120 PRINT TAB(10);"This module finds a polynomial"
130 PRINT TAB(10);"using an nth order regression."
140 PRINT:PRINT TAB(10);:INPUT"Want to see a sample
    (Y/N)";A$
150 IF A$<>"Y" AND A$<>"y"THEN 480
160 DEF FNG(X)=22-4.35*X+.3*X^2-.002*X^3-.000005*X^4
170 XMIN=0 : XMAX=100 : XSTEP=7 : GOSUB 5000
180 PRINT TAB(32);:INPUT"Press RETURN to continue.",A$
190 CLS
200 PRINT:PRINT TAB(10);:INPUT"How many points do you have
    (10 is max)";N
210 IF N>10 OR N<1 THEN PRINT:PRINT TAB(10);"Out of range.
    Please reenter.":GOTO 480
```

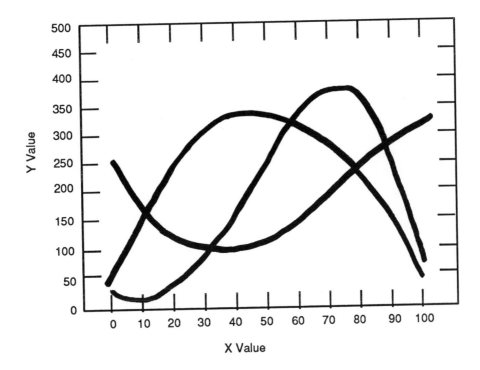

Figure A.1 A polynomial may take many shapes from a straight line to curves with several inflection points. The degree of the equation is two more than the number of inflection points.

Curve fitting Program Listings

235

```
220 D=N-1 : IF D>5 THEN D=5
230 FOR I=0 TO 12 : A(I)=0 : T(I)=0 : NEXT I
240 A(1)=N
250 PRINT
260 FOR I=1 TO N
270  PRINT TAB(20);"X,Y of point ";I;
280  INPUT ":  ",X,Y
290    FOR J=2 TO 2*D+1 : A(J)=A(J)+X^(J-1) : NEXT
300    FOR K=1 TO D+1 : R(K,D+2)=T(K)+Y*X^(K-1) :
   T(K)=T(K)+Y*X^(K-1) : NEXT
310    T(D+2)=T(D+2)+Y^2
320 NEXT I
330 FOR J=1 TO D+1
340   FOR K=1 TO D+1 : R(J,K)=A(J+K-1) : NEXT
350 NEXT J
360 FOR J=1 TO D+1
370   FOR K=J TO D+1:IF R(K,J)<>0 THEN 390: NEXT
380   PRINT TAB(10);"No unique solution. Please reenter."
   :GOTO 190
390   FOR I=1 TO D+2 : S=R(J,I):R(J,I)=R(K,I) :
   R(K,I)=S : NEXT
400   Z=1/R(J,J)
410   FOR I=1 TO D+2 : R(J,I)=Z*R(J,I) : NEXT
420     FOR K=1 TO D+1
430      IF K=J THEN 740
440      Z=-R(K,J)
450       FOR I=1 TO D+2 : R(K,I)=R(K,I)+Z*R(J,I) : NEXT
460   NEXT K
470 NEXT J
480 PRINT:PRINT TAB(27);:PRINT USING"Constant = ######,.###"
   ;R(1,D+2)
490   FOR J=1 TO D
500   PRINT TAB(14);:PRINT USING"## Degree coefficient =
   ######,.#####";J,R(J+1,D+2)
510   NEXT
520 P=0
530   FOR J=2 TO D+1 : P=P+R(J,D+2)*(T(J)-A(J)*T(1)/N) : NEXT
540 Q=T(D+2)-T(1)^2/N:Z=Q-P:I=N-D-1:J=P/Q
550 PRINT:PRINT TAB(14);:PRINT USING"Goodness of fit (R^2) =
   #.###";J
560 PRINT:PRINT TAB(10);"Want to see values
   (Y/N)?"
570 PRINT TAB(10);:INPUT"(you must calculate values to get a
   plot) ",A$
580 IF A$<>"Y" AND A$<>"y" THEN 1050
```

Curve fitting Program Listings

```
590 PRINT:PRINT TAB(10);:INPUT"Type start, end, and stepsize
    for variable X: ",A0,A1,A2
600 PRINT
610 PRINT TAB(20);"        X              Y"
620 PRINT TAB(20);STRING$(11,196);"   ";STRING$(11,196)
630 FOR X=A0 TO A1 STEP A2
640 Y=0
650  FOR J=0 TO D : Y=Y+R(J+1,D+2)*X^J : NEXT
660 PRINT TAB(20);:PRINT USING"######,.### ######, .###";X,Y
670 NEXT X
680 PRINT TAB(20);STRING$(11,196);"   ";STRING$(11,196)
690 PRINT : PRINT TAB(10);:INPUT"Another set (Y/N)";A$
700 IF A$="Y" OR A$="y" THEN 590
710 PRINT : PRINT TAB(10);:INPUT"Want to see a plot (Y/N)"
    ;A$
720 IF A$="Y" OR A$="y" THEN 730 ELSE 760
730 XMIN=A0 : XMAX=A1 : XSTEP=A2
740 DEF FNG(X)=R(1,D+2)+R(2,D+2)*X+R(3,D+2)*X^2+R(4,D+2)
    *X^3+R(5,D+2)*X^4+R(6,D+2)*X^5
750 GOSUB 5000
760 PRINT:PRINT TAB(10);:INPUT"Want to refit the curve (Y/N)
    ";A$
770 IF A$="Y" OR A$="y" THEN 190 ELSE RETURN
4990 REM
5000 REM  This subroutine plots a function on the screen.
5010 REM  Function must be passed as fng(x)
5020 REM  Range of X and steps are defined by XMIN, XMAX,
     XSTEP
5030 CLS
5040 PRINT
5050 I=-1 : YMAX=0 : YMIN=0
5060 FOR X=XMIN TO XMAX STEP XSTEP
5070 I=I+1
5080 YVAL(I)=FNG(X)
5090 IF YVAL(I)>YMAX THEN YMAX=YVAL(I)
5100 IF I=0 THEN YMIN=YVAL(I) : GOTO 5120
5110 IF YVAL(I)<YMIN THEN YMIN=YVAL(I)
5120 NEXT X
5130 IF YMIN<YMAX/10 THEN YMIN=0 ELSE YMIN=10*INT(YMIN/10)
5140 YMAX=10*INT(1.1*YMAX/10+.5)
5150 YSTEP=(YMAX-YMIN)/20
5160 IF YSTEP=0 THEN YSTEP=YMAX/20
5170 HSTEPS=INT((XMAX-XMIN)/XSTEP+.5)
5180 FOR I=0 TO HSTEPS
5190 Y1VAL(I)=INT((YVAL(I)-YMIN)/YSTEP)
5200 NEXT I
```

Curve fitting Program Listings

```
5210 XLGD$=SPACE$(7)+STR$(XMIN)
5215 XLGD$=XLGD$+SPACE$(72-LEN(STR$(XMIN))-LEN(STR$(XMAX)))
     +STR$(XMAX)
5220 MID$(XLGD$,44,1)="X"
5230 ORD$(0)=SPACE$(8-LEN(STR$(YMIN)))+STR$(YMIN)+"+"+
     STRING$(69,"-")+"+"
5240 ORD$(20)=SPACE$(8-LEN(STR$
     (YMAX)))+STR$(YMAX)+"+"+STRING$(69,"-")+"+"
5250 FOR I=1 TO 19
5260 ORD$(I)=STRING$(79," ")
5270 MID$(ORD$(I),9,1)="|" : MID$(ORD$(I),79,1)="|"
5280 NEXT I
5290 MID$(ORD$(10),7,1)="Y"
5300 FOR I=0 TO HSTEPS
5310 IF Y1VAL(I)<0 OR LEN(STR$(Y1VAL(I)))>8 THEN 5330
5320 MID$(ORD$(Y1VAL(I)),I*70/HSTEPS+9,1)="+"
5330 NEXT I
5340 FOR I=20 TO 0 STEP -1
5350 PRINT ORD$(I)
5360 NEXT I
5370 PRINT XLGD$
5380 RETURN
```

Normal Curve

The normal curve, a shape frequently found in nature and based on probability theory (Figure A.2), is usually applied to distributions of events about a mean. It is symmetrical about the mean is moved to the right or left by the value of coefficient c. The curve is horizontal (zero slope) at the mean which is also the highest point, and then curves down to an inflection point at just over 60 percent of the highest value. It then continues down in a shallow curve which is asymptotic to the X axis.

$$Y = a/\exp((X-c)^2/b)$$

Where exp is e (2.71828). The three coefficients have very specific shaping values: "a" is the highest point, "b" is two times the square of the X value at the inflection point, "c" is the horizontal offset of the highest point.

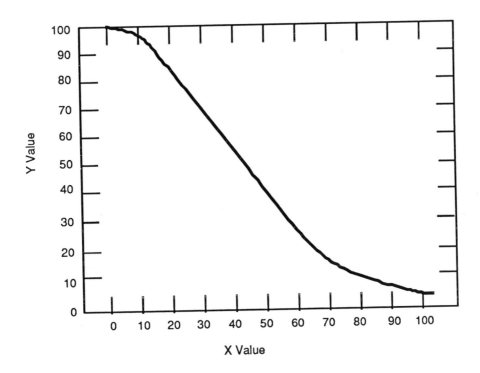

Figure A.2   A normal curve has zero slope at the highest point (here shown at the Y axis) and curves down to become asymptotic to the X axis.

Curve fitting Program Listings

239

```
2000 REM Normal Curve
2005 DIM YVAL(73), Y1VAL(73),ORD$(20)
2010 CLS
2020 PRINT:PRINT TAB(10);
2025 PRINT"This module calculates coefficients for the
     normal curve:
2030 PRINT:PRINT TAB(25);"Y = A/EXP
     ((X-C)^2/B)"
2040 PRINT:PRINT TAB(20);"Where: A is the Y intercept"
2050 PRINT TAB(27);"B is a shaping coefficient."
2055 PRINT TAB(27);"C is the horizontal offset of the
     highest point."
2060 PRINT:PRINT TAB(10);
2065 PRINT"(Note: B is 2 times the square of the inflection
     point.)"
2070 PRINT: PRINT TAB(10);:INPUT"Want to see curve
shape";A$ 2080 IF A$<>"Y" AND A$<>"y"THEN 2140
2090 DEF FNG(X)=100/EXP((X-10)^2/2600)
2100 XMIN=0 : XMAX=100 : XSTEP=6.5
2110 GOSUB 5000
2120 PRINT TAB(32);:INPUT"Type RETURN to continue.",A$
2130 CLS
2140 PRINT:PRINT TAB(10);"You need three points to
     determine the curve."
2150 PRINT:PRINT TAB(20);:INPUT"What is X,Y of point 1:
     ",X1,Y1
2160 PRINT TAB(20);:INPUT"What is X,Y of point 2: ",X2,Y2
2165 PRINT TAB(20);:INPUT"What is X,Y of point 3: ",X3,Y3
2170 IF X2=X1 OR X3=X2 OR
     X3=X1 THEN 2190
2180 IF (X2>X1 AND Y2=>Y1) OR (X3>X1 AND Y3=>Y1) THEN 2190
     ELSE 2185
2185 IF X3>X2 AND Y3=>Y2 THEN 2190 ELSE 2200
2190 PRINT:PRINT TAB(10);
2195 PRINT"Higher X must have lower Y.  Please reenter."
     :GOTO 2140
2200 IF X2 <X1 THEN SWAP X2,X1 : SWAP Y2,Y1
2202 IF X3<X2 THEN SWAP X3,X2 : SWAP Y3,Y2
2204 IF X2<X1 THEN SWAP X2,X1 : SWAP Y2,Y1
2206 C=X3
2207 FOR I=0 TO 20
2208   D=(LOG(Y1/Y2)/LOG(Y2/Y3))*((X3-C)^2-(X2-C)^2)
2209   IF (X2-C)^2-(X1-C)^2>D THEN C=C+10*X3/2^I ELSE C=C-
     10*X3/2^I
2210 NEXT I
```

```
2212 IF (X2-C)^2-(X1-C)^2-D>.01 THEN 2214 ELSE 2216
2214 PRINT TAB(10);"Can't fit a curve.  Please reenter
     data.":goto 2140
2216 B=((X2-C)^2-(X1-C)^2)/LOG(Y1/Y2)
2218 A=Y1*EXP((X1-C)^2/B)
2220 PRINT:PRINT TAB(10);"Fitted equation is:";
2230 PRINT USING"  Y = #####.###/EXP((X -#####.###)^2/#####
     .###)";A,C,B
2240 PRINT:PRINT TAB(10);"Want to see
     values (Y/N)?"
2250 PRINT TAB(10);
2255 INPUT"(You must calculate values to get a plot) ",A$
2260 IF A$<>"Y" AND A$<>"y" THEN 2400
2270 PRINT:PRINT TAB(10);
2275 INPUT"Type start, end, and stepsize for variable X:
     ",X1,X2,X3
2280 PRINT:PRINT TAB(20);"      X           Y"
2290 PRINT TAB(20);STRING$(11,196);"    ";STRING$(11,196)
2300  FOR I=X1 TO X2 STEP X3
2310  Y=A/EXP((I-C)^2/B)
2320   PRINT TAB(20);:PRINT USING"#####,.#########,.###"
     ;I,Y
2330 NEXT I
2340 PRINT TAB(20);STRING$(11,196);"    ";STRING$(11,196)
2350 PRINT:PRINT TAB(10);:INPUT"Another set (Y/N)";A$
2360 IF A$="Y" OR A$="y" THEN 2270
2370 PRINT:PRINT TAB(10);:INPUT"Want to see a plot (Y/N)"
     ;A$
2380 IF A$<>"Y" AND A$<>"y" THEN 2400
2390 DEF FNG(X)=A/EXP((X-C)^2/B) : XMIN=X1 : XMAX=X2 :
     XSTEP=X3 : GOSUB 5000
2400 PRINT:PRINT TAB(10);:INPUT"Want to refit the curve
     (Y/N)";A$
2410 IF A$="Y" OR A$="y" THEN 2130 ELSE RETURN
4990 REM
5000 REM  This subroutine plots a function on the screen.
5010 REM  Function must be passed as fng(x)
5020 REM  Range of X and steps are defined by XMIN, XMAX,
     XSTEP
5030 CLS
5040 PRINT
5050 I=-1 : YMAX=0 : YMIN=0
5060 FOR X=XMIN TO XMAX STEP XSTEP
5070 I=I+1
5080 YVAL(I)=FNG(X)
5090 IF YVAL(I)>YMAX THEN YMAX=YVAL(I)
5100 IF I=0 THEN YMIN=YVAL(I) : GOTO 5120
```

Curve fitting Program Listings

```
5110 IF YVAL(I)<YMIN THEN YMIN=YVAL(I)
5120 NEXT X
5130 IF YMIN<YMAX/10 THEN YMIN=0 ELSE YMIN=10*INT(YMIN/10)
5140 YMAX=10*INT(1.1*YMAX/10+.5)
5150 YSTEP=(YMAX-YMIN)/20
5160 IF YSTEP=0 THEN YSTEP=YMAX/20
5170 HSTEPS=INT((XMAX-XMIN)/XSTEP+.5)
5180 FOR I=0 TO HSTEPS
5190 Y1VAL(I)=INT((YVAL(I)-YMIN)/YSTEP)
5200 NEXT I
5210 XLGD$=SPACE$(7)+STR$(XMIN)
5215 XLGD$=XLGD$+SPACE$(72-LEN(STR$(XMIN))-LEN(STR$(XMAX)))
     +STR$(XMAX) 5220 MID$(XLGD$,44,1)="X"
5230 ORD$(0)=SPACE$(8-LEN(STR$(YMIN)))+STR$(YMIN)+"+"+
     STRING$(69,"-")+"+"
5240 ORD$(20)=SPACE$(8-LEN(STR$
     (YMAX)))+STR$(YMAX)+"+"+STRING$(69,"-")+"+"
5250 FOR I=1 TO 19
5260 ORD$(I)=STRING$(79," ")
5270 MID$(ORD$(I),9,1)="|" : MID$(ORD$(I),79,1)="|"
5280 NEXT I
5290 MID$(ORD$(10),7,1)="Y"
5300 FOR I=0 TO HSTEPS
5310 IF Y1VAL(I)<0 OR LEN(STR$(Y1VAL(I)))>8 THEN 5330
5320 MID$(ORD$(Y1VAL(I)),I*70/HSTEPS+9,1)="+"
5330 NEXT I
5340 FOR I=20 TO 0 STEP -1
5350 PRINT ORD$(I)
5360 NEXT I
5370 PRINT XLGD$
5380 RETURN
```

Diminishing Returns

This equation is also found frequently in nature as well as in economic and business activities (Figure A.3). It is the typical "point of diminishing returns" curve. It rises sharply, or with some curvature from—or above—the origin, toward a maximum value which it approaches asymptotically, creating a "knee" about two-thirds of the way up. The equation is written:

$$Y = a + b * (1 - 1/\exp(X/c))^d$$

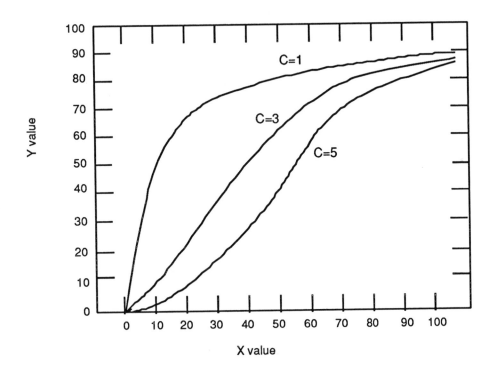

Figure A.3 A diminishing returns curve may start straight up from zero when c = 1, or curve up depending on how much above 1 the value of c. It then moves up and over a "knee" to become asymptotic to a horizontal line at Y = a + b. Coefficient a simply shifts the entire curve up off the X axis.

Curve fitting Program Listings 243

Where "a" is the Y intercept, "b" is the distance from "a" to the highest point of the curve, "c" is a shaping coefficient that determines how quickly the curve rises with increasing X, and "d" determines how much curvature there is near the origin.

```
3000 REM Diminishing returns
3005 DIM YVAL(73),Y1VAL(73),ORD$(20)
3010 CLS
3020 FOR I=1 TO 4 : PRINT : NEXT
3030 PRINT:PRINT TAB(10);"This module fits the exponential
     curve:"
3040 PRINT:PRINT TAB(20);"Y = A+B(1-1/EXP(X/C))
     ^D"
3050 PRINT:PRINT TAB(10);"Where A is the Y-axis intercept at
     X=0,"
3060 PRINT TAB(16);"(A + B) is asymptote at infinite values
     of X"
3070 PRINT TAB(16);"C controls the speed of rise"
3080 PRINT TAB(16);"D determines the curvature near the
     origin"
3090 PRINT:PRINT TAB(10);:INPUT"Want to see a sample";A$
3100 IF A$<>"Y" AND A$<>"y"THEN 3150
3110 DEF FNG(X)=9+90*(1-1/EXP(X/20))^3
3120 XMIN=0 : XMAX=100 : XSTEP=10 : GOSUB 5000
3130 PRINT TAB(32);:INPUT"Press RETURN to continue.",A$
3140 CLS
3150 PRINT:PRINT TAB(10);:INPUT"What is the value of Y when
     X is zero? ",A
3160 PRINT:PRINT TAB(10);"You need three more points to
     establish the curve."
3170 PRINT:PRINT TAB(20);:INPUT"What is X,Y of point 1:
     ",X1,Y1
3180 PRINT TAB(20);:INPUT"What is X,Y of point 2: ",X2,Y2
3190 PRINT TAB(20);:INPUT"What is X,Y of point 3: ",X3,Y3
3200 PRINT
3210 IF X2<X1 THEN SWAP X2,X1 : SWAP Y2,Y1
3220 IF X3<X2 THEN SWAP X3,X2 : SWAP Y3,Y2
3230 IF X2<X1 THEN SWAP X2,X1 : SWAP Y2,Y1
3240 IF Y2>Y1 AND Y3>Y2 THEN 3270
3250 PRINT:PRINT TAB(10);"Increasing Xs must result in
     increasing Ys."
3260 PRINT TAB(10);"Please reenter data."
     : GOTO 3150
3270 C=X3 : C1=X3
```

```
3280 IF X3<.01 OR Y1<A OR Y2<A OR Y3<A OR X1=X2 OR X1=X3 OR
     X2=X3 THEN 3380 3290 FOR I=1 TO 20
3300  R1=(1-1/EXP(X1/C))
3310  R2=(1-1/EXP(X2/C))
3320  R3=(1-1/EXP(X3/C))
3330  D1=(LOG(Y1-A)-LOG(Y2-A))/(LOG(R1)-LOG(R2))
3340  D2=(LOG(Y1-A)-LOG(Y3-A))/(LOG(R1)-LOG(R3))
3350  IF D2<D1 THEN C=C-C1/2^I ELSE C=C+C1/2^I
3360  NEXT I
3370 IF ABS(D1-D2)<D1/1000 THEN 3390
3380 PRINT:PRINT TAB(10);"Can't fit a curve.  Please reenter
     data." : GOTO 3150
3390 D=D1 : B=(Y3-A)/R3^D
3400 PRINT:PRINT TAB(20);"Equation is:" : PRINT
3410 PRINT TAB(15);:PRINT USING"Y = ####,.#+######,.#(1 -
     1/EXP(X/######,.#))^##.##";A,B,C,D
3420 PRINT:PRINT
     TAB(10);"Want to see values (Y/N)?"
3430 PRINT TAB(10);:INPUT"(You must calculate values to get
     a plot.)",A$
3440 IF A$<>"Y" AND A$<>"y" THEN 3600
3450 PRINT:PRINT TAB(10);:INPUT"Type start, end, and
     stepsize for variable x: ",X1,X2,X3
3460 PRINT:PRINT
     TAB(20);"      X              Y"
3470 PRINT TAB(20);STRING$(11,196);"    ";STRING$(11,196)
3480  FOR X=X1 TO X2 STEP X3
3490  Y=A+B*(1-1/EXP(X/C))^D
3500  PRINT TAB(20);:PRINT USING"  #####,.##
     #####,.##";X,Y
3510  NEXT X
3520 PRINT TAB(20);STRING$(11,196);"    ";STRING$(11,196)
3530 PRINT:PRINT TAB(10);:INPUT"Another set";A$
3540 IF A$="Y" OR A$="y"THEN 3450
3550 PRINT:PRINT TAB(10);:INPUT"Want to see a plot";A$
3560 IF A$<>"Y" AND A$<>"y" THEN 3600
3570 XMIN=X1 : XMAX=X2 : XSTEP=X3
3580 DEF FNG(X)=A+B*(1-1/EXP(X/C))^D
3590 GOSUB 5000
3600 PRINT:PRINT TAB(10);:INPUT"Want to refit the curve";A$
3610 IF A$="Y" OR A$="y" THEN 3140 ELSE RETURN
4990 REM
5000 REM  This subroutine plots a function on the screen.
5010 REM  Function must be passed as fng(x)
5020 REM  Range of X and steps are defined by XMIN, XMAX,
     XSTEP
```

Curve fitting Program Listings

```
5030 CLS
5040 PRINT
5050 I=-1 : YMAX=0 : YMIN=0
5060 FOR X=XMIN TO XMAX STEP XSTEP
5070 I=I+1
5080 YVAL(I)=FNG(X)
5090 IF YVAL(I)>YMAX THEN YMAX=YVAL(I)
5100 IF I=0 THEN YMIN=YVAL(I) : GOTO 5120
5110 IF YVAL(I)<YMIN THEN YMIN=YVAL(I)
5120 NEXT X
5130 IF YMIN<YMAX/10 THEN YMIN=0 ELSE YMIN=10*INT(YMIN/10)
5140 YMAX=10*INT(1.1*YMAX/10+.5)
5150 YSTEP=(YMAX-YMIN)/20
5160 IF YSTEP=0 THEN YSTEP=YMAX/20
5170 HSTEPS=INT((XMAX-XMIN)/XSTEP+.5)
5180 FOR I=0 TO HSTEPS
5190 Y1VAL(I)=INT((YVAL(I)-YMIN)/YSTEP)
5200 NEXT I
5210 XLGD$=SPACE$(7)+STR$(XMIN)
5215 XLGD$=D$+SPACE$(72-LEN (STR$(XMIN))-
     LEN(STR$(XMAX)))+STR$(XMAX)
5220 MID$(XLGD$,44,1)="X"
5230 ORD$(0)=SPACE$(8-LEN(STR$(YMIN)))+STR$(YMIN)+"+"+ STR
     ING$(69,"-")+"+"
5240 ORD$(20)=SPACE$(8-LEN(STR$(YMAX)))
     +STR$(YMAX)+"+"+STRING$(69,"-")+"+"
5250 FOR I=1 TO 19
5260 ORD$(I)=STRING$(79," ")
5270 MID$(ORD$(I),9,1)="|" : MID$(ORD$(I),79,1)="|"
5280 NEXT I
5290 MID$(ORD$(10),7,1)="Y"
5300 FOR I=0 TO HSTEPS
5310 IF Y1VAL(I)<0 OR LEN(STR$(Y1VAL(I)))>8 THEN 5330
5320 MID$(ORD$(Y1VAL(I)),I*70/HSTEPS+9,1)="+"
5330 NEXT I
5340 FOR I=20 TO 0 STEP -1
5350 PRINT ORD$(I)
5360 NEXT I
5370 PRINT XLGD$
5380 RETURN
```

Appendix B

DISCOUNT RATES FOR CASH FLOW

Throughout this book we have assumed that profits were the main objective—profits for future years as well as profits for the current year—and we have judged our success as publishers by doing a straightforward accumulation of the anticipated stream of earnings. The higher the total, the better the strategy.

This ignores a critically important aspect of financial analysis—the magic of compound interest. You will remember the essential facts about compound interest—$1,000 deposited in a money market fund is worth $1,100 one year from today if the fund pays 10 percent per year. Thus, there is an exact equivalence between the $1,100 next year and $1,000 today. A similar calculation can be applied to cash earned two, three, four, or five years in the future to find its equivalent value today. When you add all the present values of these future cash flows, you have a number that represents the entire future stream of earnings.

A money market fund is essentially risk free—it is backed by the bank and by the United States Government. A magazine's future cash flow, as we have seen, is a much less reliable investment, so an investor will demand a higher return on the investment, which translates into a higher discount rate to be applied to the magazine's earnings. I have seen venture capital companies use 20 percent, 30 percent, and even 40 percent rates when considering an investment—a range of choice that can have a very substantial effect on the present value, as shown in Table B.1.

In Table B.1 the cash flow is patterned after a magazine that has passed its break even point and promises to show substantial growth in profits, up to $500,000 a year, at which point it levels off. The magazine is assumed to have a residual value of $2 million at the end of the tenth year. Note that at the higher discount rates, the contribution of the later cash flows quickly approaches negligible values. At the 40 percent discount rate, the $500,000 in year nine contributes only $24,000 to the present value, and the entire $2,500,000 in year 10 adds only $86,000 to the present value.

This suggests that a magazine like this one with a cumulated cash flow of $6 million may be valued at anything from $3,013,000 to $738,000,

| | | Discount Rate | | | | | | | |
| | | 10% | | 20% | | 30% | | 40% | |
Year	Cashflow ($000)	PV	CPV	PV	CPV	PV	CPV	PV	CPV
1	100	91	91	83	83	77	77	71	71
2	200	165	256	139	222	118	195	102	174
3	300	225	482	174	396	137	332	109	283
4	400	273	755	193	589	140	472	104	387
5	500	311	1065	201	790	135	607	93	480
6	500	282	1348	167	957	104	710	66	546
7	500	257	1604	140	1097	80	790	47	594
8	500	233	1837	116	1213	61	851	34	628
9	500	212	2049	97	1310	47	898	24	652
10	2500	964	3013	404	1714	181	1079	86	738

Table B.1. Present Value (PV) and Cumulative Present Value (CPV) over time at a number of different discount rates.

Discounted Cash flow

depending on the discount rate. That's a wide spread, so let's take a close look at the discount rate and see if we can narrow the choice.

There are actually three components to the discount rate. The first, as we have mentioned, is the risk free return. Clearly, any magazine must earn at least what an investor could get if the money were place in a risk free investment of some kind. To be comparable to our discounted cashflow calculation, we must use as the risk free return the interest offered by a long-term investment such as 10-year government bonds which, for simplicity in the calculation, let us assume pays 10 per cent.

Second, an investment must take into account inflation in the value of dollars. Because the government bond is paid off in future (i.e. inflated) dollars, its return already incorporates inflation. For example, the deflated interest rate portion of a 10 percent nominal return is less than 4 percent if inflation in the value of the dollars is a flat 6 percent. If the projections of cash flow for our magazine use future advertising and circulation prices, and estimates of future costs, the cash flows are in future, inflated dollars.

Finally, an investment in a magazine will be expected to earn a premium over the risk free rates offered by government bonds because of the greater risk the investment entails. There are several methods used by financial theorists to estimate the risk of an investment. The most popular one measures risk in terms of the volatility of a given stock in comparison to that of one of the larger market indices, such as Standard & Poor's. Thus, if a given stock is found to be half again as volatile as the S&P Index, its riskiness (called beta in the literature) is 1.5. If it is twice as volatile, its beta is 2.0. The problem is that our magazine is probably not traded on a stock exchange—making an estimate of volatility entirely guesswork.

The Betting Odds

A better method is to use a more intuitively understandable—(and mathematically simpler)—measure of risk. I suggest that risk be measured in terms of betting odds. If you flip a coin and bet on heads, the chance of losing is one in two, or 50 percent. The return on such a bet, if you win, is 100 percent. Let's start a graph of return against risk (Figure B.1) and plot this first return percentage (100 percent) against the risk of loss (50 percent).

If you step up to a parimutuel window and bet on the favorite, the odds may be quoted as six to five. This means that if you win, you will get back

$1.20 for each dollar you bet, for a return of 20 percent. The parimutuel computer at the track keeps a count of all bets and, in this case, probably found that, for every $5 bet on the favorite there was only $1 bet on all the other horses in the race. Of course these figures exclude the percentage taken by the track management. Your theoretical Chance of Failure (loss) is only one in six, or 16.67 percent. I say theoretical, because there is no way of knowing the actual Chance of Failure on a horserace. This would take more knowledge about the horses, the weather, and so on, than we are likely to have. We can now plot a second point on our graph—a 20 percent return against a 16.67 percent Chance of Failure.

We can find the Risk Premium, as determined by the Chance of Failure, in the following formula (with all the variables expressed as decimal fractions).

$$Risk\ Premium = Chance\ of\ Failure/(1 - Chance\ of\ Failure)$$

For another example, if you estimate that the Chance of Failure of your magazine start-up is 25 percent, the Risk Premium would be:

$$Risk\ Premium = 0.25 /(1 - 0.25)$$

$$Risk\ Premium = 0.333 \quad (or\ 33.3\ percent)$$

This relationship (plotted in Figure B.2) is easier to understand and use than the beta factor. Note that at 100 percent Chance of Failure, the Risk Premium would be infinite—no one would willingly invest in any project that is certain to fail. However, we do occasionally invest small sums in something that has close to 100 percent Chance of Failure. For example, when did you last buy a lottery ticket? You spent a dollar or two in an investment that had odds of failure measured in millions to one—but the win would provide a very high return and the consequences of loss are negligible, so you took a flyer. This matter of the consequence of loss adds another dimension to the investment decision, but that is best left to a future book.

Putting it to Work

At last we are ready to make our first estimate of a present value for our magazine. It starts with a required or expected rate of return equal to the risk free return of government bonds, includes the effect of inflation, and is

Discounted Cash flow

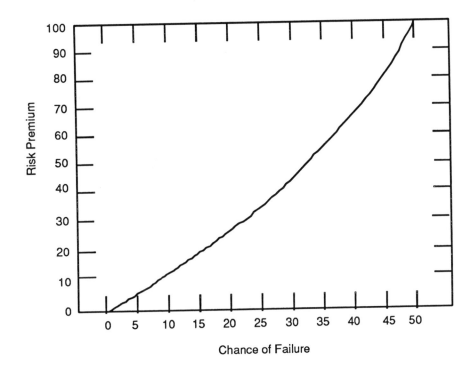

Figure B.1 To find the risk premium divide the Chance of Failure by one minus the Chance of Failure.

Discounted Cash flow

251

modified by our estimate of the riskiness of this investment. If you think the Chance of Failure of a particular magazine is about 15 percent, you multiply the risk free return by the required 17.7 percent Risk Premium from the graph or the equation, and get just over 30 percent (1.12 times 1.177 equals 1.318). If this discount rate is applied to the cash flow of Table B.1, the net present value is $1,202,000.

One further factor needs to be taken into account in this selection of a discount rate. There is no reason to expect that inflation will remain at a constant level throughout our projection, nor would the magazine present a constant risk of failure. To take the variability into account, we start again with the constant component of the risk free return. This is 6.67 percent after we deduct 5.0 percent for inflation from the bond return. Now we must list the expected inflation for each year of the projection. Similarly, as the magazine matures, one would hope that the Chance of Failure declines so the Risk Premium would be reduced. The product of risk free return, inflation, and Risk Premium is shown in Table B.2.

To calculate the net present value, the cash flows year by year must be carried down to the present through each of these discount rates, also year by year. The revenues from year three, for example, must first be discounted by 42.7 percent to find the value at the end of year two, then by 50.7 percent to find the value at the end of year one, then by 60 percent to find the current value (Table B.3).

It is interesting to note that the cumulative present value with this variable discount rate is almost identical to that calculated with a constant rate of 40 percent, even though the variable rate is above 40 percent for only three of the ten years. This emphasizes the great weight given to the revenues in the earlier years, and the relatively smaller importance of the later years when discounting.

It may be discouraging to consider that $6 million in cash earnings is only worth $730,000 today, but we are dealing with a relatively high risk venture in its earlier years and an inflation that eats away at the value of those future dollars.

And if you don't like the price you can always choose not to sell.

Discounted Cash flow

Appendix C

PACKAGED APPLICATION PROGRAMS

Five different curve fitting routines similar to those found in the listings of Appendix A, have been written by the author in Pascal and compiled for fast running speed. These include full graphics capability and the display of the curves on the screen. Curve types include the Normal Curve, the Diminishing Returns Curve, an Arctangent Curve for data that moves quickly from one level to another, a Hyperbola, and a Polynomial Curve for more variable data than fits in the other curve forms.

Budget and Strategy Models

A magazine budgeting program and a strategic modeling program have been written based on the material presented in this book.

The budgeting and strategy programs accumulate the necessary data and assumptions in a fully prompted, easy to follow data input routine. Each set of accumulated data is stored in a separate disk data file which may be printed out for later review, and is easily revised or modified as actual figures or new data become available.

The program then computes and prints statements of circulation, revenues, expenses, cash flow, and profit and loss on a monthly basis for 72 months.

When two or more magazine data files have been entered they may be consolidated into a single set of financial statements.

The strategy option gives you the ability to experiment with a full range of what-if assumptions. You can test changes in critical factors like subscription or single-copy prices, promotion levels, advertising prices, frequency and, in seconds, see the impact of these changes on cash flow and profits.

The five curve fitting routines mentioned above are built into the strategy option, so when you have entered data points the coefficients are derived and automatically stored in the data files.

The programs are called The Magazine Master. They will run on any IBM Personal Computer and are compatible with PC DOS, or MS DOS 2.1, or higher. You will need 256K of internal memory and two 360K floppy disk drives, or a single 360K floppy disk drive and a hard disk. You should have a printer capable of printing 132 columns, either in condensed or standard type width. Graphics capability is desirable for the strategy option, though not necessary.

The Magazine Master and the Five Curve fitting Routines are available from:

Sheridan Software
1031 Sheridan Road
Evanston, IL 60202

312-869-1965